The Expat Spouse

SEX. LIES. MONEY - 'til death do us part.

Mary Brown

Self-Published

UNTITLED

CHAPTER 1

The shrill ringing echoed down the wide marble hallway. The sound was unfamiliar; the home phone never rang. Making a free landline call wasn't the done thing on the compound; people thought you were cheap if you used a free-of-charge landline, since everyone owned the latest top-of-the-range mobile. Even her Mum back in the UK had disconnected her archaic landline in favour of the latest smartphone. Anji had begged her to keep it, but she explained that she only ever received cold calls from foreign call centres trying to sell her double glazing, none of whom would take no for an answer, and was far too polite to slam the phone down on any of them. If someone was calling at home, it had to be either an emergency or something very serious. Anji panicked. The first thing that popped into her head was the kids, of course. She hoped they were ok. Anji cursed as she stubbed her toe in her rush to pick up the receiver, alarm bells ringing in her head while her imagination went into overdrive, imagining the worst. She grabbed the handset while biting her bottom lip, trying to dull the searing pain that throbbed in her big toe.

"Hello?" she spluttered in a high-pitched voice. The sound seemed to come from her gut rather than her throat, which was now seizing up. Maybe she would cough up a lung if she supressed the pain any longer, she thought to herself as the agony sailed through, making

1

her stomach roll.

When no-one spoke she blurted out, "Yes? Yes?" which roughly translated as *'what the hell is wrong? Are the kids ok?'* Anji tried to focus on the call, while frantically searching for whatever it was she'd caught her foot on, feeling the blood drip from her toe as she retraced her steps in her fuddled mind.

"This is Karen. Don't say a word. I just want you to listen." Anji stood frozen to the spot.

"OK," she stammered. Karen's voice sounded so serious and unfamiliar. Anji pressed the receiver closer to her ear so she could hear properly. The pain was clouding her concentration and the pressure of the handset gave her something else to focus on.

"I heard you've been gossiping, apparently about Steve and me," began Karen. "I mean – of all people, Anji, you were the one I trusted the most. You! One of my best so called friends. You walk around here all virginal, like your shit doesn't stink. Mrs Fucking Perfect, and you're the one who wants to ruin my perfectly good marriage. All I can say is, what the fuck, Anji, what the fuck?!"

Anji stood there, stunned. Steve was Karen's gormless husband. Why would Anji be bothering herself dishing any dirt about him? He had, after all, the personality of a dry turd. She recalled a particularly tense dinner party, where Karen had to tell him to go upstairs and change his trousers because he was sporting a suspicious stain on the front, like a naughty teenager who couldn't help himself. He'd spun on his heel and marched upstairs, pounding down minutes later in clean clothes with a face like a moody fifteen-year-old.

Anji refocused her mind back on the conversation as Karen continued to rant down the phone in a tirade of shit throwing. All she could hear was the word 'fucking' ringing in her ears. Not only was there blood oozing from her toe, but now she also felt the blood draining from her whole body. She had no idea what was going on but she realised that, here, that didn't actually matter. She felt cold and shivery, her teeth chattering from the dread that suddenly gripped her. It was no longer fear over her children's wellbeing; now it was the fear of being the next victim on the compound. It was the way the compound worked. The compound's inhabitants waited like a pack of wolves for any kind of salacious gossip, information or news to jump on, to dissect and digest before bringing the person down to their knees. Rumours would start flying like trapeze artists at the circus. A frenzy of social media scandals and serious tattletales would pursue until it fizzled out, if ever, leaving your reputation in tatters.

In less than two minutes, the colour had drained from Anji's world and she couldn't utter a word. She felt as heavy as a brick, her stomach dropping along with her mood. She wasn't used to being accused of anything. She'd always kept her head down and her nose clean when it came to meaningless gossip. But by tomorrow morning, Anji knew that hers would be the name on everyone's lips; she was the bitch who'd brought down Karen's marriage. Whether it was true or not, round here gossip raged like a forest fire. A fire which was almost impossible to put out, once it had started. Anji knew, like a forest fire, it was best to let them rage until they burned themselves out, even if it took months. The problem was, even when the fiery gossip was extinguished, it would leave a pile of ashes of your reputation. Anji had seen victims on the compound being attacked for scandals like this, but she'd always stayed in the grey zone, never speaking up for either the victim or villain. That was the way she liked it; it was far easier to take the cowardly approach, standing on the side lines, having the best view to observe and be the perfect, non-playing team member. Anji knew it was the easy way out, but that's how she behaved with everyone she knew, including her family and friends. They all knew her as Anji, the good old egg.

"Are you listening, you stupid bitch? Are you?" The question knocked Anji to her senses, shaking her back to reality. She couldn't believe what she was hearing. She'd never heard Karen speak like this about anyone, let alone her.

"Karen, please, listen to me. I have no idea what's happened, can you explain? Just tell me, please! I'm your friend!" she begged, hoping that the Karen she knew would come onto the phone any minute and say this was all a bad joke. She desperately wanted to make Karen believe her, that she had no clue what she was talking about, but between her chattering teeth and non-functioning brain it was impossible to express herself properly.

At the other end of the line, Karen slammed the phone down noisily. She had clearly made her mind up already and Anji's protestations had fallen on deaf ears. Anji wanted to replace the receiver but her body was frozen to the spot with shock and she couldn't move. As she stood there with the phone still glued to her ear, she realised that Karen hadn't hung up the phone properly, as she could hear the muffled chaos at Karen's end. She'd obviously left the phone off the hook unintentionally.

"That bitch!" Karen howled. Anji, still listening, standing still like a store mannequin, dumbfounded and seriously wounded at the hideous words lashing from Karen's mouth.

"I've always been so nice to her," continued Karen, none the wiser that she could still be heard. "I even kept her from finding out about that pathetic specimen she calls her husband. Let her live in her fantasy world, with her perfect children and her fucking perfect husband!"

Anji put the phone down methodically and quietly before she could overhear more breaking news that she didn't want or need to know. She held onto the marble bench for support for a few moments not knowing what to do next. Each word that had spilled from Karen's lips had felt like a punch, winding her right in the gut. Looking down at the floor, trying to focus, Anji realised her toe didn't hurt as much as her throbbing head or her tightening chest, where her heart thundered like a friggin' freight train. She had no idea what had just happened. When her brain took over again, she walked herself and her damaged toe to the bathroom as if her limbs didn't belong to her. As she began to assess her injury, she wondered how her day could have changed so dramatically. Her foot looked even worse than it felt, but it didn't help that the rest of her body ached as if her muscles had been flash burned with acid. *This must be a mistake*, she though, hoping the situation could be patched up as quickly as her little digit.

Outsiders often described life in Saudi Arabia like living in a golden cage. Compounds were filled with expatriate families, because a man securing a job in Saudi meant the wife came along as a trailing spouse. What a title! Anji, the trailing-bloody-spouse. It was an absolute insult to any self-respecting and educated individual. Women sacrificed their lives back home to further their husband's careers. It was largely forbidden for women to work, and most women found a way to fill their days with shopping, exercising and gossiping. Many wives who couldn't find legitimate work worked illegally under the radar, lured by the extra money. Seeing those extra zeros on their bank statements was like winning the lottery for some. To friends and family back home it seemed almost too perfect; starting afresh, new exotic adventures and the lure of the extra cash. What they didn't see was all of the sacrifice: the pressure to make new friends for both you and the children; giving up your job to be the underling of your husband's career and success; constantly questioning your sense of worth, as all women were labelled as dependants on the husband's Visa. Mental health issues were rife and many of the women relied on a bottle of whatever they could get their hands on. Some even managed to find other substances to use to self-medicate. Anji knew only too well that these only made things worse, but today she had a bit more empathy for those women, wishing that she had something stronger than the bottle of wine chilling in the fridge.

Maids were a luxury in most parts of the world, but here they were the norm and almost every household had one. It was the done thing. If you didn't have one, people questioned why. The maids were expected to do all of the household chores along with most of the cooking and all of the babysitting. Anji had a maid, of course, but she couldn't quite bring herself to give up all of her responsibilities. She'd grown up in life where you had to work hard for what you had, and relying on others for your every need just didn't sit right with her. She enjoyed cooking so she generally did this herself, and left her maid, Lani – who was the envy of every other overworked maid in the compound – to do some light cleaning, ironing and occasional babysitting. Every afternoon in the gardens and community halls where children played, there would be a sea of housemaids, but most of the children's mothers were nowhere to be seen. Most expat wives had grown up in households without maids, but quickly adapted and took full advantage of the freedom that having hired help brought. But women were denied other freedoms, such as the opportunity to drive, so drivers were also a necessary part of the family. With few freedoms other than time and money, as you can imagine, came loose lips. Gossiping was a favourite pastime. Anji had indulged in listening to gossip many times, but always teetered on the edge of any chattering groups. You had to be exceptionally careful once you started walking that fine tightrope.

Slumping into the luxurious armchair by the twin basins in her bathroom, Anji began to gather her senses. It dawned on her that she'd become yet another victim of someone else's sensational rumour. She began breaking down the accusations. It was the first Anji had heard she was a home wrecker. How come she was being singled out for it? She was unsure if Karen was accusing her of sleeping with her husband – the thought of having anything to do with Steve made her want to retch into the sink – or if she was just passing on a rumour she'd heard herself. If the latter was true, Anji felt a pang of guilt for Karen and her children. She hoped it was just fabricated, farfetched bullshit like most of the news mongering that went on around here. She loved Karen in a way that you would love a sister. So vivacious and, usually, self-assured, she was the first person Anji had met in the compound who was willing to give her a chance of friendship. When Anji had arrived three years earlier, Karen introduced her to Saudi life and had made her feel positive about her move to the Kingdom; a fellow trailing spouse and, so she'd thought, a kindred spirit.

One of the things that had thrown Anji the most was how out of character Karen's phone call had been. Karen was one of those people who exuded positivity and made friends quickly, not just because she was gorgeous but also because she was beautiful inside; the kind of beautiful person who wraps her soul around everyone she meets. A head of well-styled black curls hung around her face effortlessly, and a heavy coat of red lipstick always adorned her full lips. In fact, Anji never saw Karen without her trademark red lips. Her eyes were green; not an emerald green but more like the soft green of spring, sprinkled with sunrays, set into a face with porcelain white skin and perfectly formed laughter lines decorating the side of her eyes like they were just supposed to be there. Her pale and striking appearance mesmerised the locals. Karen turned heads. Everyone noticed her; she attracted people like bees to a flower. And it wasn't just her physical appearance; it was something deeper, some kind of positive magnetism which was undeniably captivating. It was the first time Anji had found such magic in a person.

Anji began to feel tears cascade down her face at the thought of Karen being so angry and miserable because of her. It wasn't just the injustice of the gossip which upset her, but also because she felt so powerless to do anything about it. If the rumours about Steve were true – obviously not with her on the other end of the affair – then she just couldn't fathom the cruelty; you follow your husband thousands of miles to help push him up the career ladder, then – if Karen had understood things properly – he has an affair? It broke every rule in the non-existent book for expat spouses and the idea was torturous.

Then her mind flipped to something else. Had Anji heard right? Had she really heard Karen hint that Jeff, her husband, wasn't so pure and wonderful himself? Had anger and bitterness led her to make such a callous remark? But, then, Karen hadn't even realised Anji was still on the phone listening when she'd said that. Questions swirled around her mind and made her feel dizzy again. The thought of Jeff going behind her back to have an affair was absolutely absurd. He barely had time for his own family with the hours he put in at work, so the idea of extra-marital-goings-on was ridiculous. It was obvious that Karen was just being spiteful and ghastly. But did she even have those things in her? As she continued to ponder this whirlwind of questions, all of the tears Anji had been keeping inside of her over the past 3 years began to spill out, like water pouring from a broken dam. Living like a single mum on the compound while Jeff had been busy running the hotel and bringing the money home had not been part of her life plan. Had she sacrificed too much of her own freedom and choices to allow him to build a successful career? He provided them with a life that was more than comfortable, but it was at a great cost. Anji and the kids barely saw him these days. Was it worth it? Her face drenched in tears, she curled up on the chair that sat in the corner of the oversized bathroom, bringing her legs towards her chest and cried herself into a restless sleep.

She didn't know how long she'd been out for when her children startled her awake, Max and Georgina, racing into the bathroom.

"Mum!" they shouted breathlessly, "We're hungry!"

They both looked baffled to find their mum asleep during the day, especially in the bathroom armchair, and they grinned from ear to ear when Anji mumbled instructions to order some food in as she was feeling poorly. It was a real treat for them to order in from the restaurant, so they bounded back down the stairs, oblivious to their mum's suffering. Anji tried to lift her head but it felt like a dead weight and throbbed so much it was as if her brain had its own heart pulsing deep down within. She sank back down into the cushions, pinching her eyes closed, hoping that she could fall asleep again and wake up to find this had all been a bad dream.

CHAPTER 2

The following day, Anji woke to find that her toe had recovered but her mind and heart hadn't. Her head was fixed to her shoulders yet somehow seemed to be spinning in its own solar system, speculating about what was transpiring within the walls of the compound. She was hoping the call from yesterday had been one big stupid misunderstanding that could be quickly resolved. Karen would understand once Anji had explained everything.

After getting the kids ready for school in a blur, Anji walked them to the bus. She had hoped she'd see Karen; that they'd exchange smiles, have a chat and Anji could explain that the situation was nothing to do with her. Like a rainbow after a storm, the friends would hug and Karen would plant her red lips on Anji's cheek; a kiss to seal the acceptance of her friend's apology. A stupid apology for something she had no fucking clue what it was about and how or who started it, but she was ready to say sorry just to sweep the whole friggin' saga under the carpet.

Anji looked in the mirror before heading out and noticed the ugly bags hanging under her sad eyes. Pinching her cheeks, she tried to inject some colour into her face, but only a shadow gazed back. Yesterday's crying and a rough night's sleep had taken their toll and Anji quickly glanced away from her reflection.

No amount of concealer and contouring would fix this mess. It was going to be one of those days. When she reached the bus with the kids, Helen, the school monitor, was grouchy. "You're one minute late," she grumbled, with a curled lip that hinted she was more than annoyed. This sour-faced bus monitor didn't smile on a good day, so Anji simply apologised, resisting the urge to snap back, 'One minute you stupid bitch, I'll show you one minute!' as she imagined herself hitting her over the top of her miserable head with her Gucci handbag. She didn't need the negative energy or evil stares from the other pissed-off mums. She hurried the children onto the bus and managed to send them off with a smile – a wry smile, but nevertheless a smile – and, as the bus went on its way, the kids blew her kisses that warmed her soul just a little.

Most of the other mothers had disappeared, which was a blessing today. She wasn't in the mood for making polite conversation. She let out a deep sigh of relief and swung around to head back home. The sigh turned into a gasp as she found herself face to face with Karen.

"Hi Karen," she stammered, "I was hoping to see you." Anji smiled, praying that Karen was in a better mood after she'd had time to sleep on her allegations of the previous day. Anji looked round, realising it was just the two of them. She was so pleased she didn't have an audience of scandalmongers waiting for the juicy details. Karen edged right up to Anji's face. Anji felt her friend's breath on her skin; it was vinegary and stale, stinking of booze. She winced. Karen's eyes looked like two burn holes in a blanket, and Anji realised her friend had clearly had a pretty rough night too. Mustering as much courage as she could, Anji held out her arms to invite her for a hug, but before she could complete the manoeuvre, Karen was practically frothing at the mouth.

"Listen, bitch, stay away from us!" Karen spat. "The damage is already done. I just hope you can live with yourself." She turned to walk away then spun round and added, "You're in total denial; you caused the mess that your husband is in. You know Jeff's dipping his dick in more than one household round here, right?" she sneered, her lip snarling. Obviously the anger was boiling over as hot as lava. "And since you're a disloyal cow, it's about time you found out."

Taking short, shallow breaths, Anji didn't dare move. She had so many questions, but her voice box felt like it had narrowed to the width of a needle. Her nerves were shredded and she was scared she'd wet herself in fear if she tried to inch away from the confrontation; suddenly wishing her down below was as tight as her throat. By the time she had managed to gather some of her senses, Karen was gone. Anji tried to lift her feet but they were as heavy as lead. She turned to inch her way home, realising she'd never felt as alone as she did at that very moment.

Once Anji made it home, she saw that her driver, Omar, was waiting to take her to work. Anji had managed to find the perfect job for herself in Riyadh. One of the school mums ran the HR department in the ladies' only section of a small marketing company and Anji had literally begged her for the part-time role. On seeing Omar, Anji suddenly contemplated calling in sick until she realised that a day stewing in her own company would be a terrible idea. Better to keep her brain busy at work then languish at home, churning over her apparently ruined friendship and besmirched reputation. Dashing into the house, she headed to her dressing room where she hurriedly covered her eye bags again with a double layer of Chanel concealer; a luxury they could now easily afford but a far cry from the days back in the grey and damp of the UK, where Anji would fish out make-up BOGOFs and bargain bucket finds in Boots. A smile played on her pouting lips for a moment as she thought of how grateful she was for how things were now, forgetting herself for a minute. Then her pouting turned to frowning when the reality of the current situation brought her crashing back down to earth. Twisting the lid back on her lip-gloss, she waved her hand under the illuminated mirror to turn it off, and headed downstairs.

"Hello, ma'am." Omar greeted her as he always did, jumping from the driver's seat to open the door for her. She always scolded him for doing this – she was perfectly capable of opening the door for herself. For the past three years she'd told him off, but there was no argument today, and none of the usual light chatter. Anji thought it would be better to keep her mouth shut as she was teetering on the verge of tears and was afraid she'd say something, which would start her off again. She was desperate to press Omar for more information on Jeff's movements, but she knew she wasn't ready to hear any answers yet. So Anji kept her mouth firmly shut the whole way to the office. Always professional and polite, Omar smiled his usual goodbye as he drove away from the office building. Anji got into the lift and rode it to the fourth floor where she worked in the small ladies' only section. Only women and children were allowed on this side of the office, and the door was always locked to prevent any strangers – or the religious police, who were always men of course – from entering.

As Anji's computer booted up, she took off her Abaya – or black bin liner, as she called it – which was mandatory and had to cover the body from the shoulders down to the feet. A scarf fell over her shoulders, just in case the religious police asked her to cover her hair. The black sack managed to cover a multitude of sins, and on more than one occasion Anji had left her pyjamas on under it all day. She had once tried to surprise Jeff by turning up to his office with nothing but her underwear beneath it. In a screaming whisper, he threw her out of his office and she could practically see the red mist swirling above his beetroot-coloured face. It hadn't even been her idea; she'd overheard some of the ladies sharing stories about how they'd seduced their husbands and, Janice, a dowdy woman who was well into her fifties, had gone into great detail about how she had done this and explained how it had driven her husband wild. *If she could do it, so can I '*, Anji had thought. But, of course, it had backfired, and instead of passion had resulted in shame

"What the hell were you up to?" Jeff had scolded. "What if you had an accident on the way here and had to go to hospital? I could get deported for this. Could you at least try to use your small brain sometimes, if that's even possible?" She ran from the office with her confidence knocked down a few more notches; those marks on the bedpost were definitely travelling in the wrong direction. It was something they would never ever mention again, and an attempt at seduction that Anji would never repeat. The feeling of rejection was something she was becoming familiar with, but the shame on that day was something she'd wanted to bury away forever.

Jeff was very straight-laced when it came to intimacy in their relationship. He was very much the missionary man; he was in charge and didn't like to experiment with new ideas. If Anji suggested anything new he refused, demanding to know where she'd learnt or heard about it. Their sex life had always been monotonous at times, but these days she was just glad if she found him in bed in the mornings when she woke up. These days he would often sleep in the hotel if there were a late meeting or dinner, to avoid coming home in the early hours and waking everyone up. They had discussed it and both agreed that Jeff would get more sleep by having this arrangement.

'How do I know if my husband is cheating,' Anji typed into the search bar once her computer screen had flickered into life. Pages of answers followed. Anji felt better knowing she wasn't the only person Googling the same subject. Apparently it wasn't so taboo after all if the search engine was anything to go by. 'Does he smell of perfume? Is he less affectionate? Does he dress differently? Is he instigating arguments? Avoiding time together? Spending more time at work?' Anji stopped there. She could probably answer yes to all of these questions. She hardly saw Jeff these days, but didn't view it as unacceptable behaviour on his part. As General Manager of one of the top hotels in the country, it was normal for him to be out late. Saudis socialise later and eat later than Europeans, and the family had adjusted accordingly. Anji had always been expected to adapt to the country and she never complained; she saw it as part of her job as the obedient trailing-spouse. Her husband's colossal wage also helped; she couldn't deny that one.

"Hi, Anji, what are you working on this morning?" Sara suddenly piped up over her shoulder. Just when she thought her day couldn't get any worse, she found her boss looking over her head straight at her screen. A wave of heat surged to Anji's face. She felt every blood vessel enlarge, and thought if she'd had to take a lie detector test at that moment she'd have failed hands down.

"Anyone I know?" Sara enquired.

"No, just a friend back home." Anji lied almost too effortlessly. Despite being close to her boss, she didn't want to explain her current situation, as she couldn't cope with having a meltdown in the office. *Always keep your home affairs at home*, she reminded herself.

"Well then, back to work," Sara said. *Yes, get back to the job I'm paying you to do, rather than doing detective work for other people's husbands on work time...* Of course, Sara had every right, so Anji apologised and excused herself, heading out towards the bathroom to douse the fire in her cheeks. Splashing her face with cool water, but being careful not to ruin her make-up, Anji wished she could have a cold shower to refresh herself; rewind and start the whole day again. That would have to wait. Confronting herself head on, Anji looked in the mirror and chided herself. How the hell could she believe that her husband of fifteen years was a lying, cheating rat? She suddenly felt so damn stupid. Her emotions were on a perpetual roller coaster – one minute dismissing any idea of Jeff being a lousy two timer and the next minute creating big stories in her head about him fucking every woman on the compound – alternating between disappointed and downright desperate. One thing was for sure: as much as she tried to talk herself out of it, a seed of doubt had been planted in her mind and was already sprouting bright green leaves, blossoming with vigour and vitality. Anji was of course wondering if Jeff really *was* working late every night. Was he rubbing shoulders with royalty in the hotel's private dining rooms, or was he rubbing another woman's shoulders somewhere within the confines of Saudi? She hadn't given this idea much thought in the fifteen years they'd been married – after all, she trusted him – but she struggled to get that image out of her mind. She shook her head, pulling back her shoulders and standing tall as she headed back into the office.

The day flew by while Anji kept herself busy with the accounts, chasing payments and closing contracts. She was glad she'd decided to come into work, but was desperate to share her worries with someone else. She was sure by now everyone on the compound had read the gossip via WhatsApp or, hell, even seen it on the breaking news on CNN. Anji waited for Sara to go on her lunch break so she could call Lily, another of her best friends. Lily's husband worked for Jeff and, although Anji had tried to avoid any friendships formed through her husband's work, the women had become instant friends and made it a habit to talk daily. On the compound you had to be in each other's lives, like it or not, and Lily and Anji got on like a house on fire. Her friend picked up almost instantly.

"Lily, I've been wanting to call you all morning." Anji's voice became croaky as she tried to suppress her tears.

"Why? What is it?"

"I can't tell you over the phone. Can you come over later so we can talk?" Anji whimpered into the receiver, feeling her eyes prickle with tears.

"Pop by at eight o'clock," Lily offered.

"I'd prefer my place if you don't mind?" She didn't really want Lily's husband, Adam, listening in on their conversation. She certainly didn't need Jeff finding out.

"Sure. I'll pass by at eight. And please cheer up. It can't be that bad, I hope." Anji carried on Googling while Sara was out of the office. She wouldn't be stupid enough to get caught again. She found her mind drifting back to the past, when she and Jeff had first met.

Jeff was the love of Anji's life. He'd swept her off her feet; literally, at 40,000 feet. While boarding a flight to Dubai to start a new job in one of the leading Hotels, he had discovered at check-in that Business Class was overbooked and had accepted a downgrade for the extra air miles. He ended up taking a seat in economy next to Anji, who was also heading to Dubai for a new role in a well-known travel agency. He spent the entire six-hour flight entrusting her with his life story before spending the next six months pursuing her doggedly; calling her, turning up unexpectedly, and sending gifts to her office. Anji hadn't wanted a relationship at the time but this strong, ambitious perfectionist managed to make her win his heart. For her it hadn't been love at first sight, which only made Jeff more determined to make her fall for him.

One Valentine's Day, Jeff sent Anji a Cartier ring made of gold, with a tiny love heart at its centre. From that day she realised that if she accepted it, this was going to be more than a girlfriend-boyfriend relationship. Anji gave in, allowing Jeff to become her anchor, the armour protecting her from the world. Anji was too kind, too giving, and people took advantage. Jeff shrouded her from all of that and kept her shielded from people and situations where her kindness could be exploited. It took her a while to get used to, but in the end she agreed his protective nature was a divine blessing.

CHAPTER 3

That afternoon was a blur of children's activities. Max had basketball in the sports hall and Georgie attended ballet in the room above. Anji kept herself busy, watching each child's activity. As she went from one area to the other, she didn't stop to chat; she felt far too self-conscious for all of that. She felt the other mums' eyes burning holes into her back like lasers – do they know, or don't they? Everything felt too raw and surreal; she wasn't ready to protest her innocence to anyone. Chinese whispers were echoing around the whole arena, and Anji could sense mums going quiet and hushing each other every time she approached. She was totally overwhelmed; being caught up in gossip was exhausting and made her feel sick to her stomach with worry.

Putting Max and Georgie to bed that night, she told each one what she loved most about them. The two children loved this part of the evening.

"Max, I love you because you made me so proud of you today scoring three baskets".

"And Mum, I love you because… I just do"

"Georgie, I love because you are kind, giving, and you love your brother."

"No I don't," she screamed, which made them all laugh out loud.

"Mum, I love you because I just do".

Both would say the same thing every evening. It was their thing. Anji clung to the children a little longer than usual during their bedtime hugs. They were her safe port in the storm she was battling through, and she revelled in these moments of calm.

Anji was sitting in the living room, staring at the wall in thought, when she heard the key turn in the lock. "Hi Anji, I'm here!" Lily always let herself in. She was more like a sister than a neighbour and they told each other almost everything. Anji already had a bottle of white wine on ice and couldn't wait to drink the forbidden juice. All alcohol was purchased on the black market. The substandard booze was always overpriced, but beggars can't be choosers, thought Anji. Who better to share this sinful act with than with Lily, her anchor in this crazy hellhole?

Anji was rifling through the kitchen cabinets to pull out wine glasses, when she felt her friend's arms wrap around her from behind. Lily hugged Anji with all her might. Already crumbling into an emotional mess, Anji's sadness threatened to crush her, along with the unbearable weight of guilt for something she hadn't even done. She melted into her friend's tight hold, hoping Lily could shed some light on the truth behind the accusations. When Lily released her grasp, Anji was already doubled over, sobbing. She wasn't normally one for emotional expression, as her conservative upbringing didn't allow for tears. She tried to repress her sobs, but everything seemed so overpowering. Hiding her face with her hands, Anji realised she'd been holding everything in for far too long.

"It can't be that bad," cooed Lily. "Come on."

"Well it is. It's worse, honestly."

Lily frowned so hard it looked like her eyebrows were planning a vacation to another part of her face. Despite the frown, she was still stunning. Lily was a modern-day Nordic goddess, carrying herself fiercely, with eyes as cold and blue as the Baltic Sea, and thick blonde hair that was as strong as she was. Taking her cue from her friend's expression, Anji opened up and released all the angst she'd held pent up since Karen's call. The whole story hurled from her mouth like a tidal wave, crashing out in no kind of order.

"Oh Anji, you know it's all gonna blow over in a few days. You know how this compound works. Someone new always has to come under fire. This week it's your turn," explained Lily shrugging her shoulders matter-of-factly. "Get a grip! Have I taught you absolutely nothing during your time here in this bloody cage? When the hell are you going to toughen up?"

Anji looked on, gobsmacked. Like a deer caught in the headlights of a fast-moving car, she pricked up her ears to confirm she was hearing right. The tough talk jolted her back to the real world. She realised her tears had dried up suddenly as quickly as they had come. Then Lily laughed, a distressing kind of cackle, which was very weird since there was nothing particularly funny about the situation. It certainly seemed out of place and inappropriate. Flipping her blonde mane over her shoulder, Lily scoffed: "This is bullshit. I'm telling you now I'm gonna fix this. I'll talk to Karen and smooth this over. Go and have a shower and clean up before Jeff comes home." She insisted. In stunned silence, Anji dutifully nodded.

"Don't speak to Jeff yet," Lily almost barked her

order. "Let's do our homework first. You know these things tend to blow over quickly." As her friend turned to leave before they'd even opened the precious bottle of wine, Anji felt the tears returning. She was now Lily's obedient student, always the obedient verging on pathetic, little student. She could add this to her list - obedient friend, obedient wife – what next? She prayed Lily could dig her out of this mess so she could get back to her life of plain sailing, smooth and stress free.

Anji undressed wearily. The day had been exhausting to say the least. Looking at herself in the full-length mirror she wondered if she had already lost a few pounds since the news broke that she was a home wrecker and her husband a lying, cheating bastard. She brushed her blonde hair and took a deep breath, deciding then and there she'd no longer be a victim of this ridiculous situation. She would find the real culprit, if there was one, and the scandal would soon be a past memory. It was hard to imagine that Steve was capable of having an affair. He was the type of man whom, if you'd asked him to put his privates somewhere other than his underwear, he would need instructions before asking 'is it in yet?' Anji wondered how he'd managed to father two children. But they were definitely his, as they both looked the spitting image of him.

The Jeff question had very much taken root. As she prodded at the bags under her eyes, a feeling of acute awareness crept up on her like a ghost. Suddenly she felt completely isolated, like a lone shark in a huge ocean. She felt thoroughly melancholy as she remembered her once-so-perfect life. In the past, Jeff could make her laugh about everything and anything. Was he really making some other bitch laugh now? Despite feeling that she should be strong, her face contorted with pain at the thought he could be with someone else. The mental image was there now, branded with an iron rod. Was it her fault? Had she driven him to this? Anji had never felt worse in her whole life. Turning on the shower and stepping into the steam, she stood under the cleansing water and felt her shame and pain wash away, if only for a few minutes.

CHAPTER 4

"Bzzz! Bzzz! Bzzz!" Anji woke to her 6am alarm with a start. It had been a week since the rumours about Anji had started winding their way through the compound, and Anji's unwelcome new sleeping pattern had practically turned her into an owl, with the wide staring eyes to match. Staying up all night was painful, not to mention shattering. This morning though, she woke up feeling rested, having slept like a dead man. She scurried to the toilet as quietly as possible and saw Jeff's suit thrown in the bathtub. Instantly, the hairs on her neck stood up straight like a choirboy at Christmas. Something didn't smell right, and it caught her off guard.

Anyone who knew Jeff would know this was abnormal behaviour. The man was meticulous about cleanliness and detail. This was useful in his role as a luxury hotelier but frustrating in an ordinary household, as she had learned early on in their relationship when he'd arrive home from a long day at work and start organising the rooms like he was a housekeeper at the hotel. She let him, although it niggled her no end because he made her feel inadequate as a homemaker. She had tried to talk to him about this a few times, but over time it became clear that he didn't care how his behaviour made her feel. If one thing could be said about Anji, it was that she was a quick learner, and she instinctively knew which battles to choose to fight; this wasn't one of them.

Anji wondered what the hell her husband's suit was doing, just chucked into the tub. Usually his suits were neatly hung over his clothes horse, ready for the next long day at work; even if they were heading to the dry cleaners they'd still be very carefully folded. Anji fished his shirt from the bath and tentatively brought it up to her nose. There were no traces of perfume; only the sweet scent of Terre D'Hermes cologne. He'd been using it way before they met, and she loved it. She felt a pang of relief, yet her gut hung in disappointment for doubting him again. She'd have to work on these new feelings of jealousy and insecurity. Throwing the shirt back where she found it, Anji was careful not to disturb the scene because she knew Jeff would recognise if his clothes had been tampered with. She didn't want to take the risk of him noticing and asking her about it, which would no doubt lead to an argument that of course she wouldn't possibly win.

Anji bent over the bath to rearrange the clothes in a believable mess, trying to remember how she had found the pile. She buried the shirt back under the jacket and tossed the pants carelessly on top. She knew Jeff would blow a fuse when he saw his own sloppiness and would probably blame someone else for it, like he always did. Things were never his fault. As she stood up, she felt something wet and sticky on her hand. Peering into the bath to check she hadn't knocked over the bottle of bath oil which perched on the immaculately organised shelf near the taps, her eye was drawn to a small, sticky stain by the zipper of his trousers. She got back on her knees, snatched the trousers out of the bath and held them closer to her nose, already knowing what she would detect that gross smell of ammonia.

Anji's stomach lurched as intensely as if she had been hurtling down a rollercoaster. She slumped down onto the cool, tiled floor holding her head in her hands. There could only be two explanations: One – he had relieved himself out of desperation, because it had been weeks since they'd last had sex. Thought, if that was the case, surely he would have come home, undressed and done it? Or; two – he'd been with someone else, and someone who was impressive enough to make him forget about his obsession with cleanliness for a brief spell.

Her throat pulsed; she was sure her heart had managed to find its way up there which was forming the lump she couldn't swallow down. How long had it been since Jeff had last tried it on with her? She tried to recall, but she really couldn't remember. She stared at a white tile which had a tiny chip out of it. Almost in a trance, she rubbed her eyes, trying to concentrate and remember when they had last made love; well, 'had relations' would be a more accurate description, as there wasn't much passion involved these days. Jeff had always had a high libido and had always been the instigator; that was the way it was. If Anji ever tried to advance on him for a change, Jeff had a way of making her feel shameful and dirty, so she had stopped doing it. Since moving to Saudi Arabia, their intimate moments had become few and far between, but in all honesty, she hadn't really given it much thought until now. He worked late most nights and she was usually asleep when he got home. That was just the way things were.

As she contemplated the idea that she had put their relationship on the back burner, thoughts prickled at Anji's mind like pins and needles. Was this all her fault?

Was she the one to blame? She had absolutely no idea what to do next. Usually so collected, Anji's thoughts were in a jumble, a mishmash of a million speculations. She struggled to catch any threads of meaning and would need a needle to try to stitch it all back together again so things would go back to making sense. She just wanted to go back to being her old life, back in her comfortable bubble. A noise from somewhere in the house jolted Anji back into reality. She stood up and looked at herself in the mirror. She looked like she'd aged ten years in a week. She splashed her face with cold water and said to her reflection, in a whisper, 'the show must go on', then forced herself, heavy and heart and all, to go and rouse the kids for school.

Max and Georgina were already awake so Anji busied herself with preparing breakfast. To avoid having to face anyone, she delegated the task of taking the kids to the bus stop to Lani, her young housemaid. It saddened her having to do this, as this was normally one of her favourite parts of the day. She always had the best conversations with her children on the walk to the bus, and she was aware that they were getting to an age where, soon, they'd no longer want to chat with their mother in the mornings and instead would want to walk with their friends or have their heads buried in their smart phones. This thought made Anji feel even more depressed than she already felt. Anji had always put the kids first, before herself and before Jeff, since the day they were born. Her husband didn't like it, and it was the cause of many arguments. She knew children needed love, support and guidance. Anji had given Jeff the freedom to climb the career ladder while she focused on raising the kids. She took her role very seriously and was conscious that, since quitting her job back in the UK, it was the only serious work she had left. She was full of pride for her children and it had only grown stronger as they'd gotten older and developed into little, or not-so-little, people.

Anji's eldest child, Max, was eleven years old and had a wonderful way with people. His magnetism was contagious; he loved humans and they loved him. On his first day at school, he quickly won all of his teachers over and girls swarmed around him like bees to a flower. With his mop of blonde hair and already chiselled features, Max was most definitely in the popular crowd. God help him as he got older, Anji often thought.

On the day she was born, the doctor who'd delivered Georgina said he'd never seen such an alert child. Now nine, she was still very switched on and strong-willed. She was the kind of child you could throw into a lion's den and she'd walk out without a scratch. Georgina had been two weeks overdue, so maybe the extra incubation period had given her super powers. Despite the frequent arguments, Anji was grateful for her daughter's headstrong attitude, which she felt was an absolute requirement as a woman in the 21st century. Whereas Max had taken many of Anji's family traits, Georgina took after her dad with her golden hair and amber eyes, the same perfectly formed nose and a smile that could light up the world.

Today both kids were full of smiles. Watching them get ready for school lessened Anji's pain a little and helped put things into perspective. She smiled to herself; what luck to have two such amazing children. She adored them; they were so pure and perfect in her eyes. She waved them off as they chased each other up the road towards the bus, and when they went out of sight Anji trotted upstairs to get herself ready for work, already feeling her mood drop.

Jeff remained in bed, clearly in a very deep sleep. This was unusual for him. Anji was the one who slept at night; when the children were younger it was their dad who woke up if they were unwell or had a bad dream. He was such a light sleeper, it was like he could sense them. She quietly slipped onto the bed and lay beside him for a few minutes, gazing at his peaceful face, searching for some clue that he was cheating. He looked so innocent, so tranquil. Seeing him like this made her doubt all of the suspicions she'd had over this past week. She leaned in to kiss his forehead, gently, as she didn't want to wake him. Peacefully unaware, her husband didn't move.

Riding with Omar on the twenty-five minute journey to work, Anji realised she'd have to make an effort to talk to her lovely chauffeur. None of this was his fault and he didn't deserve the silent treatment, so she made polite conversation. Omar only ever spoke when spoken to. His approach to his work was a blessing in a country where having a driver was a requirement for all women. Anji loved him for the comfort he allowed her. He was always on time, always pleasant, and had the soul of an angel. Omar had once admitted he preferred driving Anji to 'Sir Jeff', because she was the nice one. At this news, they had both giggled quietly.

"Please don't tell Sir!" he had laughingly begged more than once, but it was nothing Anji didn't already know. Jeff was a perfectionist and saw errors where others didn't, so it took time for staff to warm to him.

When she arrived at her desk, Anji was relieved to see that Sara wasn't in. The last thing she needed right now was to be micro-managed. She found it impossible to concentrate on her work so she gave up and allowed her mind to wander. Her rose-tinted view of Jeff from this morning was fading and her doubts were creeping back in. Was the scant evidence on his pants enough to end things and break up their family? She'd surely be stupid to consider such a move. This trailing spouse had invested so much into this life she'd built and so had he; there was no way they would both give it up so easily. Perhaps Saudi life was getting to her; Anji could practically feel the compound walls closing in and threatening to suffocate her.

She took a deep breath and called Jeff. "Good morning sunshine!" she chirped, in her cheeriest voice. "Rise and shine... Unless you're up already?"

"What the fuck Anji?!" barked Jeff. "I need to sleep! You woke me up for what?"

Floored by his response, Anji stuttered a half-response. "Oh! I just wanted to..."

"Sorry," he softened his voice suddenly realising Anji was clearly upset. "I worked late yesterday – you understand, don't you babe?"

"It's ok, I know you're busy," she said. "But can you make some time for us soon? We miss you, really miss you." She didn't often resort to emotional blackmail like this but today she felt she had no choice; not just for her sake but for the kids too. They really needed their dad yet some days it felt like he was a figment of their imagination. She was desperate to ask him how the sticky stain had ended up on his trouser zipper, but she knew him well enough to know that blindsiding him would only make him shut down.

"Yes...yes." She sensed him sighing down the line. "This weekend I will make time, we can have lunch and a swim, ok? I'm going back to sleep now."

"Alright. I love you darling." But as Anji replied, she realised he'd already hung up. Her heart sank. She felt empty and pitiful. When did she become this shell with no substance and no soul, merely existing for the sake of her husband and children? Where was the girl with big dreams and ambitions? Whenever she asked herself these questions, a wall came up in her head to try to block the thoughts out. It was just too hard, too painful. Those dreams had been put on the backburner when she met Jeff and got caught in the slipstream of his dreams and ambitions. Now they were so far away that she felt no hope of ever reaching them. She couldn't even bring herself to go back to the School Reunion a couple of years back that would just have been too painful to explain how being a full time Mum and dutiful wife living in a golden cage was so fulfilling.

Anji thought back to the pride she'd felt at her graduation, after her classmates had voted her the student most likely to succeed. There had even been a little crown, placed on her head by the guest speaker. The crown, much like the day itself, was little more than a distant memory; hidden in a dusty box, never to surface again. She'd felt so elated that evening; the recognition fuelling her already lit flame of ambition. She hadn't felt any pressure; just a quiet confidence that she'd make a success of whatever she put her mind to. She had to give herself some credit; she'd devoted her life to being a mother, which was the best job she'd ever had, and she believed that the success of her two amazing children could at least be partly attributed to her. But she was desperate to show her children that she could be and do anything, so that when she told them that *they* could be and do anything, the words held meaning rather than being empty. If only she knew where to start.

Anji thought back to the day when Jeff announced that their lives were about to change for the better. It had come at the perfect time. She'd been dealing with the stress of a full-time job, running a household and having two small kids in crèche. Looking back, she had no idea how she'd managed it, especially since she'd been alone so much. She'd desperately wanted to spend more time with the children, but even with two full-time incomes, the couple had found it hard to make ends meet. The promise of a sweeter life had seduced them, and within a month they had rented their home out, packed up and were on a plane to Thailand to begin their adventure. Somehow, in the 12 years between then and now, the sweetness had become bitterness. She'd been willing and happy to stay at home with the children and sacrifice her career, but she hadn't intended on sacrificing so many other things too. Piece by piece, things had fallen away; firstly her career, now her relationship, following swiftly her self-esteem and self-worth. It had happened so gradually that she hadn't even noticed. If Jeff had said to her 'there's only room for one boss around here' back then, she would have told him, in no uncertain terms, where he could stick it. As it was, he had said this to her more than once in the last few years

– even gone as far as calling her deluded for thinking she could do anything for herself – yet she did nothing for the sake of her children's well being. The gradual erosion of her self-esteem meant that now, when he said these things, she believed him.

CHAPTER 5

Saturday morning arrived with a bang. It was only 7.45am and the first tantrum was already erupting. Max couldn't find his racket for his tennis lesson and Georgie wouldn't let him use hers.

"It's pink Max!" she screamed at her brother. "Your friends will think it's too girly, and Kitt will laugh at you!" She was holding the racket behind her back to keep it away from her brother. Max was about ready to smash her to pieces, let alone the racket, but Anji intervened.

"Get in here now!" she barked. "It's too hot to argue outside, and the neighbours are still asleep!" The kids did as they were told; it was rare for mum to lose her temper, so they knew she must be incredibly serious.

Anji was shattered. She'd barely slept a wink, lying awake all night wondering what Jeff was up to. He hadn't returned from work which filled her with anxiety, although part of her felt relief that he wasn't here to blame her for Max's behaviour, which he inevitably would have. It was already 35 degrees outside, and Max had turned scarlet from a mix of heat and anger. A few of his friends had turned up to meet him for practice and were enjoying the drama that was unfolding before them. Anji decided to deal with Max, knowing there'd be no reasoning with Georgina until she'd calmed down enough to give up her racket.

Anji seized Max by the arm and dragged him outside. As they made their way to the tennis courts, Max's mates trailed closely behind, solemnly silent.

"Mum, let go of my arm," her son whinged. "You're hurting me!" She knew he was embarrassed and self-conscious but if she released him she was sure he'd run off, so she gripped the fleshy part of his upper arm a little tighter. This made him try and pull away more, and suddenly they were having a tug of war with the whole of his arm.

"Why do you have to ruin my life?!" snapped Max. "You've already ruined Karen's – isn't that enough for you?" Anji stopped still in her tracks. What the fuck? Where had that come from? She knew Max was just retaliating to embarrass his mother in the same way she was embarrassing him, but this was a low blow. The worst part of it was that it meant her son had been infected by the gossip which was spreading around the campus. Still speechless and frozen to the spot, she noticed her son's friend Alex standing there, firsts clenched and giving her daggers. Ah, it made sense now. Alex was Karen's son. She felt a misplaced sense of relief that Max had heard something from Alex rather than from somewhere else. She loosened her grip on Max's arm and he struggled free. Anji turned to Alex and their eyes met for a second before he quickly looked away.

"Alex, tell me what's going on will you?" she said, attempting to sound calm and reasonable. Alex was sullen-faced, his blue eyes focused on the ground. She walked slowly over to him. The boy was slim, and was clearly his Father's son. He hadn't taken his gaze away from the floor, and Anji's gut reaction was to pull him in for a bear hug. She could feel his shoulder blades jutting out; his body seemed frail and stiff. She tried to lift his head so he'd look at her, desperate to explain that it wasn't her who was ruining his mum's life, but Alex turned his face away and wriggled away from her. She knew it was best to let him go. The poor kid was already suffering and didn't need more anguish. These pre-teen years were so important; kids struggling to find their place and connect with the world, especially third culture children. She hoped this drama wasn't going to send him over the edge. Having attended the tween talk at school, she knew all the positive parenting tips and made a mental note to look out for Alex as well as Max.

"Listen boys," Anji set out to explain. "Gossip happens around here all the time. Alex, your mum and dad are going through a rough patch. I can assure you though, I have nothing to do with it. If you need someone to talk to, I'm always here. You know that, don't you Alex?" None of them raised their faces. Max's eyes were like pools of pain and it hit home to Anji, the severity of all this gossip and how it affected everyone, not just the bored women looking for a pastime. Realising that she wasn't going to get a response, Anji looked at her watch and said,

"You're all late for your lesson, come on." They continued their walk to the tennis courts in silence.

Anji managed to scrounge a racket from Kitt, the kids' elderly tennis coach. In his day he had been quite the star – seeded number one in his home country of the Philippines. The kids loved him, as did the parents; he had the patience of a bloody saint. In England he'd be seen as a minor celebrity, but in the Philippines he was past his best so was put out to pasture, which is how he ended up in Saudi, living out his retirement in the harsh heat and teaching a bunch of spoiled brats.

Having delivered the boys safely to their lesson, Anji turned to leave, but not before reminding Max it was family day so he needed to head straight home. Her son grimaced as she tousled his hair with a goodbye; it would seem Max wasn't looking forward to spending time with his loved ones today. As Anji walked home she felt the day getting hotter by the second. Her head was swimming with this morning's events, until she heard some faint shouting in the background, which brought her back into the present with a harsh bump. She carried on without looking round, until she heard a distinct cry of, 'Home wrecker!'

Anji closed her eyes and breathed deeply. Sensing that the sound was coming from the direction she was heading in, she instead started marching towards the small Swedish school with trepidation, not knowing what she would find. The shouting got louder, and she heard a different voice this time, clearly calling out 'Dick sucker! Cock lover!" followed by hysterical laughter.

Anji stopped and turned towards the shouting. Three kids, about ten years of age, were laughing their heads off. The second they saw her approach, the trio took off at speed, and she looked on helplessly as they ran away from her and out of the school playground. She stood zero chance of catching up with them, especially in this heat. And if she could, what would she do? Beat them within an inch of their lives? She didn't think so. Anji felt her shoulders sink. Deflated, she realised she'd never find the parents of these little punks, and was ashamed that these children – who could barely know the meaning of what they'd been shouting – had aired her dirty laundry right in front of her.

Tears pricked at her eyes as she watched the kids' backs disappear into the distance. They couldn't care less if Anji has a home wrecker or not. They'd obviously heard their parents – and the rest of the compound – talking, and thought it would be funny to shout it out loud. And then it suddenly hit her; her poor kids were going to be ridiculed and bullied over this shit. *No they're fucking not.* She puffed out her chest, raised herself up to her full height and held her head high. She was ready for the fight.

CHAPTER 6

As soon as Anji walked through her front door, she grabbed her phone and dialled Lily. A red mist was forming and she was about to blow. Her friend picked up.

"Lily, I'm sorry to call so early, I hope I didn't wake you," she said in a breathy tone, "but did you find out who told Karen? Please say you did. This is just torture." It was obvious that she had woken her friend, as Lily's words were half spoken, half yawned.

"No nothing yet. But don't worry, I'll find out. Leave it with me." Anji felt a sense of annoyance mixed with desperation at Lily's flippant words.

"Please Lily, this can't carry on. A bunch of ten-year-olds just called me a cock sucker… this has gone too far!" Anji hung up without a goodbye, fingernails clawing at her lips in anxiety. Now the kids knew about it, what could she do? She had to think quickly; she couldn't have Max and Georgina implicated in the gossip. Anji had to protect them from the madding crowd. Her heart sank as she realised that it had come to a point where she'd have to share the story with Jeff. It was simply getting too big for her to handle alone. If she didn't tell him he would find out from someone else, if he hadn't already. Despite her anger and confused feelings towards Jeff right now, she knew her knight would rescue her. A smile spread across Anji's face; an instant feeling of relief that her husband would be able to fix things. He was brilliant at sorting out this kind of stuff. She planned to speak to him once he was home from work and decided she would need some help to ensure he was on her side.

She went to her dressing room, pulled out her Burberry bikini and tentatively tried it on. She stood in front of her full-length mirror feeling, if she was honest, pretty bloody pleased with herself. The bikini hadn't fit her in years, but after her recent weight loss it fit like a glove. Her mind flashed back to being pregnant with Georgie when Jeff had commented on her putting on a few pounds. He'd said she looked like the Michelin man. He'd loved her fuller breasts, but laughed at the size of her derrière. From barely being able to keep his hands off her tits, to patting her arse and calling her 'fluffy butt', a hormonal and unsure Anji was left completely confused about what was and what wasn't acceptable when it came to pregnancy weight gain.

With her new – inadvertent – slimmer figure, the bikini clung to her body in all the right places. Rubbing some tanning oil into her décolletage and legs for a little shimmer, she slicked on some lippy, tied a bandana around her hair and added a cute Missoni beach dress. Glancing in the mirror, Anji immediately felt pleased with herself. She didn't actually like this look on herself, if she was honest, but she knew Jeff would be pleased with her svelte body. That seemed to be all she did these days - try to please other people – and look where it had got her. She was still the centre of a scandal which had nothing to do with her.

An hour after she'd expected Jeff home, Anji called his phone a few times, but there was no answer. His 'last seen' on WhatsApp had been turned off, which was normal, and she figured he must be with the hotel owner or a VIP. This was quite normal so she wasn't too worried, and she silenced the tiny voice of doubt that popped into her mind. She busied herself waiting for the kids to come home, keeping her phone close by, waiting for the heads up from Jeff so she knew when to head to the compound restaurant where they would meet for lunch, as was their tradition on family days.

Max and Georgie had now arrived back, their little faces red and flushed. The heat was as hot as hell fire, but Riyadh's lack of humidity made the temperatures a little more bearable. As she greeted her children, Anji clocked her phone light up. She glanced at the screen: 'Can't explain now but will miss lunch'. Anji went from feeling a million dollars to feeling as small and insignificant as a cockroach. Today's confident, fierce Anji shrunk back to *stupid old Anji* from yesterday. She hated to admit it, but she needed Jeff to make her feel whole again.

She punched her fingers into the screen, using capitals to make her point. 'NO WORRIES, WE WILL WAIT FOR YOU. WHAT TIME CAN WE EXPECT YOU?'

'DON'T WAIT,' came the reply. He was typing in capitals, playing her at her own game. She fell backwards, sinking into an armchair in the hallway, grateful for the cooling air con as her skin flared in embarrassment and confusion. How could she have been so foolish?

Anji threw down her phone and stomped through to the kitchen, grateful the kids had disappeared upstairs to their en suite showers to cool off after their tennis practice. Heading for the fridge, she flipped her hair over shoulder, adjusting her bandana before reaching into the refrigerator to pull out an organic chicken. She didn't want to cook in this heat but, by God, she would make a beautiful home-cooked meal for her husband's return even if it choked her. The irony of her response was lost on her as she went on in a passive-aggressive auto-pilot. Sod the restaurant and the stares of the other diners at the 'table for three'. She would make the best damned roast chicken he had ever tasted.

Knife in one hand and raw bird in the other, she attempted to free it from the string ties on its footless legs. The kids loved her mum's recipe, somehow juicy and tender like back home, despite the bird being reared in Saudi. She began making incisions into the chunky flesh so she could stuff the secret spice mix in. This special mixture had been a closely-guarded family recipe for generations, so Anji's mum had claimed.

A wave of hate washed over Anji as she slashed at the bird's skin. A memory flashed in her mind of a book she'd borrowed from the English library, all about serial killers. The lines about Albert Fish caught in her throat: "I choked her to death, then cut her into small pieces so I could take the meat to my room, cook, and eat it..." Anji's breathing felt both laboured and rushed at the same time, and a wave of dizziness came over her. Before she knew it, the chicken lay slaughtered on the cold marble worktop, deader than it had been when she'd taken it out of the fridge. Bile rose in her throat and she gagged, spitting it out into the sink as she surveyed the scene around her. The punctured, bloody carcass had been subjected to a frenzied attack. There were chunks of flesh splattered up the splash backs, streaks of bloody chicken juices down the front of the cupboards and across her sundress. Resting her hands on the edge of the units and pressing her weight into the surface, she felt her head spin as she took a few deep breaths to steady herself.

What the hell had she done? She had no recollection of what had just happened. There was a fine line between sanity and insanity, and looking at the kitchen surfaces Anji found herself wondering if she was capable of murder. She had terrified herself, clueless as to what had come over her. With shaking hands, she gathered the mess into a tea towel, scooping chunks of flesh off the worktop, and dumped it all into the bin before the kids could see what she'd done. For good measure she pulled out the bin bag, tying it off frantically before running out of the house with it and dumping it in the outhouse bins. She didn't even want the housemaid to see the hideous mess. Scrubbing at her hands in the sink, she took some deep breaths to compose herself before calling up the stairs: "Lunch at the restaurant kids – let's go!" She needed to get out and see people, even if they weren't quite up to seeing her just yet.

CHAPTER 7

On the way to the restaurant, Anji's heart was hammering in her chest. *I'm in for a coronary,* she thought to herself. The cracks were beginning to show, and she could feel the pain of them intensely. Today would be really busy in the restaurant, with it being family day for everyone, and the thought of the crowds made Anji want to turn back towards the house, right back to the remains of the corpse she'd just hidden in the bin. She wondered if she should give it a burial; it was the least she could do, considering the macabre, grisly end the poor bird had faced. Maybe that would help give her some closure and she'd feel a little better. In reality, she realised that this train of thoughts only made her sanity even more questionable.

The kids hadn't once asked about their dad's whereabouts since finishing their tennis lessons. It was a relief; no extra lies to pollute their little heads.

"Let's go the supermarket way," Anji insisted. Going that way meant they could enter via the rear of the restaurant. The back door seemed appropriate for a could-be murderer.

"No way," whined Max. "I saw my friends on the other side." She didn't want to tell the kids she was too much of a coward to use the main door in. She wanted to use the back door and scurry in unnoticed, like a frightened rat. Not wanting to cause another scene with Max, she swallowed her fear, took a long deep breath into her gut and reached for the door handle, opening the door quietly and letting herself in unheard. Her discretion was for nothing, however, as the kids couldn't stay quiet and called out for their friends straightaway. The Indian waiter greeted Anji and her children warmly.

"Hello Miss Anji!" beamed Mohammad. He knew everything about everyone on the compound, and of course he was in the know about the latest gossip, but his gleaming white smile hid any hint of judgement he might be feeling. Stepping into the restaurant, Anji decided to leave her sunglasses on. The glares of every man, woman and child turning to look at her were blinding. Everyone wanted an eyeful of the compound's resident home wrecker. She felt like screaming 'Fuck you all, I'm guilty! Are you happy now?' But she didn't, because she had the children with her. And besides, she wasn't guilty of anything. Nothing they knew about, anyway.

Mohammad wafted about, making polite conversation about how lucky Anji was to get the last empty table. Anji walked with her head down, avoiding any eye contact or conflict. She could still hear their whispers all around her and could feel the other diners' stares burning into the back of her head and as she went to take her seat at the table, Anji felt a tap on her shoulder. As she looked up, fearing the worst, she saw it was Bonnie. Bonnie was a robust little lady in her sixties, who leaned in closely to embrace her friend.

"Hi Anji! I haven't seen you in a while!" Anji was taken aback by the display of affection and felt her face redden as everyone still had one eye on her.

"You'll never guess where I've been?" Bonnie didn't wait for a response. "That's right, back to the States! My daughter had a little baby boy so I went home to help her out," she explained in her Southern drawl. "He is so handsome he looks just like Grandpa Jack over there".

Anji quickly did the maths and realised Bonnie was only talking to her because she hadn't been back in Saudi Arabia long enough to have heard the news.

"Wow, congratulations!" Anji replied, acting politely but knowing full well that Bonnie would know everything within a few minutes. "How is the new mum doing?" She smiled, still reeling from the rare sight of a friendly face.

"Bonnie, Bonnie! Over here!" Daniela called from across the crowded room. "You're having lunch here with us," she said, patting the empty seat next to her. "Got lots to tell you!" Daniela caught Anji's eye. Her lips pursed and one eyebrow cranked up, as if to say, 'we're going to tell her everything, just you wait'.

"Sorry Anji, I'll catch you later," smiled Bonnie as she headed over towards the table. Anji's hopes sank as she realised that this was the way things were going to play out from now on. She may as well just place an advert on the compound bulletin board, or maybe even in the main lobby:

Professional Home wrecker
Anji, experienced home wrecker available for rent. Can break up any home – no job too big or too small! For an extra fee, can also cut husband up into pieces and erase any trace with a tea towel. Tea towel included with sale.

Nose diving back down to earth, Anji gave their food order to Mohammad, who was waiting patiently with a smile, palms pressed together and ready to help. Anji watched Max and Georgie run off towards their friends.

"Call us when the food comes please Mum!" Anji felt lost as the kids disappeared; they would have kept her distracted from the anxious feeling in the pit of her stomach. The poor kids didn't deserve to be used that way though, thought Anji with a pang of guilt. Fumbling in her bag, she pulled out her phone to keep her busy while she waited for her Fish and Chips to arrive.

Unlocking her phone and beginning the mindless scroll through Facebook, Anji felt her jaw drop to the table as she opened the app. What the fuck? 'Anji Harris is a home wrecking whore' read the caption alongside the image; a photo of Anji taken on her fortieth birthday. Instead of seeing the glamorous shot and being reminded of the happiness she'd felt at her surprise birthday party, Anji saw the image plastered with the word BITCH in a bold, white font.

Obviously someone had taken the photo from her own profile, doctored it and used it as their own profile pic, tagging every one of Anji's hundreds of online friends in the process. Her shaking hands fumbled to click on the profile where the photo came from but found that they'd changed their own screen name, so she had no idea who this impostor was. Anji felt her heart bang in her chest and her airways closing as she spotted the only comment beneath the photo. 'Who is this? Do I know you?' it read. Anji's mother wrote it. It was the last thing Anji remembered before everything went black.

CHAPTER 8

Anji was aware of people around her. She could hear a gentle beeping sound but couldn't quite place it. She tried to open her eyelids, but they felt heavy as lead. Focusing all of her energy, she managed to peel her eyes open, one at a time. From her vantage point, lying down, she could see a state of the art television, a small cabinet and one chair. She could smell antiseptic. The panic started to rise inside her as she realised where she was, and the gentle beeping she could hear became louder and more urgent.

A flurry of nurses came bounding into the room. One of the nurses – a stern-looking lady who must've been in her seventies – was tapping something into the monitor screen. In the UK she'd have retired a long ago, but here she was, still working her socks off. *Good for her*, thought Anji.

"Relax dear, just relax...We don't want another episode, do we?" Her voice was softer than her features. Anji tried to push herself off the bed in a panic but found that couldn't.

"Why aren't my legs working?" she demanded, frantically, "I want to know why my legs won't –"

"Calm down now, calm down." The older nurse laid her hands on Anji, firmly but reassuringly. "We gave you a sedative dear, a fairly high dose. It will wear off soon enough dear." *If she calls me dear one more time,* thought Anji. Though there'd be no ass kicking, since her legs didn't work.

"I just need to know if my kids are ok," pleaded Anji, her voice wavering.

"Ok, ok, dear I will get your phone out and you can call...." Anji practically snatched her mobile out of the lady's hands but found herself fiddling with her phone, almost unsure how to work it. Initially confused as to who she should call first, instinct kicked in and she remembered to dial Jeff. The phone rang and rang; no answer. She scrolled down and dialled the next person she thought of.

"Lily!" she panicked "I'm in hospital. Have you –?"

"Anji, it's ok." Anji was relieved to hear her friend's voice on the line, calm and controlled. "Max and Georgina are with me. I told them they will see you tomorrow. What happened with you?"

"I was hoping you could tell me; I can't remember a damn thing. Maybe it's the medication they gave me?" Anji lied. She could remember everything, but she didn't have the energy to explain. She'd be checking her phone to remind herself of the post as soon as she hung up the call, and she was pretty sure Lily would already know about it anyway. She'd probably even been tagged in it.

"You've lost so much weight. You must eat, Anji. If this has happened because of this ridiculous situation then it's time to move on. I'll talk to you when I see you." Lily seemed genuinely concerned and Anji felt grateful towards her friend.

"Could you bring me my toothbrush and stuff later on? And kiss the kids for me please and tell them not to worry. I will see them tomorrow." She finished with a little white lie. "I am feeling better."

That was bullshit, she felt horrendous and the guilt was killing her, despite the fact that she had no reason to feel guilty. She wondered if Karen was feeling the same, since she'd condemned Anji to ridicule and gossip over a crime that she'd never even committed.

By seven o'clock, Anji still hadn't had any visitors or any phone calls. The nurses were wonderful but they weren't her friends, and she needed a familiar, kind face. She felt so alone. As she wriggled down in her bed to get comfortable for a nap, she picked up on a male voice. She opened one eye and saw an olive-skinned, honey-eyed Adonis in a white coat. Anji wondered if it was just her doped-up brain playing tricks on her and giving her something beautiful to focus on amongst her train-wreck of a life right now.

He wasn't a typical kind of gorgeous, or the kind of sleek, smooth man Anji would usually be drawn to. He was rugged looking, with a five o'clock shadow and tired eyes, but with some kind of aura about him. It was mesmerising.

"Hello, I'm Doctor Hassan," he said, smiling right at her, as the skin around his eyes crinkled. Anji felt a sudden self-consciousness; what sort of state was her hair in, and did she need a touch of blush? She pretended to rub her cheeks, secretly pinching them in hope it would give her a little colour.

"So, you had an anxiety attack. Do you know what that is?" She was still hanging onto his last word, her eyes following the shapes his mouth made as he spoke. Was it the drugs? She hadn't even realised he'd asked a question and was waiting for an answer. Anji felt herself blushing and blinked to clear her head in a bid to regain some clarity and dignity.

"I'm sorry, this wasn't in your notes," the doctor apologised. "Are you mute and communicating with me through your eyes? I wasn't told this, please forgive me." Doctor Hassan laughed and Anji was relieved to see he wasn't being serious. Those eye crinkles were back and Anji felt her insides melt a little. "Ok," he teased. "Blink once for yes, and twice for no."

Anji mouthed self consciously "Ok" with a crooked grin. It was a poor attempt but she didn't want her efforts to go unnoticed.

"Ok that's better. So, an anxiety attack is an episode of shortness of breath, tight chest, nausea, dizziness and sometimes even passing out in severe cases. It's always short-lived and usually brought on by worry – stressful situations basically." He looked at Anji to check she understood before continuing. "The main thing is to try to understand what triggers it. Then you can avoid it or learn what to do when you feel it happening."

She could have listened to his voice forever. It was sweet and warm, and she was feeling embarrassed because she was actually turned on. Was she that desperate for some attention? In truth, she'd never so much as looked at another man since meeting Jeff. Trying to rationalise her thoughts, Anji dismissed her strange feelings and blamed them on the medication she'd been given. It would pass.

Stifling a yawn and faking tiredness, she hoped the doctor would understand and leave her and her murky thoughts in peace.

"Well my name is Doctor Hassan and this is my card. The hospital number is on there. I'll pass by tomorrow morning – if everything is ok and your vitals are back to normal, we can send you home don't worry."

"Thank you doctor," Anji could feel herself blush. "Goodnight."

The very moment he left the room, Anji's fingers started to venture beneath the bed sheets. But she suddenly thought better of it; pleasuring herself in the hospital wasn't a good idea, and seemed more than a little sordid. Plus, what if there were cameras in her room? She could see it now – social media would be plastered with candid videos of lonely Anji masturbating on her sickbed. Thinking of the shame, she pulled her hands out of the blanket and placed her arms stiffly on either side of her body. She prayed this would be nothing but a weird dream when she woke up in the morning.

As the minutes passed and there was no sign of any visitors, and certainly no sign of Jeff, Anji started to feel low sinking in her own self pity. Telling everyone and herself that she was fine when inside she felt fucked up suffering in silence. Stuck in Saudi, no real friends, her mum thousands of miles away and all on her own in a hospital bed. She wanted out. She felt ready. After all, Jeff had made his fortune, and with his boss the Sheikh being so generous, she was sure he'd leave with a brilliant reference and perhaps even a golden handshake. He could leave. He wouldn't need a job immediately thanks to all those new zeros at the end of his bank balance, and they could all relocate together. She'd had enough of life in Saudi Arabia. As a woman, you had so few rights compared to life in the West. The idea of leaving excited her and ignited a fire in her belly. She decided she would propose it to Jeff as soon as she saw him.

Finally, just before nine o'clock Lily tiptoed in with a tiny bag of belongings; a toothbrush, some toothpaste and a pair of pyjamas. She felt a little disheartened at the lack of anything personal or any little treats to make her feel better.

"Hey hey," she whispered as she kissed Anji's cheek. She gave no explanation for being late, but she supposed that she had been busy looking after the kids. "The children are great, don't worry. If you're still here tomorrow, I'll bring them after school."

"I really am so grateful to have you, thank you," Anji acknowledged tearfully as a croak in her throat threatened to erupt and burst into tears. "Did you happen to speak to Jeff?" Anji probed.

"No. Adam has tried to call him but he must be with the Sheikh. No one has seen him and he wasn't at work today," explained Lily.

Lily held Anji's hand, squeezing it tightly to reassure her. "Look, don't worry, please," she implored. "No one cares about you or me; how you might be feeling. They care about a good story. You're the headlines right now. Jeff is a good man; you know he wouldn't destroy everything by having an affair. And he knows that even being in a car with a woman who's not a relative can get you deported. He's smarter than that. And believe me when I say he loves you."

"I know," sighed Anji. "You're right. Maybe it's time to leave this place, a sign. I'm just trying to make sense of all this, that's all. We were never meant to be here forever. Jeff told us two years at most when he took the job."

Lily stood up to leave and kissed Anji's forehead like she would a sick child. The small act of kindness brought her a little comfort.

Sometime later, though she had no idea how long, the nurse came by to give Anji a sleeping pill. *It must be night time*, she thought, squinting towards the window. She had no idea how she had passed the time today as it was all a bit of a blur. She gulped the pill down with a glass of water. No way would she be going into work tomorrow; she couldn't face the stares and she still felt very wobbly. Before she drifted off to sleep, she sent a text to her boss, Sara: 'I won't be in tomorrow, sorry. Not feeling well'. She had barely pressed the send button as her heavy-lidded eyes closed for the night.

CHAPTER 9

"Good morning!" His husky voice vibrated as the room filled with early morning light. He pulled open the curtains and moved towards the bed. Up close, his eyes were like honey; a soft hazel brown with flecks of green. The sunlight bounced off her naked torso and glinted off the white teeth in his smiling mouth. He was ready and aroused, planting sensual kisses on her breastbone. One touch from him and its intoxicating. Hormones were running riot, as the temperature in the room seemed to increase. She yearned for him between her legs, but he was in no hurry. He was a slow eater, taking pleasure with every bite. He made his way down her chest, nuzzling between her breasts, biting each nipple on his way down, feeling the rest of the way with his fingers feeling her clitoris pulsating away his finger tips are electric. Her back arches in anticipation. She was wild she loved the feeling of being the centre of attention. Entering her, he grinds away managing to get deeper and deeper with each and every thrust moving together at his rhythm. Anji feeling the full intensity allows herself to scream in untamed, unadulterated pleasure.

"Hello – good morning I said," the doctor repeated. "Your pulse has regulated and all your vital signs are back to normal." Anji's mood deflated as she gradually opened her eyes and realised that the best session of her life had all been a phenomenal dream. She felt ashamed that all it had taken was for a man to show her a glimmer of humanity for her mind to flip to imagining herself in bed with him, dirtying the sheets. As if she didn't have enough to feel shit about already, she now felt disgusted with herself, hoping she hadn't been moaning sensually in her sleep while he'd been in the room waiting for her to stir. With that thought in mind her face burned, the blood rushing to her cheeks as fast as a freaking freight train. She glanced at him to see if he looked as embarrassed as she felt. There was no way he could possibly know about the dream, but still she felt like she'd been caught red handed.

"You're definitely well enough to go home. I do think stress was the main cause. I hope in the future you can manage the triggers, before you have another full-blown attack."

Still wet from her dream and unable to look him in the eye, she patted her blanket straight. Doctor Hassan stared at her as she flattened the sheets. He was waiting for a response, which he soon realised, was never going to come.

"I think you should come back in a week," he proposed, "just for a check-up. You might have some questions once you've had time to digest this situation. Don't underestimate the gravity of it." He called the nurse through, asking for the paperwork to discharge Anji, and she let out a trembling sigh as Doctor Hassan left the room.

Anji turned on her phone and was elated to find 23 missed calls from Jeff. Her initial joy soon turned to anger as she realised that they'd all been from this morning. He hadn't tried to contact her at all yesterday; what kind of man doesn't notice his wife and children aren't at home for a whole night? Her immediate reaction was to call him back, but then she thought she'd let him sweat it out. She wouldn't call him back, even if it meant she'd pay the price for it later. Right now, she didn't really give a shit how pissed off he was.

After composing herself in the en suite bathroom and having secured her ride home with Omar, she pulled her Missoni dress over her aching body. She wanted to leave unnoticed, but realised she had no Abaya to cover herself with to leave the ward. Anji really wanted to leave quietly, rather than being plastered across all the Saudi TV channels in a gaudy coloured mini dress, it could actually happen. She asked a passing nurse, who gave her a paper cloak, which she donned to cover her modesty. It didn't do much for blending in; being bright green, but it would have to do until she got into the car.

Anji handed all the necessary documents to the front counter, wishing she could just sit in the waiting room and let someone else check her out. But as no one had come to take her home, she had to do it all herself. With her head aching and no energy, she rubbed her temples and struggled to stay upright, resting her elbows on the desk and closing her eyes.

"Insurance or cash?" barked the receptionist on the other side of the counter, stunning Anji out of her semi-sleep. Without opening her eyes, she handed him her credit card, which she had prepared earlier.

"Insurance or cash?" he demanded again.

"What do you think, if I've handed you my credit card?" she counterclaimed, her tone snappy and cantankerous. She wasn't used to handling stuff like this on her own. Jeff was always so concerned and authoritative in matters like this, so Anji had just let him get on with it. Even though it usually bugged her, she wished he were here now to take over dealing with all the paperwork and payments, when all she wanted to do was head back to her room and lie under the crisp white sheets. Anji restrained her urge to shout at the Indian receptionist, like she really wanted to, and instead she took a deep breath. He was just doing his job, and the poor guy was probably overworked and underpaid, like so many workers in the Middle East.

"Thank you, madam," he said as he handed her back her card. "I truly hope you feel better soon, have a nice day." She took a mental note of his name, suddenly feeling guilty for her snappiness towards him.

Anji was making her way to the revolving doors when she felt a hand on her shoulder. Spinning around, she came face to face with the handsome doctor. Her insides did a full 360. The pang of shame came back to her from earlier. She wondered if she was desperate, falling for the first guy in months to show her any attention. She scolded herself, reminding herself that he was only doing it as part of his job.

"Sorry to make you jump. I just wanted to say you can call me anytime. I mean it." He gave her a small smile and an understanding nod, almost as if he had known the contents of her dream.

"Thank you," she managed, her voice a tiny squeak, as she went through the doors and felt a surge of relief to see the lovely Omar waiting for her.

CHAPTER 10

Anji languished in bed, drained after a morning of chaotic thoughts zooming around her mind; of the kids, of Jeff, of the Doctor unbelievably, the hope of leaving Saudi... Lily had popped by not long after Omar had dropped her home, bringing a beautiful pot roast round. It smelled amazing, reminding her of Sunday roasts in the UK, and making her even more homesick. Lily had helped Anji up to bed, explaining she'd see to the kids today and not to worry. A couple of sleeping pills had knocked her into cloud cuckoo land, and she had no sense of time as she drifted off.

An intense pressure on her legs woke her abruptly. Was she dreaming or awake? It felt so surreal. She yelped out in pain, fumbling for the light switch before she realised it was just Jeff sitting on her legs with his full weight, completely unaware, and was trying to pull off his shoes sloppily. Extricating herself from under his load, she made a fuss of rubbing her legs. Jeff swung his head around and the stench of cigarettes and whisky hit Anji full force. "Where the fuck were you?" he slurred. "I tried to call you!" He grabbed for her arm, raising his voice: "I'm talking to you!"

Usually Anji kept her emotions firmly in check, especially when Jeff had had a few too many, but this time she couldn't hold back.

"What do you want? An obedient wife who speaks only when she is spoken to?" Anji could practically feel the bloody boiling point in her veins. "When I call you, you never answer! I don't say a word because I –"

Before she could finish her sentence, he brought his fist to rest on her lips. Almost in slow motion, the fractured punch didn't make contact but the backs of his hairy fingers perched on her mouth, ready to block any more words tumbling out. He hadn't hit her; he was threatening her. Leaving his hand in place, he brought his forehead to hers and looked straight into her eyes. She struggled not to show fear, but her heart was racing and she felt adrenaline coursing through her body. She could sense the wild rage that was pulsing through his. Spit formed at the corners of his mouth while his teeth clenched and his face got redder and redder. He didn't look like Jeff. He looked like a monster. For the first time in their fifteen-year marriage, she was petrified.

"You listen to me!" he bellowed, "If I call, you answer. That's the fucking rule around here. If you call and I don't answer, that's not my problem. But if I call and you don't answer, that *is* my problem!"

Anji tried to make her voice sound stable but she could feel her throat quiver as she spoke, his fist still by her mouth. "You're talking absolute shit. You're drunk – how the hell did you get home?"

"I drove." He said matter-of-factly, almost gloating.

"You're crazy, drink driving in Saudi! What a joke you're becoming," she berated him bravely. "Did you even know that I was in hospital? I could have died, do you know that? You never answer your phone anymore," she sniffled, struggling to keep her emotions from spilling out.

"Stop the fucking over-dramatic actress effort with me! You're becoming a liability. I called the hospital when you didn't answer *your* phone and – did I really hear them right? – a friggin' anxiety attack. I almost pissed myself laughing." He scowled at his wife. "How precious you are! That shit has to stop right now, you hear me? Or I'll have you on the next plane home away from my kids."

Anji reeled in shock. She grabbed the sides of his face, pulling his bloodshot eyes in line with her tear-filled ones. "Where is the man who was my protector, the man I adored and admired? Where is he?" She was blubbering now, tears streaming down her face. She couldn't hold it in any longer. She'd never felt so alone and abandoned as she had last night. But as the words fell from her mouth, she felt like a huge weight had been lifted. The rock that had dwelled deep in her chest for the last few weeks was instantaneously hoisted out. She wanted him to spill the beans, to tell him everything.

Jeff pulled himself away from her and stormed out of the bedroom, reeking of booze and unable to handle his wife's emotional outburst. Anji was still crying, and shaking from the adrenaline surging through her body. She sat waiting for him to return, and as the minutes crept by her sadness turned to anger. After ten minutes had passed and he hadn't returned, she couldn't hold her rage in any longer and decided to go and find him, to finish what she had started. She went to go downstairs as she heard a loud snort from the spare room. The door was wide open and Jeff was lying face down on the bed - he had passed out. The anguish bubbled up inside her as she thought of how unfair this was; she still had things to say, things to resolve, yet he was able to forget everything and sleep through her misery. Tears prickled her eyes again, but this time they were tears of frustration and resentment. She went downstairs and grabbed a bottle of wine and a glass from her secret stash, then stormed back up to her bedroom with them. On the way, she checked on the kids and found they were fast asleep and blissfully unaware of all this – thank god.

What had she ever done wrong? Anji sat up in bed, a glass of Sauvignon Blanc in hand, and wondered where it had all gone wrong. She'd always tried to please him, supporting him in his every endeavour. With everything she did, she consulted him first and loved to hear his advice, even if she didn't always like what he had to say. She was totally selfless when it came to Jeff. She'd realised early on in their relationship that if Jeff was happy, everyone else was allowed to be. It was Anji's job to keep the household a contented, balanced environment – it was her number one priority in life. So what had happened? Hugging her knees to her chest, she stashed the empty glass and bottle under the bed and hunkered down into a foetal position. The only thing she could do now was cry herself to sleep once more.

She was woken by the sound of the shower. The salt from her tears had half-glued her eyes together. She fumbled for the alarm to check the time: she still had one hour before she had to wake the kids. The bathroom door creaked open and Anji sensed Jeff was trying his best not to make any noise. She heard him creep around; the hairs on her bare skin standing to attention, worrying what his next move would be. Was he still angry, or had he forgotten everything in his stupor of the night before? Anji kept her eyes closed, pretending to be asleep. He slowly crept back into bed and his hands began feeling for her breasts. She clenched her eyes tightly shut. She was still so upset with him that the thought of him touching her repulsed her, yet at the same time she yearned for him. He tugged at her t-shirt, trying to pull it over her head. Sensing he was struggling, Anji roused herself from her pretend sleep to help him remove the unflattering, baggy top. He tossed it on the floor, using his fingertips to send shockwaves of desire through her body. His mouth and tongue were hard and greedy, kissing her nipples and navel. She enjoyed the warmth of his body on top of her. Anji breathed in to reveal her svelte belly and slightly protruding ribs, as his tongue moved southwards.

"Oh my god!" she shuddered, reaching orgasm almost immediately. It seemed one lick and all was forgiven. She loved the power he had over her in the bedroom. As he pulled her legs back, he penetrated deeply – every inch of him inside her. With every thrust her worries disappeared. She felt herself recharged and, with a current surging through their bodies, they came together. As he released himself she felt the warmth of his seed inside her and for a few moments she considered a baby could be a good idea. Lots of women in Saudi who were over 40 seemed to be having babies, since they couldn't work and had little else to do. Maybe she'd mention it once she'd thought about it a little bit longer.

"I love you Jeff," she mumbled to him. She so desperately wanted to hear him say it back, but he never replied. Maybe he hadn't heard. "I love you," she repeated more loudly, as he rose from the bed and headed to the bathroom.

"I love your pussy!" he smiled at her and laughed.

His words were bitter sweet but, still tingling from her orgasms, she smiled. So he still loved her pussy. She watched him walk butt naked, pondering how she could ever live without this man.

Anji made a promise to herself that life was going to get better from today. It wasn't her fault that Karen and her husband weren't happy. Jeff had just made love to her and, of course, he loved her too – he was just stressed from work. She was going to try and be a much better wife; the kind that her husband would be proud of. She was glad Jeff didn't know anything about the accusations. He didn't need the added headache, and she would certainly keep it that way for now.

CHAPTER 11

"This is a very important account for us," Sara explained. "We have to be the main provider or we'll lose it." Sara and Anji were in the office chatting about potential candidates for key positions in a prominent bank. Time was of the essence and Sara's face clouded with seriousness as they discussed applicants' character traits and experience. "We don't need anyone with anxiety!" Sara cackled before letting out a snort.

Anji looked at her boss sideways. Was that a dig? It must've been – Sara couldn't look Anji in the eye. She was focusing on the CVs in front of her, but Anji could tell she wasn't reading them; her eyes darted up and down the pages whilst she subtly tried to catch Anji's reaction.

"Who told you?" Anji demanded as she looked at Sara.

"Jeff told me," Sara said, matter-of-factly. "But only because he was so worried about you," she stumbled over her words, lowering her voice.

"Well, if you know so much, why didn't you ask how I was?" Anji was gutted. Her boss had known about the anxiety attack all along.

The air in the meeting room hung heavy with silence. Anji's brain was working like a sewing machine; small needle pricks of thought coming together to sew up the story. Only the bobbin didn't have any thread on it. Why the hell would Jeff call Sara when he never even called his own wife anymore? The thought hurt Anji, so she blurted out the question, sounding pained.

"Why would Jeff call you about me going into hospital?"

"Don't you think that's what any worried husband who cares about his wife would do?" retorted Sara. "You are one very lucky woman in my opinion."

"Noted, thanks for your opinion!" Anji was seething. "But the workplace isn't somewhere I want to discuss my personal life." declared Anji. She shuffled a CV in a pile of papers, "As you can see, the candidate has confirmed he is in all-round perfect health!" She knew she was being overly defensive, but she wasn't ready to share any details about her relationship with anyone, let alone with Sara. Anji felt like she was becoming irrational, and knew she couldn't afford another episode. Jeff had made his concerns around that very clear. She remembered the lovely doctor telling her to find a bag to breathe into before she found herself back in a hospital bed. She felt her pulse banging in her ear as loud as a jackhammer. "I'll call the candidate now," she mumbled; a perfect excuse to exit out of the room where it felt like the walls were drawing in around her.

She sat quietly, trying to compose herself enough to call the potential candidate without losing it. Anji was absolutely positive that Sara was watching her every move. She kept replaying their conversation in her head, kicking herself for losing it and making herself look a complete and utter fool. She scrunched up her face, rubbed her eyes and pushed all the weird thoughts out of her head as she picked up the receiver.

Anji expressed her feelings to Lily later that day as they sat by the pool. She explained how she'd sacrificed so much to let Jeff progress in his career, knowing Lily would understand; after all, her husband was also a part-timer since most of his days were spent at the same establishment as Jeff.

Lily had brought a lovely white wine with her and, as the alcohol was taking effect, Anji began opening up more and more. She was desperate to offload to someone. Lily kept filling her glass again and again, nodding and squeezing her hand at the right moments, reinforcing to Anji that she was her rock.

"I hear you Anji. You know we're in a similar boat," confided Lily. "I may have to leave Saudi too." Lily's tone was melancholy, subtly crying out for sympathy and attention. As predicted, Anji immediately perked up to ask why. She wasn't ready to lose her only friend. Lily relished the chance to divulge: "You know we've been here five years but we're only entitled to a two-bedroomed house." She looked over to check that Anji was listening and, finding she was, slumped over and rested her head in one hand. "It's becoming a nightmare with the kids having to share a room, so I've told Adam if the house situation doesn't change then I'm off."

Anji suddenly felt very selfish for having bothered Lily with all her issues and was pleased to concentrate on something else for a change. Her attention refocused, she sat up on her sun lounger and looked her friend in the eye. "Yes, I can see the problem," agreed Anji. "I do think you'd benefit from a bigger home. Has Adam asked yet if there might be a larger place available to you? I guess I could always ask Jeff if he can pull any strings…" Anji had always been a fixer and didn't think twice about helping out her only friend. Plus there was no way in hell she was going to let Lily abandon her now. Even if she was thinking selfishly, she was damned well going to try her best to stop Lily from leaving.

"Thanks Anji, you're the best." Lily replied in a sickly sweet tone. Anji was happy to see that Lily had perked up immediately and was smiling again.

Anji enjoyed the last few drops of wine from her glass and felt her worries melt away. Standing up and feeling a rush of blood to the head, she stretched and smiled, calling the kids out of the pool and enjoying the warmth of the sun on her skin with a relaxed smile on her face. Anji felt like the gravity of earth had shifted, and a new spirit was ignited inside her. Helping her friend would give her a worthwhile project to work on and help her to break out of her recent negative spiral. When the kids came over she put her arms round them both for a hug.

CHAPTER 12

'Hi honey, I miss you.' Anji sent Jeff a WhatsApp before she went to bed, hoping that it would help her sleep. She imagined him nuzzling his chiselled chin into her collarbone, his muscular arms pulling her closer towards his body. She thought about how his soft snore used to help her get to sleep; the rhythm and reassurance of it lulling her into relaxation. She had never felt trapped by his strong arms; only safe, snug and secure. He had made her feel like a delicate pearl, protected against the world in his embrace.

Those days seemed like a distant memory, now, as Anji spread out like a starfish in their giant bed, which felt as empty as a politician's promise she mused as if she knew anything that was happening in the world living inside this enclosure. She missed the tenderness of the man she had married, but these days, for the first time in her life, she seemed to prefer her own company.

After getting no response from Jeff, she messaged again to ask if she might have a moment of his time. She felt like a member of his staff, asking for a small window in his full schedule, but perhaps this was the best way in at the moment, him being so busy and all. Doubting she'd hear back from him tonight, her mind returned to her thoughts. She pondered ways that she could help Lily; she thought of Sara's sneer about her anxiety attack; she remembered Jeff's cold, hard words to her when he was drunk the other night...No. She wouldn't think about this. It didn't do any good. Instead, she decided to go back downstairs to get a glass of wine to help her sleep. She brought up a bottle and a glass and enjoyed the warm, relaxing feeling it gave her as she finished each glass, before stashing them away with the others and falling into a dreamless sleep.

The next morning, Anji rose from the bed and saw that Jeff's side hadn't been slept in. She could hear him in the shower and, checking to see if he'd slept in the guest suite – which was also untouched – realised he must have only just come in from work and got straight in the shower.

The kids gave a shout across the hall, "Goodbye Daddy!" Despite the running water, he'd no doubt have heard them through the cheap wooden doors around the house. These villas were so beautiful to look at but the finish really was bargain basement. Anji guessed that the construction company had charged top dollar but had provided the cheapest of everything, leaving with millions in their pockets. It was the same across the whole compound and, perhaps, the whole of Saudi.

Before they heard his reply, the children were already down the stairs and out of the front door, running to the bus stop. They'd spoken to Anji this morning about making their own way to the bus stop and, as Anji wanted them to have their bit of independence – and also avoid the gossiping mothers – she had agreed. However, she hadn't expected them to just leave! She ran after them in her flip-flops but she couldn't keep up, so once she'd seen them reach the bus she turned back and headed home. As she entered the front door, she slipped on the white marble floor and fell face first, feeling sandy grit graze her cheeks as she hit the ground. "Bloody sandstorms!" she cursed. It was a regular occurrence in Saudi to have night storms, and sand would creep into every crevice. She pulled herself onto her bum, gasping as though she'd been winded, and clutched at her arm, which had taken the brunt of the fall.

"Still drunk from last night I suppose?" Jeff sneered sarcastically. Anji was startled. She looked up to see him sitting in the living room, fully dressed in his suit.

"I smelled booze on your rancid breath," he said, shooting her an accusing look. "I come home wanting to sleep next to my lovely wife and she smells like a bloody pub." Anji was so shocked she laughed, feeling embarrassed and unsure what to make of what Jeff was saying. "It's not a joke Anji. I asked myself this morning, is this the woman I really married? You'd better buck up your ideas. I don't want my kids living with a drunk for a Mother! If you're going through some kind of fucking mid-life crisis, then you'd better get yourself some help."

She hadn't expected a tirade of insults so early in the day. She actually thought she was holding up very well, considering the circumstances. Though, she supposed, he probably still didn't know that Karen had ostracised her from everyone she knew, tarred her with the title of housebreaker and pulled her name through the mud.

"I had a drink with Lily, that's all," she responded. "You want me to be happy – how can I be? I'm always here for you and the kids, but the problem is you are never here for us are you?" She had so much more pent-up anger she could've spewed out at him, but her arm was nagging with pain and she was still catching her breath from the fall.

His face unexpectedly contorted from a raging storm to a softer version of Jeff. There was almost a look of guilt on his face.

"You know, I never expected to be here all alone doing this, Jeff." She didn't want to plead with him, but she knew it would appeal to his delicate masculinity. "Sometimes I need you. I need you as my other half, my lover, my best friend."

He paused then stood up from the settee and made his way towards Anji, extending his hand to help her up from the cold marble floor. She stood in front of him and he leaned in to plant a tender kiss on her forehead – something he hadn't done in an age. He then kissed the side of her nose, just under her eye, and Anji's memory flashed back to when he'd said that was his favourite place on her face. The move was so sweet that all her animosity melted away momentarily. The last time he'd done that was probably when she agreed to move to Saudi. He had held her hands and kissed her forehead. It was a lot to ask of Anji and the children, but she would do it because she was ready to follow him any-where. He'd actually kissed her like that so infrequently that she was able to remember each and every time; one for each time she'd given birth to their kids, and one on their wedding day. This was the man who'd told her on their first date the names of both his future children: Max if it's a boy and Georgina if it's a girl. Anji felt safe. She remembered that he was the man she had always loved, needed and adored.

"Can I speak to you for a minute about Lily and

Adam?" She decided to take advantage of his sudden good mood and, without hesitation, explained their need for a bigger villa.

Jeff looked relieved, as though he'd been expecting another argument, and for a few seconds he fumbled with his words. His face softened even more, and he started to look more like the Jeff that Anji was so crazy about.

CHAPTER 13

"Anji, it's all true!" exclaimed Lily over the phone a few days later. "Karen's husband is in fact having a full-blown affair with – wait for it – you're never going to believe it…!" Anji hadn't been expecting this news and was instantly taken aback. In one way she felt a wave of relief, like there was a chance that finally she would be out of the spotlight. But she also felt angry that something which had caused her so much pain was being trivialised like this.

"So who is it?" she asked, tersely.

"Their Pilipino housemaid! Can you believe it? He's so in love with her apparently that he's declared it to the world, just like Tom Cruise did on the Oprah Winfrey show when he got together with the woman from Dawson's Creek. I think he even wants to parade her in front of everyone at the springtime party!" The compound held regular events for the residents throughout the year, and the springtime party was a highlight of their social calendar. Fancy cheating on your wife with the house maid then taking her along to that?! She felt awful for Karen, but also, secretly; glad that she would have to live through some of the shame that she had forced Anji to experience.

"This is bullshit," said Anji. "He's probably having some kind of mid-life crisis. He'll run back to Karen with his tail between his legs, begging for forgiveness.

Such a selfish prick! What about his two lovely kids?"

If the rumours about Steve and the maid were true, Anji wouldn't be surprised. The Pilipino were an attractive bunch; most of them in Saudi were young and had come over for work. It was well known that bagging a foreigner was like a meal ticket, enabling them to provide for their family and kids back home. The women always seemed to wear full make-up and skinny jeans, and boasted lovely black glossy hair. Karen's housemaid certainly fitted into that category. Lani, their own housemaid, had started working for them when she was 24, and had arrived with a mouth full of rotten teeth. She remembered opening the door to her for the first time and, as she smiled her first hello to the family, little black stumps of decomposing teeth peered out from behind her perfect lips. Jeff's immediate reaction was to send her back to the agency who provided her; his concern was that if her own hygiene was below par, how could she keep the standards up in their home? Anji convinced him to give her a chance and, as it turned out, Lani was a great housekeeper. Nineteen visits to the dentist later and she ended up with a flawless Hollywood smile.

After hanging up the call, Anji made her way to see the compound representative. Christine was a rather hard-nosed woman with a pinched face and crooked teeth, but she was a godsend around the compound. She was responsible for all the themed parties and children's activities, and Max and Georgie were enrolled in almost every activity she managed.

"Hi Christine, can I ask you a favour?" Anji asked.

"Sure," replied Christine, looking up from the art activity she was planning for the kids' recreation session that afternoon. "Shoot – but it may cost you," she joked in her Aussie accent.

Anji had come to this decision almost immediately after speaking to Lily. She wasn't sure if it was the loyalty in her or whether she hoped it would be her ticket to Karen's forgiveness, but she had to try.

"Please...don't sell spring party tickets to Steve. I heard he'll be bringing his new girlfriend, and Karen is a friend of all of us, right?" Knowing money talked with Christine, she offered to pay for the cost of the two tickets, which she was being asked not to sell. Christine gladly accepted, taking Anji's credit card and not asking questions.

"Won't you be attending, Anji? It's gonna be a blast."

Anji stood thinking about it for a few moments. Why not? She and Jeff could do with having a bit of fun, and it would be a good opportunity to show everyone that she was, and would always be, happily married to Jeff. She pulled out her card again and paid for four more tickets. That would get her and Jeff, plus Lily and Adam, into the party of the year.

Making a rapid exit before she bumped into anyone – despite the new round of gossip, she didn't know if she was out of the firing line yet – Anji rushed to the corner shop. Coming towards her she spotted Amal. She was usually a lovely, friendly lady, but the second she saw Anji she turned her face away. Anji was getting used to being blanked, but it still hurt. Anji lowered her head and quickened her pace.

"Hi Anji," Amal said, giving Anji a bolt out of the blue. This friendliness seemed to have come out of nowhere. "Anji..." said Amal, now hanging *her* head down.

"I'm truly sorry." Anji looked at Amal blankly, who continued, "I didn't mean to tell Karen that it was you who told me about Steve." Anji unconsciously took a step backwards and opened her eyes wide. As if reading her thoughts, Amal rushed her next words. "I was confused at the time – I...I mistakenly told her that it was you who had dished the dirt." Amal reached a manicured fingernail under her mirrored sunglasses to wipe a tear away. "I saw him kissing someone in his car, but they were so into it they hadn't seen me, and...and, well, I just kind of blurted it out to Karen."

Anji continued to stare, eyes wide, at Amal. Her legs had turned to jelly and she had to remember to breathe deeply to calm the rising panic in her chest. She surprised herself with her next words.

"Tell her now that it wasn't me, call her!" she didn't even care right now that she was standing face-to-face with the instigator of her recent hell. Her priority was making sure Karen knew the truth. "I've tried telling her, but she won't believe a word I say now." She somehow resisted tagging on the end, *'Thanks to you!'* "She even had the audacity to tell me that it's my husband who's having the affair," Anji explained.

"I spoke to Lily at the time and told her I wanted to call you, but she talked me out of it. You don't know how many times I dialled your number, only to not go through with it. I feel awful but I'm so relieved it's off my chest now." Amal was talking fast without taking a breath. Now she'd opened the floodgates, words were gushing out of her. "Now it's too late to say anything to Karen because the truth is out and the moment passed and I can't do it now – I'm so sorry!" Amal burst into sobbing tears. Anji was torn between her natural instinct to help – to put her arms round Amal and tell her it was ok – and her indignant rage at what Amal had done, so she just stood there, staring into the distance.

Coming back to Earth, she grabbed her phone in her handbag, like she was reaching for some kind of secret weapon. It would take one quick call to solve everything. She would tell Karen it wasn't her, and they could get all the lives on the compound together and make them kiss Anji's ass, with an apology for the hell they'd been putting her through. They'd round on Amal like a pack of wolves, and Anji would be in the clear. Only, she couldn't make the call. Amal was right – it was too late. She longed to hear a friendly voice but, not only had she lost Karen, but she now couldn't call Lily either since it seemed she was some sort of accessory to the crime. Anji felt more isolated than ever.

Amal was still standing there, now dabbing at her eyes with a tissue. Even though she hated Amal at that very moment, it wasn't her fault that she'd caught the pair in the car. And even though she couldn't see what had possessed her to tell Karen it was her she did seem truly distraught about what she had done. Anji touched her on the elbow then turned and walked away. She wouldn't wish the hostility and loathing from the women on this compound on anyone.

CHAPTER 14

"Hi Chris, how are you? It's been way too long." Anji was trying to keep her voice light.

"Hi darling, all fine here. I miss you!" Chris responded in her chirpy voice.

Chris was a friend from Anji's time in Thailand. She was a pure-hearted angel, with a humble soul; one of those people who managed to stay grounded whatever life threw at her, with her head firmly on her shoulders. Chris's husband had a wonderful job as the CEO of an affluent billionaire who owned half of the fast food chains in Thailand. He, like Jeff, worked extremely hard, so both wives had become inseparable during Anji's two-year stint in the beautiful, crazy city of Bangkok. Anji had seen many women change when their husbands achieved any kind of career success. Many of them became morbidly jealous and possessive, and suddenly they were too good to mix with the 'plebs', wanting only to rub shoulders in their newly acquired social group, but not Chris. She had remained true to herself despite the newfound freedom that her wealth had enabled her to enjoy.

Chris and Anji had always been close and although physical distance was no object, they hadn't spoken in a while. Now she needed her friend's support more than ever, she knew Chris would be there for her. Chris was probably the only person besides her own mother that Anji truly trusted and, as Anji wasn't quite ready to worry her mum yet with this, she knew Chris would be there for her through this crisis.

Though she felt guilty at first, as they hadn't spoken in so long, Anji couldn't help but let rip whilst she was on the phone. All her angst came flowing out as she dug deep and shared her innermost feelings, suspicions and fears. She talked and talked, crying until her voice was hoarse. She even thought she had lost connection twice because Chris was so quiet on the other end, but Chris was just listening and digesting the information, trying to find the right advice. Once Anji had nothing left in her to say, she waited patiently for Chris to respond.

"Anji, I love you and Jeff," Chris began. "You're a wonderful couple. I can't help but feel so sad about what you're saying." Anji could tell by the tone of her friend's voice that she was affected by what she'd revealed. "Remember, you have two lovely, adorable kids. Please don't be rash. If your suspicions turn out to be right, I think you should get yourself back to the UK and discuss your rights with a lawyer. I don't think you can get that advice where you are currently, right?" Chris was always one step ahead of the game and so smart. "You're not doing it because you want a divorce, you're just being a strong woman, ok?" she added with authority.

How Anji wished she could go back in time to when she'd lived in Bangkok. People there were so kind and sweet. It had been really rewarding working with Chris in an association to help underprivileged children. She had mingled amongst local rich and famous people, but they were humble humans rich in humanity and rich in heart. She'd loved the hospitality of that country and had felt so free. Everything was so colourful – in stark contrast to the black and white covers outside the walls of her Saudi cage. Walking down the street in Bangkok was an undertaking, with every colourful step reminding you that you were alive. Anji had a flashback of waking up on the forty-first floor of a high-rise tower with views overlooking the Chao Phraya River, looking down towards people who were as small as ants, busy making a living. Whatever time she looked out of the window, people were busy being industrious; unlike the bland confines of Saudi.

Chris spoke in such a careful, considered manner that Anji began to regain her composure and see the situation more objectively. Suddenly the whole affair didn't seem quite so intense and unhinged. She closed her eyes, taking a deep breath and gathering some clarity. Anji's first task was to get Jeff to the compound party, get him drunk and get him to agree to a trip to the UK. She was so grateful to Chris for giving her some clarity and direction. Helping her clear through the mental chatter and jumble in her head to forge her own path.

CHAPTER 15

Life was quiet for Anji in the lead up to the compound springtime party. Though she was no longer at the centre of the rumour mill, no one, other than Amal, had confronted her about their mistake or attempted to make amends. When she saw others around the compound, they mainly averted their eyes – probably through embarrassment – and Anji didn't have the energy to pick a fight. She had picked up the phone a few times to call Karen but couldn't bring herself to do it. When she'd seen Lily in passing it was like nothing had happened, and Jeff had continued to be almost like his old self; though he was rarely around his usual excuse was so busy at work. By some miracle, Jeff had however managed to make time to attend the springtime party. For that she was immensely excited. It had been months since they'd been anywhere together and, as well as hopefully having some fun for the first time in a while, she desperately wanted to show the others on the compound that she was actually happily married living in marital bliss. She also wanted to secure her trip to the UK; he would have to accept tonight or she was going to burst. Lily and Adam were also coming along, and Anji's boss Sara and her husband Fadi had tickets too. Because alcohol was served at compound events, it was often the case that a lot of expats – even those who didn't live on the compound, like Sara – would be sniffing around for tickets.

Anji hoped that Christine had kept to her word and not sold tickets to Steve and his new girlfriend, the dirty tramp and housemaid Martha. She guessed they were still together and that he and Karen hadn't got back together; she hadn't heard otherwise, since Karen still wasn't talking to Anji. The couple's marriage seemed beyond salvageable now anyway, especially since Steve would no doubt be accustomed to Martha waking him up with a daily blowjob and opening her legs at the drop of a pair of trousers.

Anji looked breath taking, if she said so herself, in an emerald green dress, which had a plunging neckline that revealed just enough to keep it modest. Her hair was absolutely perfect in a stunning high tail, revealing her gorgeous freckled face, and her legs were toned and bronzed. Anji had had her hair and make-up done by the male stylist at the salon on the compound; ironically, outside the walls of the compound it was a criminal offence for a man to do this sort of work on women anyway, and if he'd done it anywhere else he'd have been deported back to his home country of Lebanon.

Jeff had noticed how incredible Anji looked and was looking somewhat uneasy as she clipped her long Christian Dior earrings into place they had been a gift from Jeff. She opened a new bottle of perfume by Ellie Saab another gift and sprayed the scent onto her wrist and throat, she'd been wafting intoxicating hints of orange blossom and gardenia around. He was always bringing her little presents like that. To the untrained eye, he was the perfect husband; though the trained eye may have noticed the airport price tags on the packages of the gifts, where they'd been bought as an excuse to chat up the pretty sales ladies.

Finding himself aroused by his wife's appearance, Jeff began fiddling with his cufflinks. She ran to rescue him and put them effortlessly into the buttonholes, clicking them into place. He stole a glance at her cleavage before pulling her in tight and inhaling the scent of her. She felt him harden, pushing his cock into her groin. She smiled inside, happy that she could still turn him on, but also wary not to use this card too early when she had to keep him in a good mood for later.

"Shall we?" He motioned to the bed.

Anji wasn't ready to be ruffled up. She had spent so much time getting ready, plus the kids were running around the house with their friends. She let him down gently, promising, seductively, to make it up to him after the party. She instantly felt guilty but managed to keep to her word, leaving Jeff feeling frustrated and unspent. He was so used to getting his own way. Not so long ago, Anji would have just pulled her underwear down so he could just relieve himself, but not today. It wasn't part of her plan, plus her dress was silk and she didn't want it ruined before the party had even started. She kissed his cheek and clip-clopped down the stairs, leaving a trail of delicious scent behind her.

As Anji and Jeff walked into the room, the couple could feel all eyes on them. Jeff took his wife's hand and led her towards their seats; she felt herself grow two inches taller, her ponytail swishing even higher as her chest swelled up with pride. Let them stare, for here was a couple truly in love with one another she thought to herself.

Jeff noticed how the men turned in their seats to

get a glimpse of his foxy good-looking wife. He held her close to him, ignoring the greedy eyes boring holes in his back. He leant in as they laughed together, taking their seats. He looked proud of his trophy wife, and Anji revelled in his attention. If the wolves were out to get her, she was safe from them while she was with Jeff.

Sara came over to greet Anji, giving her one, two, three kisses. Having travelled and lived in many different places, Anji found it difficult to keep up with the appropriate number of kisses for the culture she was in. She had always felt this Lebanese way was too much – one kiss was enough, surely? As the wine started flowing and the two began to mingle with the other guests, Jeff told Anji he needed to speak to Lily about something. Anji wasn't too happy about this, as Lily was not on her good list at the moment, but being the loyal wife and wanting to prove the gossipers wrong, she doused her suspicions with another gulp of vino and smiled innocently at her husband.

As she watched Jeff and Lily head outside to the palm trees strung with glinting fairy lights, she grudgingly turned her attention towards Adam. A wonderful, hardworking, dedicated husband and family man, he was also the most boring person she'd ever met. Anji pondered if he was blessed in other departments, because conversation certainly wasn't his strong point. But at that moment, Anji was just happy to have some company to keep the vultures at bay because they were circling, waiting for a window of opportunity. She could sense it.

After listening to another of Adam's dull anecdotes and pretending to laugh for the umpteenth time, Anji craned her neck around, looking for Jeff and Lily. Where had they got to now? People were beginning to hit the dance floor and, now alone under the swirling party lights, Anji's thoughts began to whirl round her head. She saw dowdy Janice walking the warpath, coming directly towards her with a face of fury. Fear rose in Anji's throat. What could it be? She looked towards Adam to divert her attention but he wasn't there; they'd stopped talking when the music had got too loud, but she hadn't realised he had deserted her. She put her head down in preparation for whatever verbal abuse was about to come.

Thankfully, as Janice reached her, so did Lily. Anji looked up, relief washing over her face. Lily had defused the ticking time bomb. Janice mouthed 'LATER' with a threatening look on her face as she turned back to the group of women who were avidly watching and waiting for the sequel to unravel. Like a cackle of hyenas, they were all giggly and jittery on the fermented grape juice, like vultures swooping waiting to scavenge from the demise of someone else.

"Thank you so much!" yelped Lily above the pounding of the music.

Anji tried quietening her heart, she felt like it was beating louder and harder than the track the DJ was playing. Lily had her hand over her mouth and her eyes were dancing around the place.

"What? What is it?" Anji cross-examined, eagerly awaiting her explanation.

"Jeff has organised for us to have the type B villa, just like yours! He really wants us to be happy here in Saudi!" She leaned in with a great big bear hug. "Anji," she carried on breathlessly, "if you only knew what this means to us."

"I really am so happy for you," Anji announced, a big grin spreading across her face. "If anyone deserves it, it's you." And then Anji thought of Jeff, and the wisps of suspicion, which had been swirling in her head whilst he was away with Lily. Now she knew he was answering Lily's prayers. He'd really heard Anji's request to help her friend out. What a kind, generous man he was. At that moment she wanted to rush back home to their marital bed and reward him with what she had promised earlier.

"Where is Jeff now?" Anji probed.

"Oh, we were outside by the private function room because it was quiet there," she explained, still on a high from the news. Head held high, Anji attempted to walk confidently past the pack of rumourmongers hoping none of them got up and followed her, ready to find and thank her wonderful compassionate husband.

CHAPTER 16

"I want to be with you now, I need you. I felt so jealous seeing you and her together tonight." A woman's voice travelled across the silent courtyard.

"It won't be long, be patient," Anji heard a man whisper.

As she cut across the courtyard towards the function room to find Jeff, Anji continued to hear muffled voices. She walked slowly past them, trying not to make a sound. They were busy having more than a conversation, and she caught sight of a flash of bare shoulder in the darkness. Anji panicked, moving towards the rusty door of the electrical room, desperate not to be seen by them. She tried not to let out a sound as her sandaled feet squelched in something damp and mouldy-smelling. She held her breath, thinking that her reputation was already in tatters so if she got caught now things couldn't get much worse.

There was a sudden scuffling of feet and out of the shadows came a familiar outline of a figure she knew. Anji's heart was knocking on her tonsils; waiting for her to let out a scream that would be so loud it would shake the compound walls. She swallowed it down as hard as she could, as bile rose in her gullet.

Sara was pulling her top down over her big, pert, splendiferous breasts. What lovely creations they were; Anji couldn't help but admire their perfect formation.

When God was giving out those, he'd been extremely kind and generous to Sara. Anji certainly hadn't been blessed in the same way. She often asked Jeff if he was sad she didn't have big boobs, and he always had the same reply: "More than a handful is too much." She had been stupid enough to believe him. Now he was munching on Sara's Mont Blancs while his own wife's bee sting tits lay dormant under her exquisite green dress.

What a lying, no good, fucker! So, the rumours were actually true. That realisation alone was enough to make her crumble like a house of sand, smashing into a trillion granules. She didn't scream, attack them or even make a scene to her own amazement. She didn't cry or go crazy like she'd seen in videos showing mad, jealous women having fistfights in public over their cheating other halves. She stayed frozen to the spot, unable to do a damn thing. She could feel the electricity between them; it was dangerous and exciting. He had a lust in his eye she had never seen when he looked at her. She never realised that feelings of betrayal could penetrate so deep, like a knife digging around in her chest, searching for the aorta to sever. Irreparable. Fatally wounded.

Now it all made perfect sense; Karen had been telling the truth. Beautiful women always surrounded Jeff; it was the nature of his job. But Anji had trusted Jeff and, until recently, had never had a reason not to. Just like that her house of cards was all burnt to cinders in the blink of an eye. Anji watched from the mushy alcove of the door, which began to stink more of something dead decomposing the more her feet squirmed in the sludge. Watching from the shadows as Sara put her breasts back into that black top and patted herself down, trying to look more respectable. A few seconds ago the same top had been exposing those huge knockers, and her skirt had been well above her waist.

Anji managed to creep out from the dirty hiding spot, her feet covered in a black gunk. She quick-footed it to the nearest hiding place she could find; as luck would have it, it was a bathroom so she could also try and clean her feet. As she stood there she saw her reflection in the mirror. She felt transparent and hollow. Everyone knew her as the wife of Jeff or the mother of Max and Georgie. But now Anji didn't even know who she was anymore. In fact, the stark truth was that she had lost herself a long, long time ago. She was broken, fragile, and at that moment her soul felt wafer thin in splinters. Nothing more than a delicate glass figurine perfect to the eye but inside ever so hollow.

She remembered how Jeff had chased her in hot pursuit so long ago. How he would never take no for an answer, not ever, and how she had loved his persistence. How determined he was and how hungry he had been for her. Now he was hungry again; not for Anji, but for fresh prey. Her life flashed before her. Something was firing in her soul. Maybe she wasn't so frangible after all.

She heard the ringing of her phone echoing around the tiled bathroom. Answering, she heard Jeff shout, "Where the hell are you?"

Pulling her heels on hurriedly, she stomped back to the party, and grabbed Jeff by the hand, leading him on to the already-crowded dance floor. In any other circumstance, it would be a gorgeous setting; booze flowing freely, lights twinkling against the dark sky, the scent of exotic flowers in the air and the glints of light reflecting off the luxury pool adding a sense of romance and whimsy to the evening. Anji swallowed down her growing rage and showed nothing but happiness to the bastard, tossing her mane back like a thoroughbred and moving her hips in a mesmerising dance. Jeff liked what he was seeing; it had been a long time since he'd seen Anji look so in control and so hot. Anji caught Sara looking at Jeff, a glint of envy in her eye no doubt. Only a few moments ago he'd been fingering her and handling her weapons. Anji caught her eye and, ignoring her queasiness, beckoned her and Fadi to the dance floor. She was already hatching an impromptu plan.

She headed towards Fadi and took his hand, leaving Jeff with Sara. Using well-orchestrated moves, she and Fadi dance-shuffled to the edge of the dance floor as Jeff swung Sara awkwardly to avoid Anji. Anji managed to eke her foot out. It was just enough to make Sara lose her balance and trip like an overly ambitious ballerina straight into the swimming pool. The tables were about to turn and the humiliation would be Sara's.

It was almost like it had happened in slow motion. Fadi stood stock still, distressed, apologising profusely to his slut of a wife, even though it wasn't his fault she'd gone in. Jeff reached a hand in to wrench Sara out, her mouth gasping like a dying fish as her drenched hair plastered across her face and her mascara attempted a new paint job down her cheeks. Anji stifled a giggle. Poor Sara; she looked more like a drowned rat than a Miss Wet T-shirt contestant.

The whole incident had spurred other partygoers to jump in too. They were laughing and splashing each other in the pool. Sara on the other hand was furious, with Jeff fussing around her, Fadi not knowing what to do with himself the witless prick and Anji quietly amused and pleased with herself pretending to look overly concerned

Fadi was calling the buggy to take them to the car. For them, the evening was over. *What a damn shame,* Anji mused. Under her breath she muttered "Good riddance and fuck off." Anji's night was only just getting started as she swanned past a shocked-looking Jeff and joined Lily on the dance floor. Two single guys jumped at the chance to dance with them, while Adam looked on with a dopey smile and Jeff wiped his wet arms with a napkin. The guy with Anji laid his hands over her hips and swayed closely with her. Jeff's face was so flushed he looked like he might explode; he stood up and dragged Anji from the grip of the younger, hot looking guy. She knew he hated his property being manhandled. But she also knew that approximately thirty minutes ago, the contract that they'd undertaken together fifteen years earlier was now irrefutably broken. The man who had promised to be 'blood of my blood' and 'bone of my bone', in his own words; to be with Anji wherever the journey may lead them; to be together forever. It crossed her mind that there'd been no mention of faithfulness or loyalty in their vows; maybe he already knew he couldn't be that man. Anji had stuck with the traditional wording of love, honour and obey, which she had taken very seriously up until that moment.

As they walked back to the villa after the final song had ended, the scent of jasmine filled the mild air. The atmosphere between the two of them wasn't quite so sweet. Jeff strode ahead, no doubt expecting Anji to follow behind like she was his obedient Jack Russell. He was checking his phone of course, probably hoping to hear from his mistress. She watched him as he walked, tall and masculine, running his fingers through his hair in a move she used to find ultra sexy. She ran a few steps forward and reached out to take his hand – part of her plan involved acting normally – but he released her grip, immediately shaking her away angrily.

Once in the villa, they reached the bedroom and he stood outside to let her go in first. It would be the only gentlemanly thing he'd do for the rest of the night. Closing the door and making a point of locking it behind him, he suddenly pushed her roughly onto the bed without uttering a word. As he pulled off Anji's shoes, she hoped he wouldn't see her dirty feet. He'd have been disgusted. He yanked her dress up above her waist and pulled her G-string to one side, while using his other hand to undo his belt. Releasing himself, he entered her forcefully, his trousers around his knees and his shirt still buttoned. He pushed her legs back, her feet over her shoulders, each thrust going deeper and deeper until he relieved himself inside her. He pulled out immediately and left to clean up. There was no kissing, no lovemaking the whole affair lasting but a few minutes. He was simply doing what he'd done many times before when he wanted to punish his wife for her behaviour; marking his territory just like a dog would. Demonstrating ownership of his bitch.

For the first time, everything became clear to Anji. She hurried to the spare room to use the shower to wash his smell from out of her, feeling sordid and degraded as she tried to rinse his semen from her insides. She walked back into the bedroom with her soft robe on and her wet hair dripping onto the floor. Jeff was already asleep on his side of the bed. She hated herself for doing it, but laid down next to him on their bed, curling up in a foetal position on top of the covers. It made her skin crawl, and not from the cool air of the air-con. Her mind unravelled as she imagined all the different scenarios. How many other women had there been, or was Sara the first? How had she been so blind? How had she not seen the signs; seen or heard the warning bells? Thinking about him fucking her then going to fuck Sara. How many times had been with her and then come home to take her to bed? Even at times when she was left unsatisfied and frustrated after sex, she'd put it down to her wonderful husband being tired and overworked. Thinking back, she'd been making endless excuses for him and had justified it by saying to herself *'well as long as he was satisfied…'* God, she felt so pathetic. She'd seen with her own eyes how he was getting his kicks. She didn't want him anymore, and there was no way in hell she would fight for him. In her head it was well and truly over.

She looked over in the half-darkness, wondering how he could sleep so peacefully. There was no grinding of teeth, night sweats or furrowed brow; no stress worrying about how to keep two women happy. She felt rage building up inside, and wondered if revenge would be the way forward. She could alert the religious police. He would be beaten, and face instant deportation after his humiliation. He'd lose his job and his pride. Now that would be so satisfying. She'd heard stories of what had happened to other cheaters in Saudi, how they'd been hung within an inch of their lives, and worse. Even if the stories had been fabricated, it was scary enough to put most men off. Not Jeff though, but she couldn't do it, for the sake of Max and Georgina. They'd have enough to contend with given the current situation; she didn't need them to be inflicted with any more damage.

Anji closed her eyes and relived the details of the 'accidental' falling in the pool, thinking about how her quick action had paid off. She now needed to concoct a plan that would be fool proof. She needed to get back to the UK and do some groundwork so she could play him like he'd played her. She didn't know she had the strength to win after all she'd been hanging on by a bare thread for weeks already but it was definitely game on.

CHAPTER 17

Two days after the party, Anji knew life would never be the same again. Her perfect bubble had well and truly burst, but she had to carry on as normal. No one could know that she was aware of the truth behind Karen's accusations about Jeff.

Work was a nightmare, having to be polite and act normal with Sara when really she wanted to run her down with her office wheelie chair, or launch at her from behind, hands around her throat at the water cooler. Of course they never mentioned the incident in the pool. It was just too embarrassing for them both. And Anji still bore the bruises on her arms and legs from when Jeff had pinned her to the bed. For once she was grateful for the full coverage of the Abaya, but her body ached almost as much as her heart.

Anji had made a plan with her mum, Jacky, asking her to call her mobile at 10 o'clock. Her mum had asked for an explanation, but Anji reassured her that all would become clear soon. Tick tock, tick tock. Anji found herself checking the time every few minutes. As the phone rang, Anji jumped in her seat. She let the phone ring a few times to make sure Sara would be annoyed and look up from her desk.

"Hi Mum, what's up?" asked Anji innocently.

"Anji, what is this? I nearly put the phone down! Don't ask me to call at a set time then take an age to answer," her mother berated her. "I'm parked up on some random embankment just so I could call you on time!"

"Oh no Mum, really?" Anji feigned shock. "Listen, I'll get myself over to you immediately. I'll sort my ticket and get there. Tell dad not to worry." She'd rehearsed this sentence about a hundred times yesterday, so it rolled off her tongue effortlessly like a dream.

"What the hell are you on about?" asked Anji's mum, confused.

"Yes, yes, don't worry. The kids will be fine. I'll call you later, don't worry." Anji's cheeks flushed; she didn't like lying but needs must.

Sara looked over the top of her reading glasses at Anji, obviously wanting to know the full story. Anji stood up from her desk, walking towards her boss and explaining that her mum had had a fall so she'd need to fly home and help her, and would a week off be ok? She realised she was babbling and hoped it wasn't obvious she was lying, but wasn't too worried; Sara would relay the message to Jeff faster than his own wife could. Of course Sara agreed to the time off instantly, no doubt making plans with Jeff in her head. Anji may as well have already been on the plane, given Sara's preoccupied expression.

Anji left a voicemail on Jeff's phone. She saw he'd listened to it immediately but didn't bother getting back in touch with his wife. Her next line of attack was his PA, Rita.

"Hi Mrs Harris," chirruped Rita, answering quickly. "I hope you are good today."

"Fine Rita, and you?" asked Anji in haste. "I'm trying to call Jeff, there's an emergency at home. Please arrange a flight and letter so I can travel alone." It angered

Anji that she needed a document to travel without her husband, while he could do whatever he damn well pleased and was.

Rita was far too reserved to ask what was going on, and courteously wished Anji a safe journey. "Remember Rita," Anji instructed. "It's urgent. If I could leave tomorrow that would be better. Thank you." Anji's plan was working well. Maybe too well, she worried. She just had to remember what she'd said to whom.

There was still no word from Jeff but Anji imagined he'd received the message and was as pleased as punch. She imagined the two of them planning the week together. Hopefully Sara wouldn't end up in their marital bed. Anji hoped he'd spend some time with the children, which would put a spanner in the works for Sara. Anji felt she couldn't delay it any longer. She needed to leave, as she was desperate to know where she stood and what her rights were. She found herself dialling Rita again to chase the flight details.

CHAPTER 18

After arriving at Heathrow, Anji got in a taxi and headed straight for a hotel in central London.

"The Mandarin Oriental Hyde Park, please," she said politely to the spotty young Uber driver. He looked young enough to be her son, and clearly didn't want to make any polite conversation. Neither did she, so for that she was genuinely grateful. The hotel was the first name that had popped into her head – she'd always loved the majestic look of the place and, since this was her chance to enjoy some Anji time, she might as well choose somewhere nice to spend it. She could have picked a dirty little hovel somewhere, trying to economise, but she decided that she deserved a little luxury.

As the cab pulled up outside the hotel's grand façade, Anji took a deep breath. This felt like the start of something. Checking in, she knew the price tag would be steep, but she was past caring. She'd only be staying two nights, so used her UK Visa card to secure the room since she was the only one who had access to the statements, and she'd pay the balance in cash to ensure there was no paper trail,. She didn't want to leave any traces of deceit.

The bellboy wheeled her small suitcase out of the lift and showed her to her room. It was a courtyard room, and Anji immediately felt at home. Over in Saudi, everything was over-the-top; huge, garish gold furniture, ugly wall art, giant plants everywhere. In the haven of her hotel room she discovered neutral decor, tasteful paintings hanging on the walls, and bronze sculptures of regal stags on the bookcase. It all felt so wonderfully British.

She sat on the bed and let out a sigh, feeling enveloped in its cushiony softness. First things first: a long bath, fluffy bathrobe and room service. Once she'd had a swim in the bath – it seemed that big – she returned to the bed to wait for her dinner to arrive, and started Googling. First thing tomorrow morning she needed to make an appointment with a solicitor about her impending divorce and future settlement. She'd already made up her mind and there was no going back. She could see his lies came too easily, and she couldn't spend the rest of her life worrying if he was or if he wasn't. Jumping on the hotel Wi-Fi and beginning her search, she found a female solicitor specialising in divorce and family law. She wanted a woman. Hopefully she would understand the situation, plus Anji would feel more comfortable divulging all the details to a 'her'. Watson and Partners LLP offered an initial consultation for free, so Anji decided to chance it and show up at her door in the morning. This was all happening so fast but she knew it had to be done.

Anji wanted to feel prepared, so she laid out her clothes for the next day's early appointment. Thinking a suit would've been a good choice if she had thought that far ahead– after all, she meant business – so Anji chose the next best thing. A smart, colourful jacket and simple DKNY trousers now hung off the wardrobe door, ready for the next morning. She didn't want to look like a downtrodden victim of adultery, and hoped that she'd come across in a good light during the meeting. If she even got in that was; Anji was nervous they might not be able to see her, but in a sudden burst of confidence she realised her determination was what counted, plus she had a clear-cut case. *They'd be mad not to take me on,* she thought as she drifted off to sleep.

CHAPTER 19

Still feeling tired the next morning, and filled with nerves, Anji couldn't stomach breakfast so sat in the plush velvet armchair in her room sipping a coffee. She decided that walking to Kensington High Street was a good idea; maybe she could clear her head a little. It felt as foggy as the bathroom mirror after her long shower that morning. The spring weather was glorious. What a contrast to thirty-five degree heat in Saudi. She felt free and alive; the colourful shop fronts, produce displays and budding trees along the road surrounded her and she took it all in, like a small child experiencing things for the very first time. She instantly liked the vibe of Kensington. The High Street was full of restaurants, bars, and wholefood markets. Culturally vibrant and full of life, this bustling road of shops and boutiques was right up Anji's street.

The hotel receptionist had said it would be a good thirty-five minute walk to the legal offices but, with a spring in her step, Anji managed it in thirty. Above the wholefood market was a sign for Watson and Partners LLP. Although she could see the name, Anji couldn't see the entrance so popped into Karous Organic Wholefood Store, since it seemed impossible to enter from anywhere other than in the store itself.

"Hello," said Anji, admiring the displays of plump dates and figs, which had probably been grown in the same place she'd left just yesterday. "I'm looking for that place." She pointed awkwardly at the sign, smiling at the shop owner who was showing off his big white teeth.

"Hey darling, you're not the only one," said the Greek guy with a smile that made his eyes dance. "You have to go around the back," he advised, leading Anji towards the rear of the shop. "Another divorce, what a shame. I'll offer you a great deal on the mangoes – they'll make you feel better," he joked gently.

Anji smiled at him, appreciating his cheeky sense of humour. She felt like telling him all about her husband and his affair with her boss, but her time in Saudi had made her wary of airing her laundry to others. They arrived at a black door and he pressed the intercom button, which was quickly answered with a buzz.

"Hello," Anji spoke into the white plastic box. "I'm Mrs Harris, I have an appointment," she lied. She knew they wouldn't let her up if she was a cold caller.

"I'm sorry," replied a chirpy voice, "we don't have you in our diary, but if you would like to come up we can make an appointment for you. Please come to the first floor." With that, the door clicked open and Anji made her way up the stairs.

The receptionist was a bright girl, no more than twenty-five; a bit of a plain Jane but cheerful. As soon as Anji reached the front desk she felt a rush of emotion at having to lie about the appointment. Tears began to form in her eyes then she suddenly started sobbing like a baby. Her guard was down and reality had hit. "You don't understand," she began babbling, "I flew in yesterday. I have to see someone today. I promise you won't be crazy to take up my case. I can pay, please!" Stumbling over her words, the receptionist came over and calmly led her to a chair, offering Anji a scented tissue and pouting with concern.

"It's ok," the girl said gently, picking up the phone on her tidy desk. "I'll see what I can do." She paused, waiting for the phone to be picked up at the other end. "Hello Mrs Watson, can you see a lady now? A Mrs Harris. I've overlooked her by mistake, it was my fault." She winked at Anji as she continued to talk, then almost instantaneously a frosted glass door opened, revealing a slight woman with scraped-back dark hair, a grey pinstripe suit and little black court shoes.

"Come on in Mrs Harris, please take a seat". She spoke in an authoritative tone which made Anji feel both reassured and slightly intimidated. Anji walked into the room, head bowed down low with a crumpled up tissue balled in her hand. She perched on the edge of the comfy leather armchair and patted her eyes with the tissue.

"I really appreciate this," Anji admitted. "I'm sure you are so busy." Part of her wished that the armchair would swallow her up; she had never for one moment thought she would end up in a divorce solicitor's office. She remembered her wedding day and feeling so confident that they would be this happy forever. At this thought, tears began to prickle her eyes again. Watson gave her a nod of acknowledgement.

"So," said Watson, spreading her fingers out across the table top, authoritatively. "We both know why you are here."

Anji nodded in agreement, wondering how and where to begin. She sat there like she had left the house and forgotten something, but couldn't quite remember what it was. She felt distracted; it was hard to focus with her emotions all over the place. Watson sensed this and went on to explain how this would all work. She ended her spiel by highlighting her fees, matter-of-factly, with no shame or embarrassment.

"The reason I'm starting with this is because I want the absolute best for you, do you understand?" Anji nodded at her slowly. "Divorce can be brutal, especially when money and children are involved. So we always aim for the best route for you. Do you have children?"

"Yes. Two." Anji managed to eke out. It was time for Anji to compose herself and share her side of the story. With a tissue in her hand, a croak in her voice and a sniffly nose, she divulged the details of the last few weeks and her wish for a divorce. Telling the details to a stranger was harder than she'd imagined, and every time Anji mentioned the betrayal the tears began to fall again.

"Well, Mrs Harris..." Watson contemplated her response for a moment, as if Anji's time was up and there were conclusions to be made. "If you want this divorce on the grounds of adultery then his word against yours isn't enough. We can work with it of course, but the woman you mentioned lives in Saudi Arabia too, therefore I'm sure your husband won't be admitting or denying anything." She certainly wasn't sugar-coating things. "Do you think you'd be able to get any proof? Photos, videos, voice recordings? All of these can be submitted as evidence. Anything that gives us proof of adultery. We need to know that sexual intercourse took place – are you sure it did take place?" She was on a roll now. Before Anji had chance to explain, she continued.

"We have to convince the judges it was a sexual affair. Cheating spouses usually keep a very low profile," she rationalised, being business-like and pragmatic. "We also need to know his net worth. I'm sorry to have to pry into these details, but it's important. We have to know what to divide, whose name his assets are in – if there are any assets...?" Watson paused and looked at Anji expectantly.

"I honestly don't know anything," admitted Anji, feeling a little pathetic. "All I know is we are very comfortable. Jeff handles all of the money, our finances – everything."

"This is international divorce. It's more complicated, messier," Watson warned. Anji's thoughts were suddenly consumed by the enormity of her current situation. "Or you could persuade him to move back here then take him for half of everything!" She said this flippantly, holding her hands in the air with a smile on her face. "Seriously, though," Watson leaned in closely, "do not under any circumstances file for divorce over there. At best, they will laugh in your face. So please think this through, don't do anything rash." The colour had drained from Anji's face; she had made a terrible mistake. This was all too complicated, too much to think about. She could just stay with Jeff and avoid all of this mess. She was on the verge of thanking Watson for her time and making a beeline for the door when Watson spoke.

"I know this all probably sounds terrifying and like you're completely out of your depth. I have a lot of women come in here convinced they want a divorce, then when I tell them what it entails they don't come back. Well, not for another year or so when things have got much worse and they're even more downtrodden than when I first met them. This is scary, it is a big deal. But from what you've told me, this is what you want. It's always your choice, I can only advise, but I want to give you the best advice I can. Play a clever game. Keep your life together. You're in a strong position at the moment; he has no clue you know anything. Use that to your advantage."

Anji thought for a few seconds. She knew Jeff would play ugly and would use her lack of financial independence against her. She had no money of her own; she gave it up when she quit her job to support her husband in his career. When they first married, she put all her savings and earnings into the mortgage. She'd never thought to put anything aside; after all, they were a partnership. Wasn't that what marriage was all about? She thought about every laugh, every kiss, every vacation that they had all shared. How he'd almost punched the stars when the kids were born. Now she was face to face with the bare facts. Her perfect life was crumbling around her.

Could she live alone? Be a single mum? Could she do this by herself, or should she bite the bullet and stay with Jeff, spending her days worrying about who he was fucking? Anji already knew the answers, and she knew that she wanted Watson on her team.

Wrapping up their meeting and promising to do everything she could to gather the evidence required, Anji said her thank yous and headed down the stairs into the fresh air. A walk would do her good, and being outdoors felt like a relief from the confines of the office where she'd had to peel layers off of herself and fully expose her thoughts and feelings. Drawing in lungfuls of fresh air, Anji's mood began to simmer down, and she found herself walking past well-manicured gardens and uniform buildings with painted front doors and white-rimmed windows. She loved the look of these homes. The place was familiar in a way she couldn't explain, but she could see herself living here with Georgie and Max. Anji envisioned herself walking the children to school, perhaps heading to some sort of part-time job after drop-off.

As she made her way back to the hotel, her thoughts turned inward. One minute she was a happily married expat wife, the next she would be a poor divorcee with a cheating ex-husband and not a penny to her name. Anji felt a sense of self-hatred well up inside for a few moments. She had allowed herself to be so controlled and so dumb; she'd let this man take her for a ride. She'd been kept in the dark all this time. She should have spoken up and insisted on a joint bank account. She now had a sense of urgency now in her steps. Desperate to use a computer, before even going back to her room, she made her way to the hotel's business centre and tapped into the search bar: 'How to trap an adulterous spouse'. She regretted it immediately, as she found herself scrolling through a sea of forums of angry women - and some men – telling their sob stories and their plans for revenge. Anji refused to align herself with these people. She tried again, this time typing in: 'How can I prove my spouse is having an affair?' Along the top, before the forums of angry and vengeful spouses, was a row of items which had come up under the 'Shopping' category. Some of these devices looked alien to Anji, but some were familiar. She spotted a picture of a normal looking camera and clicked onto it. It took Anji to a website full of images of electrical equipment. Anji felt overwhelmed - everything looked so bloody complicated – so she clicked on a button which said 'surveillance'. The first thing to come up was a 'Surveillance starter kit' which included:

- 'Keyring, voice activated recorder'
- 'iPod hidden camera – records 128 hours of video footage'
- 'Tracking key GPS logger. Battery powered, just plug into your computer and see where it's been.'

Keen to get off of this website – she felt guilty just looking at it – she added this kit to her basket and checked out using her UK card, paying extra for next day delivery to her mother's address. She would pick them up from there when she popped into see her before her flight. She felt a mix of dread and relief about seeing her mother, but reasoned with herself that she didn't actually have to tell her anything if she didn't want to. She felt her phone vibrate with an email receipt, and as she headed for the lift she quickly deleted it from her inbox before emptying her email trash. She exhaled dramatically, feeling like she'd been holding her breath the entire time.

\

CHAPTER 20

Anji struggled to concentrate as she sat quietly on the commuter train to Brighton the following morning. It could've been the stench of the egg sandwiches the guy opposite was eating, but she guessed it was more likely to be because there was so much crammed into the same tiny brain that barely a week ago had barely been used for the past decade. Calculating how to catch Jeff and Sara at it was now at the top of Anji's agenda. Despite the anger and disgust she felt towards Jeff, imagining life without him was a strangely tough and frightening thought. These conflicting feelings came in waves, crashing into each other in her already overflowing mind.

Gazing out of the window, Anji noticed a sea of green trees bearing luscious leaves. There were horses, sheep and cows littering the fields and farmland. The scenery was something she'd taken for granted when she lived over here, but it was now pulling her in and making her crave life in the UK. Her fellow passengers were reading books, tapping away on laptops, flipping through glossy magazines; all busy with their own lives, inadvertently making Saudi look colourless and boring. Over there, there was no music allowed in public areas, no buzzing nightlife, no cinemas – nothing interesting going on. Of course in the compound such restrictions were lifted, but a realisation had dawned on Anji over the past few weeks: when you know something is for-bidden, after the initial excitement of the danger, the rope around your neck starts to grip tighter and the enjoyment becomes tainted with an undertone of guilt and unease.

Sipping water from a bottle, Anji was fighting off waves of nausea as she reached her final stop. She was dreading the moment she'd have to tell her mum about all of this, and could feel a headache teasing the edges of her brain. She had contemplated making her ex-cuses and catching an early flight home but, as much as she didn't want to have to face up to her parents, she yearned to see them and be told that everything was going to be ok. Besides, she had a parcel to collect which, according to an email which she'd hastily de-leted, had arrived at her parent's home. Alighting the train and taking in the familiar – though almost from another life – atmosphere, she didn't have to wait for a taxi as they were all lined up, ready to collect passen-gers. The taxi driver at the front of the queue hopped out and put her suitcase into the boot, then jogged back round to the driver's door. Anji was still standing there next to the back door, so used to doors being opened for her that she'd forgotten that she could just get into the car herself. It felt strangely liberating, opening the door and climbing into the back seat of the taxi. She told the driver the address and took in the familiar, nostalgic sights on the route back to her parents' home.

Starting as she meant to go on, she paid the taxi driver then took her own luggage out of the boot and headed up the path with it. Spotting her dad tinkering outside in the garden, Anji's face lit up. Her parents were the safe port in her storm and she adored them. She felt guilty that she was about to lumber them with this huge burden in their advancing years, but she knew that they would want to know and would be there for her. She trusted no one else like she trusted them. When her dad caught sight of her, he smiled as he put down his tools and walked slowly over to her. She took a little jog towards him and gave him a huge hug. He still had the same smell that she remembered as a child, though had never really noticed since until now. She pulled, away, tears streaming down her cheeks, and looked at him. He looked old and it made her feel sad. She had missed so much since she'd been away. Before she had time to speak, her dad said,

"You'd better go in and see your mum. She's been worrying about you." Before she could protest, he had picked up her suitcase handle and started wheeling it in towards the house, gesturing for Anji to go first. She couldn't help but do a little run to get there, and when she did she dived through the front door and into the arms of her awaiting mother, sobbing tears of relief, sadness and happiness all at the same time.

After a long time hugging and crying – Anji's dad had given up waiting and gone to put the kettle on – Anji's mum pulled back and held her at arms' length.

"Oh my God Anji, you look so thin!" Her mum was frowning clearly worried as she wiped the tears from her eyes and cheeks. "Sit down, sit down. Tell me what's going on. Why are you being so secretive?"

"Not now Mum, later – please, just let me enjoy you both."

Anji looked around the two-bedroomed bungalow. It

was a far cry from the large house she had grown up in, but retirement had brought her parents to a smaller place which was easier to maintain. Fifty years of family history were all around, with photos of Max and Georgie and their toothless smiles taking pride of place in the living room. There was a beautiful framed photo of Anji and Jeff on their wedding day; Anji looked so elegant in her beautiful white dress, wrapped in happiness and dreams. At the bridal boutique, Anji had chosen the dress that looked effortlessly simple. She found it sandwiched between the puffy meringue styles, which looked like rejects from My Big Fat Gypsy Wedding. It was the only dress she bothered to try on, and she bought it that same day. It had fitted perfectly, hugging her figure exactly where it should. Unlike many of the old photos of her in the house, which looked dated and made Anij cringe, this one looked both timeless and regal; Anji's make-up was flawless and Jeff looked impeccable in his designer three-piece suit. Just like the photo, the wedding day had been magical. It was a small affair of 150 people gathered in a little church, which dated back to Saxon times. Jeff wanted a civil ceremony but Anji had said it was her dream to walk down a church aisle with her father. After a few sleepless nights, he had relented. She didn't know what had changed his mind, but it had made her love him a little bit more. The evening of the wedding, they'd enjoyed a reception in the garden of a beautiful country home, filling the huge marquee with music, laughter and the tinkling of champagne flutes being kept topped up. Her wedding was something Anji would never regret. When he had asked her to marry him, she had said yes in the same breath. The day he proposed, Jeff had announced the date for the wedding day, which was four months later in May. There would be no hanging about, no delaying the wonderful union. She'd felt ecstatic tingles of euphoria, and that rush lasted for the next two years until she was blessed with the news that she was pregnant.

Anji snapped herself out of her reverie. "Mum, can we go for a drive, just you and me?" she asked. "We'll bring you back some of your favourite cake," she said, nodding in her father's direction. Her dad knew better than to ask what was going on, and didn't even raise an eyebrow. She was sure he knew something was up but he'd probably ask her mum later. He was definitely a man's man who didn't handle emotion very well. He was also very protective and if he found out about the cheating he'd phone Jeff and threaten to kill him. Although she appreciated his protection and loyalty, it would ruin her plans and make the divorce process much more complicated.

After a short drive and a rather stressful parking experience, the pair chose a bench on the prom by Brighton beach and sat together, enjoying the spring sunshine on their faces. As they watched the happy families walk by, Anji told her mum everything. Her mother sat in silence, taking it all in. She was a resilient person in every sense of the word – tough and strong. Her concerns were more about the children and she said she'd support Anji in anything, as long as the kids were protected.

"We love Jeff like a son," she admitted. "This is the horrendous news, but the children are what's most important here."

"I know Mum. I went to see a solicitor and she told

me what my next steps should be," Anji explained as her mum listened intently.

"I know you will do what's right Anji. I have no doubt about that." She took Anji's hand in her own. Anji noticed the paper-thin skin on her mother's hand and squeezed a little tighter. "You know you're always welcome to move into our house if you need somewhere. I know it's small, but me and your father can take a smaller place." Her mother had always been a practical person and seemed to have a solution to everything. It made Anji feel safe. She turned to look at her mum. *Offering her their home at their age? What an amazing woman.* Anji began to well up again. Were all parents as amazing as hers?

"We are right here for you Anji, and for those lovely grandchildren of ours. Whatever you need us to do, we are right by your side." All of Anji's emotions rose up in her chest and spilled out of her as she began to sob again. Her mother kept a hand across her shoulders, letting her release all the pent-up anger she'd been harbouring, without saying a word. With no judgment or criticism, she was just what Anji needed; a solid pillar of reinforcement and strength.

CHAPTER 21

Anji woke up bright and early. She wanted to spend as much time with her parents as possible before she headed back to Saudi. She desperately missed her children and wished they were here with her and with their grandparents. Her dad was busying himself with the door, which had seized up over the winter. Anji buried her head in the newspaper, enjoying the little luxury of the daily news and headlines – something she always indulged in when back in the UK – while her dad swung the door back and forth.

"You know," he began, "I often wonder, do you ever miss the UK Anji?"

"I do," Anji admitted for the first time out loud. "You can't imagine the small things I miss, like having the paper to read, you two crazy people, of course, and the freedom of living life how I want to live it." She paused, unsure whether to voice something she had been thinking for a while. "I'm thinking I might move back...I might move to London." Her dad looked up after slamming the door for the tenth time.

"You're going to break that door, not fix it!" Anji joked.

"Interesting..." said her father, still focused on the door. "It's funny you say that. I was just talking to Bill – you remember Bill? Bill and Margaret? – Well, Margaret just passed away. It was awful; he didn't cope well with it at all it was really sudden. They lived in Kensington and when she...wasn't there anymore...he didn't want to live there alone so he moved in with his daughter down this way. He wants to get his own place down here so he's going to be selling the Kensington house. Cheap too. It needs a fair bit of work..."

Anji sat straight up with excitement. "My God, Dad, that's exactly what I want!" She realised how insensitive she must have sounded so back tracked. "Sorry to hear about Margaret. She was a nice lady."

"Bill said she was a bit of a pain in the arse, but she was his pain in the arse, you know? Not like your mother. She's a saint." Anji's mind jumped to when she had felt like that about Jeff; like she was the luckiest woman alive. Imagine feeling like that after 50+ years with someone. A small part of her was still telling her that she and Jeff could feel that way again. She wondered if things would have been different if they'd stayed in the UK. Then she remembered what she'd overheard between him and Sara.

"Do you think you could speak to Bill for me?" Anji asked her dad. Her dad nodded, then turned back to work on the door.

She wasn't sure if she was ready to live anywhere alone, but she had got this far and this opportunity sounded too good to miss. It also gave her some focus. She couldn't afford to buy a house herself – Jeff controlled all of their money – so she would need him to buy the house for her. She had no idea how she would get them back to the UK and convince him to buy a house which he wouldn't be welcome to live in, but she was going to try her absolute best to do it. She would find a way, and this Kensington opportunity could be it;

she could tell Jeff about the place and this could be her starting point, allowing her take her first tentative steps back home to the UK.

She watched her dad packing away his wood plane and screwdrivers. He had deep brown eyes, weathered by creases, and a head of messy grey hair. His hands were well worn from years of hard graft. Industrious and reliable, that's what her dad was. She watched him as he triumphed with the door, which was back to full working order, with a curt nod and short smile.

Anji headed to the small box room bedroom to pack her small suitcase, taking the recently delivered spy equipment out of its boxes and putting the instructions in a secret slip pocket in her luggage. She had always wondered why there was a secret pocket and now she knew; it was for all those women who were trying to catch out their lying, cheating other halves.

"Hey Andrew," Anji heard her mum call to her dad. "I'm off to Saudi to visit the grandkids." Her mum popped her head round the door and winked at a bemused Anji. "You didn't think I'd let you do this alone, did you?"

Anji called Rita right away to get her mum's Visa for Saudi arranged through the embassy, then all she'd need to do would be to send her passport to the office in London. She would be ready to fly in about a week and Anji would stay here until then and fly back with her. She didn't bother to call Jeff to let him know; he hadn't called her once since she'd been away. Once upon a time he would have called at least five times a day, checking in on her every move. If she were honest with herself, she was glad for the lack of scrutiny. She spent the next week making plans and reconnecting with her family and homeland. Other than the kids, she felt no desire to go back to Saudi. She remembered how excited she'd been at the prospect of moving over there; the glamour, the luxury, the weather... It all seemed fake, dull and lifeless to her now. She wished she could just fly the kids over here tomorrow and never have to return; but it wasn't that simple. She had to see this through. She had to be brave. Thankfully, a week in her parent's home with a cool breeze on her face, her stresses behind and in front of her, and some freedom and independence, had given her more strength than she had felt in years.

On the fight home she went over the plan, scrawling it on a paper napkin which the cabin crew would soon sweep away:

    1. Get back home for Easter

    2. Buy a house

    3. Check out schools

    4. Get pictures, voice recordings, anything that could prove what he was up to.

She was amazed at how suddenly she'd started seeing England as home again, but as the plane journeyed through the clouds, closer to their destination, her positivity began to fade. *What had Jeff been up to whilst she was gone? Did he love Sara? Would he leave his family for her?* Anji couldn't forget how he'd looked at her that night. He was hungry for her, it was obvious. He had never, ever looked at his wife in that way. She felt an instant pang of jealousy in her stomach and it crushed her. Sadness, anger and resentment raged away in her heart, and her insides were a mess, making her want to vomit. She realised she would need to push these feelings down and learn how to hide them quickly if she was going to carry on pretending to be the perfect wife to her cheating husband. With the sound of the plane's engine drowning everything else out, and her mother next to her fast asleep, Anji let herself feel everything for one last time. Her lips began to tremble and she felt the tears come.

CHAPTER 22

"Yes! Granny is here too," Max and Georgie chorused in unison as Anji and Jacky came in through the front door. They wrapped their arms around their Mum and Granny tightly as they always did. The joy in their faces was priceless. Gifts emerged from Granny's bag one after another before she'd even sat down. The kids' naivety was comforting; they didn't question why granny was here at all, distracted by the Toblerone and other goodies she'd purchased at Duty Free. Anji hoped they would stay this way when she was a divorced, single mother of two, and not succumb to broken home syndrome. She couldn't help fretting about their futures when she looked into their innocent eyes.

When Jeff came home later, he effortlessly played the part of the loving, wonderful, devout husband that everyone thought he was.

"Wasn't easy to arrange your Visa you know," he joked with Anji's mum. "It's lucky I like you, or you'd still be waiting in Heathrow! They're getting tougher on visitors, even immediate family." Anji and Jacky smiled nervously, not looking at each other. They knew Jeff was smart and would have noticed something was off. Jacky did a great job of acting normally, initiating some small talk about his work and life in Saudi. He didn't stay long, apologising and excusing himself, blaming work commitments.

A few days later as the kids disappeared to play with their newly-acquired iPhones – an early Easter gift from Granny and Grandad – Anji explained to her mum in great detail how she had planted the spy equipment whilst she had been catching up with her Grandkids and unpacking. Under the pretence of popping out to get some essentials, she had smuggled the equipment to Jeff's workplace, after confirming with Omar that his boss was elsewhere. She had been able to get into his office without raising suspicion, explaining to Rita that she would wait for Jeff in there because she needed to speak to him about something going on at school, and had planted the hidden iPod camera which she'd set up earlier.

"Oh Mum, my heart was in my throat, I swear!" Anji explained. "Fiddling with the bloody iPod… I'm not an expert when it comes to computer stuff, but I think it was working when I left it. I was scared to death of getting caught." With some underlying guilt, Anji had given the keyring to Max to gift to his dad. She felt awful involving the kids, but the fob was an ugly thing that Jeff would never have used if she had given it to him; if he received it as a gift from his son, however, he'd feel obliged to attach it to his keys.

Anji's mum began giggling, already a little ball of nervous energy. They set each other off, both feeling a little overwhelmed. Once they'd calmed down, wiping a tear from her eye, Jacky explained,

"Look Anji. Your dad and I have chatted, ok? You do whatever it takes and the worst-case scenario is you take our bungalow. We've discussed it. We have enough, and everything is for you in the end anyway. If you just want to come home now then you can." Anji burst into tears. Tempted as she was to leave everything and go back to the safe home of her parents, she couldn't do this to them. They'd given her everything; she couldn't keep taking from them. Their support was enough to spur her on. She was determined that she could do this, and with her mother by her side, she felt stronger every day.

As Anji dabbed at her eyes, the doorknocker sounded. It was Lily, arriving unannounced.

"Hi Mrs Brown," she chirped. "How are you? I let you have a few days with your family before I came around but I wanted you to know I've arranged a brunch for you tomorrow. I haven't seen you since last year and I missed you!" she said as she reached in to give her the three same kisses she gave everyone.

"Oh wow," said Anji, feeling deflated by her friend's sudden interruption. "Erm...Yes, ok, we will be there," she muttered. She wondered how Lily even knew that Jacky was here.

"Anji hasn't been herself of late Mrs Brown," divulged Lily. "We're all worried about her, especially after the episode in the hospital." Lily looked sideways at Anji as she said this, and Anji got the impression that she was trying to catch her out somehow. Jacky clearly got the same impression and wasn't having any of it.

"Yes, we were all so worried. But, she's a tough cookie. As you know I had a small fall recently and Anji flew straight out to be with me," she lied skilfully. "I don't know what I'd do without her". She gave Anji a squeeze. Anji was impressed by the way her mother had retaliated so gracefully to the subtle dig at her daughter. She had the impression that her mum had never liked Lily anyway. She had met her a few times during her visits to Saudi and had always been cautious around her. Not that she had ever said anything about this to Anji; she never liked to stick her nose into other people's business.

After a few seconds of awkward silence, Lily seemed uncomfortable and began to look around the room and pick at her nails. After a few more seconds she chirped, "Well I'll leave you to it ladies, see you tomorrow." She let herself out.

As the door shut behind Lily, Jacky looked over at Anji, willing her for an explanation of what had just happened. Reluctantly, Anji explained to her mum about how Lily was somehow responsible for her new reputation as a homewrecker.

"But you know Mum, somehow if this hadn't happened I would still be the stupid fool I was," Anji admitted. "This whole situation opened my eyes, so in a way I'm grateful. Or maybe I'm just looking for excuses for it all. I don't know."

"You don't need to justify yourself, Anji," her mum reassured. "Let's go and put the kettle on. What do you have for dinner out here?"

Jeff was home today by seven o'clock earlier than usual and sat in the living room chatting with the kids and his mother-in-law like a perfectly conscientious, faithful husband. Anji had to bite her tongue and supress all of her bubbling emotions. She didn't want him there. She needed her mum all to herself, and he was here demanding all of her attention. Typical selfish arse that he was. He was being extra nice to her mum, attentively offering to refill her glass of wine whenever it got low. Jeff was keenly questioning Jacky about her fall and the condition of her leg, which Anji could tell was making her mum feel uncomfortable; she could lie if she had to, but it wasn't in her nature, especially after a few glasses of wine. Anji changed the subject by mentioning the up and coming brunch the next day.

"You're on your own!" he said, wrongly assuming that this was an invitation for him to join them. "You know Friday is brunch at the hotel and it's the busiest day of the week due to a lot of VIPs coming in." Anji felt relieved. She'd already known he wouldn't attend anyway, but it was nice to know that he was being kept busy elsewhere.

Anji stifled a fake yawn and her mum followed suit. "You know what Jeff?" Me and Mum are shattered must be jet lag, I think we might turn in for the night."

"Come on Mum I will put the hot water on for you" Anji followed her mum up the stairs, and wished that she could stay in her room with her tonight rather than having to go back to the marital bed. *Remember, you have a plan.* After saying goodnight to her mother, and peeping into each of the children's rooms to check they were asleep, Anji went into her own bedroom. A lump formed in her throat at the thought of having to sleep next to Jeff; as it happened, she didn't need to worry as Jeff didn't come to bed that night.

CHAPTER 23

The summer heat of Riyadh was fierce. It was stiflingly dry and the temperature was way above usual at thirty-nine degrees. Jacky basked in the heat, enjoying the sensation of summer. It had been a long winter in the UK this year, so the heat was perfect and the sun oiled her old bones. Walking with Anji through the compound to get to Lily's house, Jacky admired the gardens. They were in full colour, exotic flowers blooming in glorious shades, with the grass lush and green. Anji explained that in a few short weeks everything would be dead, as nothing would grow in this heat, even with gardeners watering everything twice a day. As the compound had a mass exodus of women and children at the end of June when school was finally done, the gardeners accepted the fate of the vegetation and conceded to the ritual of replanting everything by September when the families came back ready for school.

In the summer months, the compound was filled mainly with men who stayed on to work. They were the main breadwinners and, left to their own devices, they usually played poker five times a week and congregated at the restaurant for their evening meals. Jeff had never involved himself in this tradition and for the first time the realisation of why clicked in Anji's mind; another group of people joined the compound during the summer months: beautiful, slim, young air hostesses working for private jets, who had undeniably been chosen for more than just their people skills. Jeff had obviously had better things to do than to play poker with the guys.

As they arrived at her villa, Lily welcomed Anji and her mum with flutes of bubbling bucks fizz. Anji sipped the fizzy cool drink, which slipped down her throat quickly in this heat. Another full glass soon appeared out of nowhere, and Lily motioned for her to drink up. Lily was a great and generous hostess but, with no food in her stomach, the second glass was making Anji nauseous. She headed to the kitchen to help herself to a piece of fruit.

"We are moving out next week to the bigger villa," said Lily, cornering her near the fridge. "I can't wait! The kids are ecstatic, as you can imagine. But," she added limply, "Sam needs to go to another school." Gone were the dancing eyes from when she had been told the news they were allowed the bigger home, and gone was the smile that could have lit up anyone's darkest day. She explained how Sam was in the Swedish school, which only taught kids up to the age of thirteen. After this, the children had to study online. Sam wasn't the kind of child who was capable of this on his own, so he would have to go to the American school in Riyadh. But, Lily explained, they couldn't afford it – after all, it was the most expensive school in Saudi – so unless a miracle occurred they may have to move back to Sweden to attend a school there. Feeling a bit giddy from the alcohol, and out of a loyalty which she felt bound to, Lily balanced her bucks fizz on the countertop, and started composing a message to Jeff. Anji knew Lily was telling the truth; it was well-known that the school had a very small campus and could only teach up to a certain age.

The American school would be the best and closest system for Sam to transfer to. As she typed, she considered the situation – the brunch, the alcohol – and couldn't help but feel a little used. Had Lily been betting on Anji wanting her children to able to go to the most prestigious school? Had she hoped Anji could call in a few favours and organise a scholarship or tuition transfer, just like she had been able to help with getting them the bigger villa? Anji always wanted to see the best in people, and even if Lily had buttered her up to ask her this, wasn't that what friends did – help each other out?

"Thanks, Anj, you're the best!" Lily hugged her tightly then walked outside again to chat with Jacky. With her phone still in her hand, Anji felt the strength she had built up within herself start to leach away, leaving her feeling empty and worthless.

CHAPTER 24

Today was the day Anji had been anticipating with fear and dread; the day to see if the spy gear had collected the evidence she needed. Jacky had agreed to go through everything with Anji for moral support. The kids were getting ready to go to their activities. Georgina had begged her Granny to go along too, but Anji promised her she'd go and watch next time. She certainly wasn't ready to deal with this shit alone.

The minutes passed by excruciatingly slowly, but as soon as the children were out of the door Anji and her mother sat down immediately. They opened the laptop and followed the step-by-step instructions for operating the key ring recording device.

"You need a PhD to understand this gobbledegook," Jacky chirped after reading the first few lines. Anji took over and managed to decipher the instructions clumsily.

"Be prepared darling," her mum instructed. "Either way, you know what you are going to do." She looked into her daughter's eyes. It was hard not to see the pain reflecting from her soul. It ripped her heart open. She secretly prayed for an honourable outcome, but had little faith her prayers would be answered. Anji looked anxious and scared as they each placed headphones over their ears. Sitting side by side, Anji's mum held her daughter's leg in a tight grip. The doors were locked and the keys left in place; they didn't need anyone bursting in on them. Anji began downloading the hours of recordings which took a deathly slow twenty minutes, so in the meantime they sifted through the iPod recordings, which were much easier to access but they couldn't seem to get any video recordings only voice audios. This was monotonous, boring stuff that neither of them were interested in. Her mother stifled a yawn as she listened to chatter about hotel meal services and issues with housekeeping. Then suddenly, Jeff's voice: "Rita, please keep Wednesday at four o'clock free. No meetings. I have a VIP client in, so keep everything clear. I don't need to be interrupted for any reason at all." Their ears pricked up; this could be a potential lead.

They fast forwarded, using the time code on the iPad recording to guess how far on they'd have to go to reach Wednesday afternoon.

'Hello Sir, Madam Najda is here for your meeting.' Rita's voice trilled out from the laptop.

"This must be it!" said Jacky, excitedly. Both women fell silent as they continued to play the recording. Geoff's voice came on now.

'Send her right in, and please do not disturb under any circumstances. She is very important to us.' There was a sound of the door closing and keys jangling.

In a whispering voice, Jeff said, breathlessly: 'Get over here now, you dirty bitch.' More heavy breathing. 'I want to know that your wet pussy has been right here on my desk – give me something to think about in my morning meetings. I haven't been able to think about anything else. Get on my desk now, you naughty girl.'

Anji's face drained of colour now looking as pale as a ghost.

'Yes, Sir,' a voice purred. It was obviously Sara's, and Anji's hand flew to her mouth; relief that it wasn't yet another woman, but shock that they had been at it in his office.

'I love this look, the professional businesswoman act; behind that beautiful face and body you're just a dirty whore. Do you know how I've fallen for you? I'm crazy about all this.'

"Najda" was moaning softly, with Jeff grunting at a steady tempo. Anji could picture exactly what was going on; he'd entered her a thousand times before, making the same sounds. Anji had never felt so mortified; not only filled with shame but also with embarrassment that her mum was listening to all of this with her. She was so very grateful that she hadn't set up the Video properly when she planted the equipment in his office.

'Your pussy is so wet. It's begging for me to be inside you.' Sara went from gentle moaning to 'ah, ah, ah' as he seemed to be thrusting deeper.

Anji and her mother were transfixed on the recording like they were listening to a box set and the plot twist had finally been revealed. Neither Anji nor her mum made a sound; instead, they sat in awkward, stunned silence. All her mothers' hopes and prayers hadn't worked after all. Anji had never experienced such a strange mix of emotions. There was the anger and sadness at the realisation she had caught him in the act, making the same noises she knew only too well. Then there was the feeling of emptiness, which began by gnawing at the pit of her stomach and ended by creating by a hairline fracture in her heart. Then there was the stab of jealousy, moments of genuine hate, and even fleeting thoughts of ending it all. Life as she knew it had changed forever.

"I can't listen to any more," said Jacky, shaking her head and looking disgusted as she removed the head-phones from her aching ears. "I feel like I've done ten rounds with Mike Tyson." Anji noted fleetingly that this was a strange comparison, but was too wound up into this alternate reality, which was apparently her life, to think any more of it.

"We have enough for that lawyer of yours I think, don't you?" A small tear crept out from her eye and Anji could see her hands shaking.

"No," Anji replied, staring at nothing in particular. "Mrs Watson said I need photos and videos." She was speaking on autopilot, unable to focus.

This was a devastating blow for Jacky. Revelations of a sordid affair were bad enough; this happened to other peoples' kids, not her own. Tears fell from her eyes but Anji had no words of solace for her mum. A fire was raging through her body. She felt so unbelievably angry. She was so tempted to play dirty and have him deported by reporting him to the religious police. They would have a field day with him. But she knew it would start a hate war between them and she hoped she was clev-erer than that. She needed his reputation intact for the sake of the kids. She wanted her house in Kensington, she wanted the kids to attend a decent school, and she wanted money in the bank. She could start a new life and he could continue his job in Saudi and fuck whoever he could get his hands on.

She had to be smart and stick to the plan. She de-cided then and there that she wasn't going to do any begging. If she was skilful enough, she'd calculate her moves and manage to deal with Jeff while remaining emotionally detached. Jeff was no fool either; if he could do it, so could she. But it would be easier said than done.

"We've got to listen to the keyring recording." Anji took a deep breath and opened the now downloaded audio file.

'Wow you look amazing habibti,' they heard Jeff saying. Habibti was an Arabic word for darling; so he was even using her language now.

'It's going to be awkward in the car, but just lift up your Abaya. I'll have to be fast, but I'll make it up to you later. I promise.'

He was doing the same with Sara that he did with his wife; just using her to relieve himself. What a selfish prick. She was sure Sara wouldn't put up with that for long.

'Oh fuck, you are so tight and delicious.'

'Is it better than hers?' Sara murmured.

'My God, are you trying to make me lose my hard on? You know you turn me on. Look at this for validation if you really need it!'

Listening to this was like a chainsaw being sawn into Anji's chest. She felt it make its way into her abdomen, even feeling the guttural vibrations of its motor as it shredded her guts. Feelings of shame saturated every cell in her body. She skipped forward through the recording in a bid to avoid the inevitable noises. Anji thought she'd throw up if she had to listen to that.

The unmistakable sound of a zipper, and lots of rustling. Then her voice: 'You know if you love me, you'll have to convert to marry me,' Sara said. Of course, she was a Muslim. Anji couldn't believe her ears. 'If you don't have a prenup, you'll keep your fortune. And you have rights with the kids if you want to keep them. So if the shit hits the fan anytime soon you'll be a protected man.' It was disturbing hearing Sara chatting more like a businesswoman now, not a floozy who'd just been screwed in a car.

'I've told you before, I have millions in the bank,' Jeff's voice reassured. 'She won't get her hands on it, that I can guarantee you. She doesn't even know how much I have. The dumb cow never asked. That money is for our kids – yours and mine.' Anji's jaw dropped and her gut lurched as she thought she might chuck up. 'And I'm not religious, Sara. I've told you before. When the time comes, we'll have to elope somewhere and have a civil marriage.'

Without taking their eyes off the black screen, Jacky grabbed Anji's shaking hand.

'Fadi will take the kids as per my religion,' spoke Sara. 'But they're older now. They'll be fine. And I won't give you up for them....'

Anji and her mother both gasped in shock at what they'd just heard. A mother giving up her children for her lover seemed unthinkable in any religion or culture.

Anji stopped the audio recording and turned to her mother. The pair of them looked like they had been through a natural disaster. Jacky's face was swollen from the tears she'd been crying, and Anji was ashen from the shock; it was like a ton of bricks had fallen out of the sky straight on to their heads. After a few minutes, Anji broke the silence.

"Punch me Mum, I might wake up." Anji goaded, trying to find some humour in this unbelievable situation. Despite the temperature outside, Jacky got up to put the kettle on; it seemed like the only thing she could do right now.

Anji's mind was a whirlwind of thoughts, feelings and sounds which were crashing into each other and pounding into the sides of her brain. A thread surfaced which she clung onto – maybe because it was less painful than the others. *'I have millions in the bank. She won't get her hands on it. She doesn't even know how much I have.'* It dawned on Anji that she had never asked him how much he was worth. She knew he had a large sum and was comfortable, but had never really needed to know the details before now. *'That money is for our kids – yours and mine.'* HOW DARE HE?! She could fathom him keeping his money from her, but from Georgie and Max? Who was this person she was married to?! She felt distraught; distraught for her kids, who deserved so much more than this sorry excuse for a father. Anger boiled up inside her and a sense of determination washed over her.

"I have to get photographic evidence." She said it to herself, but Jacky had walked back into the room at that point with the tea.

"Why don't you speak to your lawyer? I'm sure this will be enough..." Anji cut her off.

"It's not enough mum," said Anji, bluntly. "She told me. He's going to fight me all the way and I can't have any risk of this getting thrown out for being inconclusive. I need photos, or videos if I can." Jacky nodded. Before she could ask the inevitable, Anji said,

"I'll have to follow him. I can't risk getting someone else to do this for me as I don't know who I can trust. It's got to be me."

Anji and Jacky spent the rest of the afternoon devising a plan for how Anji could get the evidence she desperately needed. Jacky kept encouraging Anji to take a break but Anji was determined. She just wanted to get it done.

The plan, Anji decided, would be executed the very next day if possible before they had time to change their minds. With women still being barred from driving in Saudi Arabia, she would have to conceal her gender and dress as a man to drive a car and follow Jeff. She knew this was risky; she would be breaking more than one law. Anji considered asking Omar to drive them so she wouldn't have to pretend to be a man, but she knew that she couldn't involve him. She couldn't risk the consequences of him following Jeff and getting caught, and refused to put him in the position where this was even a possibility. Jacky insisted that she should be in the car too, to reduce the chances of her daughter being pulled over. The police were less likely to stop a man driving around an old woman. She would dress in her abaya with a head cover shrouding her face. From this point, as they didn't know where Jeff would go or what he would do, anything could happen and they would have to be prepared to deal with what was thrown at them. It wasn't an ideal plan, but it was the best they had.

CHAPTER 25

'Hi Jeff. Any news on the Lily school situation?' Anji sent the message to Jeff, having not had an answer from her previous message. She hated having to text him anything other than, *'How could you?! You cheating, lying son-of-a-bitch?!'* but, somehow, she thought, that wouldn't help her to get out of this situation in one piece. She couldn't wait for this charade to be over.

Anji and her mum had barely slept since yesterday's quite literal, blow-by-blow account of the affair. Outside her mind, life carried on as normal; she woke the kids, fed them and got them to the bus. With so much else on her mind, she'd managed to ignore everyone on the compound, but she knew the gossip was worse than ever. Everywhere she looked, there were women engaged in the latest whispering campaign. It was torture; Anji had no one to turn to and felt trapped inside her own head, constantly fighting with the enemy that lived between her ears. Self-doubt crept in at the weirdest times and she often had to remind herself that this hadn't been a choice. *Life is unpredictable, Anji; shit happens.* She was on the verge of completely burning herself out with self-sabotage, which wasn't helping her current predicament. No-one seemed to notice or care, except for her mother of course.

On the way to work, a message pinged up on Anji's phone: 'I've asked already. I sent a request. I'm not doing anything that jeopardises my position.' *That's damn rich*, she thought to herself, as she envisioned him banging Sara on his office table with his trousers rattling round his ankles. After yesterday's revelations, she was walking around as if every nerve ending in her body was exposed. She felt raw and vulnerable, imagining it would only be a matter of time before everything got too much and she exploded. She felt the bile rising up into her throat as she walked towards the door of her office, knowing that her husband's lover was going to be on the other side. She swallowed it down, took a breath and pushed open the door.

"Good morning Sara! How are you?" Anji trilled, a little too enthusiastically, as she stepped over the threshold.

"You know, life is great. Really great!" her boss replied. *I bet it is*, thought Anji. Who wouldn't be ecstatic having two men – her husband and her lover – running around after her? Before Anji had chance to reply, she felt her bag vibrate. She took out her phone, which flashed up 'Hospital' on the screen. She looked at her phone, confused. She wasn't expecting a call but she hastily answered, worried that something may be up.

"Good morning Mrs Harris. This is the office of Doctor Hassan. He has asked us to call you, as you didn't turn up to your appointment. Could you pass by at four o'clock to discuss your results?" a soft-toned lady enquired. *Crap!* Her mind was so full that she'd forgotten she had her follow up appointment. This was the last thing she needed.

"Could you please just tell me over the phone? I don't really have time to pop by, my mother is visiting." Anji asked, an edge to her voice.

"Unfortunately not. Doctor Hassan stressed that he needs to see you in person. But it will only take a few minutes of your time," she urged.

"Ok, four o'clock," Anji agreed and put the phone down. She already felt guilty leaving her mum in the mornings, and now she'd have to leave her in the afternoon while she headed to the hospital. Deep down she knew that Jacky loved the peace and quiet of the villa and could handle being along for a few hours; it was Anji who wanted to spend as much time as she could with her mother. She was her safe space.

Anji wasn't going to let the small fact that her boss was fucking her husband get in the way of her doing her job. Despite everything, she smashed through her to do list and felt an inner sense of pride at her achievements that day. It felt good. Anji decided to pop to the hospital on her way home from work, rather than wait until 4pm. When she arrived, she was escorted into an empty room. The plaque on the door read 'Doctor Azeez'. This made Anji nervous. Why would she be waiting for a doctor called Azeez?

"The doctor will be in shortly. Wait here," said the Indian lady with glasses about three sizes too small. This was probably the only place where women didn't have to wear abayas. Instead they wore crisp white trouser uniforms. Anji wished she was wearing trousers; her abaya had got twisted on the door knob somehow when she'd entered the room, and when she'd tugged to release it, she'd heard it rip. Gazing over at the strip of torn black fabric on the floor, she shrugged. Oh well. She hated wearing the damn things anyway. Deep in thought, her eyes remained transfixed on the cloth until she heard the familiar tones of the handsome doctor she remembered.

"Hello Mrs Harris." Dr Hassan spoke gently, entering the room. "I've been worried about you. You didn't turn up for your appointment," he announced as he closed the door behind him. Anji noted that this was something a male doctor would never usually do in Saudi when attending a female patient, unless she had a chaperone.

"I'm so sorry doctor," Anji apologised. "I rushed off to the UK, I've had so many things on my mind." Dr Hassan gave her a small, forgiving smile.

"Now, the reason I've called you here is..." There was a long pause.

Suddenly it dawned on her; maybe she had a life-threatening disease? Maybe it was incurable? Jeff would end up getting exactly what he wanted – her out of the picture. His wife would die and he would get the kids, money and his mistress ruling the roost. What an absolutely perfect fucking ending. Her children would have a new mum. She grew very hot under the collar and was feeling a little frazzled. She tugged at the neck of the cloak to allow her some space to breathe.

"What is it?" she demanded.

"This is very difficult for me and extremely unorthodox. Please let me apologise for what I'm about to say."

"No apologies needed, just tell me. Am I sick?" she urged

"No, no, no that's not it. Listen, please. I...I can't stop thinking about you." Anji's thoughts stopped sharply, derailed from their high-speed journey. "From the moment I met you in Accident and Emergency,

I haven't stopped thinking about you. I feel like I've known you for years. I just had to see you again." He sounded like a love-struck teenager. "I'm so sorry if this has offended you Anji, but I just had to tell you," he confessed. "I have never felt like this about anyone."

Anji sat there. Her body was still, no words came from her mouth. She had been shocked into silence, feeling flattered and embarrassed all at the same time. It had been months since she'd received any kind of attention from Jeff, and she was feeling needy. Her mind flashed back to the last time her husband had used her to mark his territory. It had been harsh and foul, and she'd failed at her attempts to erase it from her memory. Now she was being reminded again of how lonely she really was. She imagined the doctor taking her in his arms and kissing her tenderly. Appreciating her as she was – imperfections and all – and feeling sexually desired by him as he whispered sweet, tender words in her ear. She roused herself from her daydream realising he was still talking.

"I had to tell you now because I'm leaving Saudi. I've had an offer to work in London, running my own practice in Harley Street. I was born and raised in the UK and now I'm going home. I've had a million arguments in my head, trying to talk myself out of telling you this... but since I'm leaving I felt I had to be courageous or foolish I don't even know what you would call it." He was building up to something. "Did you feel it too Anji? Did you?" His eyes pleaded with her, searching for a yes.

There was absolutely no denying that they did have a connection, a spark of something. But Anji couldn't handle any complications and she wasn't stupid enough to embark on a relationship when she was still with her husband. She even considered it was Jeff trying to trap her, She couldn't think straight and it was too much.

In the UK, he would have been struck off for such revelations, or faced a disciplinary from the General Medical Council. But in Saudi Arabia, they wouldn't have taken a complaint from a woman seriously – not that Anji was thinking of reporting him; she was secretly flattered by the so needed attention.

"Do you know I am married with two children, doctor?" Anji ventured.

"I just thought... Well, I just had to tell you. That's all. Life is too short not to get on and live it." He spoke in muted tones, looking towards the white tiles of the hospital floor, deflated and disappointed.

He opened the door for her; no words, no handshakes, no goodbyes. Anji left in a blur of emotions.

CHAPTER 26

In Saudi Arabia, Friday was the day of rest the Sunday of the West. It was a family day and since Anji's mum was in town, they were all going for brunch at Jeff's Hotel. Anji couldn't remember the last time they had all been together. Things certainly felt much different to the last time, when they'd been a secure family unit. Or at least Anji had believed them to be.

At the last minute, however, Jeff decided to take them to the Kempinski rather than 'his' hotel. He said his mother-in-law deserved a treat and she should at least see the competition. Anji now sadly doubted everything she heard coming out of his mouth from the smallest thing, but she was starving and just glad to be getting some food.

They all clambered into the car, Anji allowing her mum to take the front seat next to Jeff. She could see from the back seat that it aggravated him, noticing a displeased frown cloaking his face in the rear view mirror. This of course dispersed immediately when he turned to look at Jacky, showing her a quick grin the Hoteliers face. The journey was tense and quiet until they entered the ostentatious grounds. The hotel was beyond opulent, with fountains and lion statues lining the entrance. If they had been anywhere else, they'd have been in awe. But in Saudi it was just another outlandish place to go and visit.

The kids were overjoyed. Their faces lit up when they saw the choice of food on offer. Everything was beautifully displayed; so lavish and extravagant. From whole lobsters to exquisitely-carved watermelons; there was so much to choose from. The children's expressions were an absolute picture as they watched the extra-large ladies bustle around the buffet, overfilling their plates. They were totally captivated, and at one stage Anji had to have a quiet word with them to discourage them from staring; for one thing it was rude, and secondly, it was quite embarrassing.

Anji and her mum took a walk around, looking at the hundreds of items on the huge buffet. They picked out their favourite seafood while Jacky gave her daughter a quiet lecture on when to approach the subject of moving back home. It was something the pair of them had been talking about for days now. Anji had been so confident when she was discussing it with her mother, but now her throat was tight and she was apprehensive. She panicked that this bout of stage fright would give her cold feet, but she knew it had to be done soon. It was now or never and she couldn't fluff her lines now; she was way too invested.

As they delved into the food, Anji attempted to take a bite out of the crayfish. She, at that moment realized she had no appetite, and the bulging eyes stared at her urging her on, she cleared her throat. "I'm thinking of taking the kids back to the UK this summer." She blurted it out quickly. Before Jeff had a chance to speak, she continued. "We can get a small place in London. The kids can go to school there. You can commute from there. Long-term, Saudi isn't a good place to be since the kids will be teenagers soon." She said this second part without taking a breath, but was so relieved that the words had tumbled out with no hesitation. She focused on the crayfish, its eyes still intact. She felt like it was mocking her, but it was most definitely dead.

Jeff remained stone cold silent, muted, staring down at his plate and pushing his food around with his fork. Max and Georgie had both stopped eating and were looking back and forward between their parents. Max started to speak but Georgie kicked him under the table. Anji tried to clear the air.

"Jeff, they don't even know how to cross a road. They need roots. They need to belong somewhere. You have to agree with me on that," she pushed.

"They belong with their parents," he scowled. Anji could see that she'd made him insanely mad. His ears had turned bright red. But she knew him well enough to know that he wasn't going to lose his cool in front of her mum or the General Manager he personally knew too well. He straightened up, planting a false smile on his face.

"So tell me when you thought up this little plan Anji; was it all by yourself? Even your mother can tell you, I give you a life any woman would dream of!" He looked straight at Jacky, but she was too flustered to respond, and busied herself fiddling with her Abaya under the table.

Anji suddenly remembered what she'd heard Jeff telling Sara while he was fucking her. He'd said he wanted Anji back in the UK so the two of them could play happy families. She wasn't sure whether he was just playing a game, or perhaps he was upset because she had broached the subject first. Either way, she had planted a seed and, if she was clever enough, she could make him feel like it was his idea. How the hell she was going to do that was beyond her, but she was going to give it all she bloody had.

"Dad told me there's a property coming up cheap in Kensington. It would be an amazing investment for you. Needs a little work, but it'll pay you back dividends. And we always wanted a home in London, right? For the kids eventually..." Money had always held Jeff's interest, as well as his legacy.

The children had remained quiet during the whole conversation, nibbling away at their food like church mice. They were alarmed by their dad's sudden out-burst, and they couldn't miss his ears burning bright red; the vein bulging angrily in his forehead. Anji car-ried on, telling him to strike while the iron was hot, in the interests of the children. She realised she was using the kids as pawns in the scenario, but decided the ends justified the means. She suggested to him that the school holiday in May would provide the perfect oppor-tunity to return to look at the house.

"We'll miss you terribly, don't misunderstand Jeff." she offered, "But sometimes we have to make sacrifices for our family. We both knew that it would come to this eventually; we've discussed this before." They hadn't discussed it ever before, but she knew Jeff wouldn't ask when and where they'd talked about it, since he hadn't heard a word she'd said in months.

Jeff looked over at Jacky, who smiled graciously at him. "OK. I'll take a look. But I'm not promising any-thing," he asserted. He needed time to weigh up the pros and cons. Maybe it was a good idea, he deduced, but he still needed to decide whether it was in his best inter-ests.

Max and Georgie could barely contain their excitement. They'd been waiting for their cue to be able to speak, and couldn't keep it in any longer. Jumping up to squeeze their dad, they squealed, "Yes! We're going to the UK!" Jeff hugged them back, while giving Anji an evil sideways glance. He made a point of saying they'd only be going back for a holiday at this stage, but Anji took this as a win, one step forward. Jeff could now have Sara all to himself; he'd be free to do whatever he wanted, whenever he wanted. The truth was, Sara would rule him with an iron fist. She'd make his life miserable. Anji knew Jeff better than anyone and she had become used to his weird and wonderful behaviour, but Sara would never accept his eccentricities. Sara would try and change him, mould him. He would understand later what he had taken on, but Anji wasn't worried anymore. She was on a mission to get out of there as fast as she could.

How stupid men are, she thought, so blindsided by pussy. And as for Sara, taking on a man with baggage – a wife and two kids – at the cost of her own sons. Anji knew the millions in Jeff's bank account had everything to do with it.

In the car on the journey back to the compound, Anji had decided to ride up front. She didn't want to infuriate Jeff more than she already had. Max and Georgie were busy making plans about their trip back home. Granny was encouraging them, which excited them that little bit more. Jeff remained hushed, probably reasoning with himself that getting Anji out of the picture would make his life much easier. Or so she hoped.

Anji smiled faux-sweetly in Jeff's direction. She gulped some air as a wave of panic washed over her. Her mind was thinking 'man up prick!' she then envisioned a huge L tattooed on his forehead. Her lips continued smiling smoothly, but her mouth said nothing.

CHAPTER 27

Anji donned a beanie, tucking her hair up neatly inside it. She'd found it in a dirt-cheap shop on the outskirts of the compound. She had looked for pants and a shirt there also, but had no luck they had nothing that would help her pass as a driver of one of the privileged expat families, so she took one of Jeff's shirts and paired it with her own jeans. Finally, she smudged a little black eyeliner under her eyes and around her chin. That would have to do as a five o'clock shadow. Most of the drivers looked permanently exhausted since they worked so many hours, so her natural demeanour should fit the bill nicely. Anji studied her reflection in the mirror – she looked beyond ridiculous, but it was the best she could do. It would be very easy to lose her nerve at this point, especially since she had to drag her mum along with her, but the thought of the kids kept her fearless and unflinching.

Anji's mum looked perfect in a black Abaya and black face veil. All that was visible was her piercing blue eyes. Anji looked at her and burst out laughing in normal circumstances she would have taken a picture for the holiday album but this wasn't a souvenir they wanted to remember or re-capture. They were both feeling a little volatile, so

Jacky stood in stunned silence, unsure of how to react to her jittering daughter and their crazy situation.

"Look Anji," Jacky began. "Are you ready to do this? If not, we can devise another plan. You don't look ready at all to be honest with you. I can't see what you find funny. I'm a nervous wreck!" she confessed.

Anji sobered up quick smart when she thought about her nerves. They were about to commit a crime. At this time of the evening, the kids were at the cinema on the compound watching the latest Spiderman movie, while most of the menfolk had already arrived home from work after making their way up the long, palm-fringed road that led into the compound. She hoped there was no one around to see them both in their farcical outfits.

Anji climbed into the driver's seat. Her feet reached nervously for the pedals, and she could feel everything shaking; her hands and her legs quivering. Both she and her mother gripped with terror. With racing hearts and shallow breaths, a sense of nervousness penetrated their every cell. They didn't speak – there was nothing to say.

The unlikely duo, were relieved to get through security without a word, thinking themselves dreadfully lucky. They were also glad of tinted windows, which were difficult to see through especially since it was getting dark outside. The guards just waved them on. The difficulty would be when they arrived back – if they made it that far. The plan was for Anji to drive to the office and wait for Sara to leave work. They would then follow her. Anji was on edge already. Driving in Saudi was madness, so she concentrated on the road whilst her heart banged like a blacksmith's hammer in her chest.

By 6.30pm, they were nearing the office. Jacky sat fiddling with the camera, checking it was working. As they pulled up near the building, they watched Anji's colleagues Meera and Rowena leave. Their husbands were waiting in the parking lot across from the office for them, and as they gave each other a wave goodbye and stepped into their respective vehicles, Anji and her mum swivelled their heads back towards the door. Sara swept out of the building gracefully, her hair on show and looking ready for a night out having locked up for the night. When Anji had left the office earlier, her boss hadn't had a scrap of make-up on. Now it was a different story. She looked like phenomenal even decked out in her black Abaya.

JEFF WAS PULLING UP RIGHT UP BESIDE HER.

"Fucking hell Mum! Bingo!" said Anji, much more loudly than she had anticipated. "He is so fucking predictable." Sara was looking around quickly, before ducking her head and getting into Jeff's car.

Anji put the car into drive and they followed the couple. Her foot trembling as she pressed on the accelerator. She made sure there were at least two other cars between them as they drove, so they didn't draw attention to themselves especially since Jeff would recognise the car. Probably his hand was way up her Abaya now and had other things on his mind anyway, like banging his bit of fluff. Anji kept her gaze fixed on their car, since they were taking side roads now they pulled up into a small side street slowly trying to find a place to park. Jeff and Sara then emerged from the car Jeff grabbing hold of her hand looking more like a married couple rather than a pair having a straycation. They made their way to a large gated house surrounded by a high red brick wall.

Anji decided in that moment to park slightly out of eyes view. She took a few deep breaths before climbing out of the car. She told her mum to stay in the car and pretend to sleep. Under no circumstances was she to get out of the car; that was a strict order. She was sure her mum had aged two years with the stress of the last few weeks, and no doubt Anji had aged even more.

Her hands shook as she passed through the unlocked gate, closing it gradually to avoid any creaking or banging. She then walked around the perimeter of the house. It was dark – Anji was grateful for that. The outside was paved, and she had to be careful with every step in case she fell over something and caused a racket. She realised she was getting good at this sneaking around lark, and was thinking way ahead of the game. The windows at the front of the house had iron bars decorated with pretty flowers. The bars covered the entire window, and the curtains were drawn so there was no way she would see inside. Hoping she'd have better luck elsewhere, Anji dropped to her hands and knees to creep undetected to the back of the house through the side alley way. The light around the luxurious swimming pool helped her to see a little more as she spotted light coming from a ground floor window.

At this point, she considered running back to the car and forgetting about it. It all seemed so sordid and sleazy plus her knees and hands hurt for scraping them along the concrete and grazing them on the small sharp pebbles. Then she imagined herself struggling on a minimum wage job in a council house, and not being able to cover the bills. It spurred her on. She was panting now, like a dog on all fours. The pulse in her ears was drumming so loud, and her heartbeat raced so fast she wondered if she was going to make it out alive.

She laid back trying to catch her breath and noticed an outhouse for the generator which she slowly crept over to and leaned up against it. Taking two more deep breaths, Anji steeled herself, building up the courage to peer out. Sara was in full view removing her Abaya. She was stark naked under it, not even underwear. Dirty Bitch thought Anji to herself as she watched Jeff fiddling with his zipper his eyes boring into her the whole time intensely. She then sat naked beautifully naked, with the body of a twenty something precautious on the bed as he was already hard, put his 9 inches into her mouth without kissing her, touching her or even trying to tease her. Good old selfish Jeff shaking her head in disappointment. Sara on the other hand certainly knew what she was doing; she was definitely a pro, going at it like a dog with a bone her salivary glands producing enough fluid to paralyze Jeff with ecstasy. His eyes rolling back drunkenly, intoxicated by the seventh heaven he was experiencing. He grabbed her hair from the back to stop her sucking his cock,she obeyed. Next he laid back on the bed before she jumped up from her seated position straddled and rode him as you would a wild stallion her breasts moving in a perfect figure of eight motion mesmerizing, dazzling really.

Anji had always been the submissive one in their relationship, and Jeff was the boss in that department. It was clear as day that Sara was the boss in their liaisons. How did Jeff like that, Anji wondered. He'd made his position very clear from the start of their relationship; taking her in missionary position, fully in control. She'd loved the feeling of his bulk on top of her, and was more than happy since it was the only position that Anji could really reach orgasm as he hit her g-spot – not every time, but some of the time. She felt so betrayed. Why hadn't he spoken up? She would have been more adventurous and even tried harder in the sack. He obviously wanted his wife to be the obedient subject and his mistress the unbridled stallion so he could keep her in check.

He gently moved Sara over after all her buccaneering and fucked her ever so slowly. Their lovemaking was sensual and burning with desire. Anji was completely transfixed. It was as if she was watching a full-on sex movie; even she couldn't help feeling slightly aroused. She wished she were able to handle herself the same way. Sara threw back her hair and her body tantalised every taste bud in Jeff's mouth. She knew Sara would see the euphoria in his face, and she felt sad knowing that she could never bring her own husband to that level of elation.

"Oh fuck, got to take pictures!" Anji cursed under her breath she had forgotten the camera in her haste in the car so would have to take them on her mobile forward them to her Mum and delete from her camera roll ASAP.

Making sure there was no flash, Anji began zooming into their faces so they'd be visible in the pictures. It wasn't easy – all she could see was legs and arse. She tried her best resting her body on her knees gaining a little height and was grateful she'd never have to do this again, especially while she watched them snog so passionately. Jeff had told her that he didn't kiss other people on the mouth she was the chosen one, because other people's germs disgusted him, yet here he was, almost swallowing the bitch.

Snapping away she certainly had plenty of evidence now. She took a couple of breaths before slowly crawling again back to the closed gate and quietly opening the door she did a sprint back to the car, a sprint that Hussein Bolt would have been proud of. The hot air filled Anji's deflated chest and she felt like she was ready to puke. It had all been so surreal. She jumped in the driver's seat, gasping, her lungs burning. Her mum looked over and gave her a stern look: "Take a minute for goodness' sake – you'll black out in that state and kill us both!"

Anji gulped some air. She wished she could lie down, but she really needed to get back to the security of the compound. A tingling sensation ran up and down her arms and legs, she felt disconnected while she panicked about the whole situation. Focus, I can do this, she repeated to herself; I can do this. Doctor Hassan had taught her to use the mantra when she was struggling. Taking a deep breath, she pulled the car out of the street and headed home; grateful for Sat Nav, since she had no idea where they had ended up. Her mother held up the camera "I wanted to bring this to you but I was so scared I'm so sorry".

Anji explained she had her mobile and gave it to her mum to scroll through as they drove back in silence listening to google maps. They parked up outside the compound and Anji put on her Abaya that she had cleverly remembered. She couldn't get back in without security taking note of the new driver, and she didn't want to raise any suspicions. She wiped her face with its generous sleeve, trying to take off the stubble she had attempted to paint on earlier. She let her hair loose and they walked through security bowing their heads, exhausted and silent as the men gave them a wave, not knowing what the duo had just unbelievably pulled off – without a hitch.

CHAPTER 28

Jacky had packed her suitcase and was ready to fly home. They had hardly mentioned the day's previous events. They were worried in case they too were being taped. Since she had planted the spy equipment, she realised how easy it was to do, and had become suspicious of her own home being planted with any devices. Every time they wanted to talk, they locked themselves in the bathroom and whispered to each other. Even then, Anji wasn't 100 per cent secure that they weren't being watched.

"Look Anji," Jacky had told her daughter, "Don't let this ruin you. The children need you to be strong and in a good place mentally. Give me the videos and photos and I'll send them to your solicitor. I'm so proud of you. I know you'll do what's best for your family. You have your father and I; we can support you all for a while until you get yourself on your feet."

Anji didn't know where she was going to find enough strength, but she was damned if she was going to give up now. The feeling of being alone without her mum was daunting, but she needed her to deliver the evidence; it would certainly swing everything in her favour. She always had her parents' support if shit hit the fan, and that she was grateful for. Anji hugged her mum so tight and thanked her quietly, as she pressed tighter. Tears pinched both their eyes and they were unable to look at each other any longer. It was agonising knowing that the next few months ahead would be torturous for Anji as she tried to keep everything together.

That night as she lay in bed, she closed her eyes and watched the porno movie of her husband and his bit on the side play across her eyelids, as it did every night. She couldn't get it out of her head. Anji had always been self-conscious and shy in bed, but Sara was confident; basking in glory as she mounted her ride, sending Jeff over the edge, rotating her hips while handling his balls. She felt sick knowing she had stayed too long and seen too much. But she'd had to, to gather the evidence.

It hurt because she knew she would never be able to seduce Jeff the way Sara had. The way he kissed Sara when he'd told his wife he could never do that. When they'd had sex there was no lying in the pool of sexual juices after intercourse, no hugging in his arms her face pressed against his chest, no legs laced together and entwined as they slept after climaxing. There'd never been any pillow talk, expressing their hopes and fears, sharing funny stories and staring into each other's eyes. Jeff would rather jump straight from the bed to the toilet to have his shower and return fully clothed. There was no gentle kiss goodnight. Jeff got into bed and immediately turned his back to Anji. She would try and hold his torso, and he would lift her hand off and place it on his hip. He didn't want her hands around his waist. In the early days, Anji had hoped for more. But over the years, she'd tried to understand him and his peculiarities. And as his affair came to light, she realised that a lot of his peculiarities were in fact just another way for him to control her. As her awareness and strength grew, she started to notice the shackles of their marriage.

Lying in bed, she reviewed the rest of her plan in her head; she wasn't able to write anything down so hoped she could remember everything. There was no room for mistakes, so Anji had to keep it simple in order to remember all her lies and schemes. She needed to cut her emotional ties to him, and she'd embark on her plan the very next day. Realising she was capable of a lot more than she had ever given herself credit for, Anji felt she could breathe more easily. As the weight lifted, she drifted into a dreamless sleep.

CHAPTER 29

The following morning, Anji trailed behind the kids, who were playing tag on their way to the bus. She let them run ahead and was relieved to have a little time to herself so she could think about her plan. She'd have to strike today before the nerves got the better of her and hysteria sunk in. She was glad to avoid the vile bitches who were out to give her dirty looks, though, truth be told, she was well on her way to not giving a shit. The bus whisked past and she managed to blow a kiss to Georgie who was waving fiercely.

Approaching her on the pavement was Bonnie, out walking her little terrier before the tarmac got too hot. Anji quite liked Bonnie; she hadn't had any grief from her. Not yet, anyway.

"Good morning lovely, I saw Jeff yesterday with a blonde in Gucci at the mall," Bonnie revealed. "He told me he was getting a gift for your birthday. Lucky girl – hope I didn't spoil the surprise!"

"Ah, I'll pretend I didn't hear anything then!" said Anji as she carried on walking, hot footing it back home so she could get to work without getting entangled in dog leads or niceties. A blonde? Was he really flaunting his multiple infidelities so blatantly? Mind you, nothing would surprise Anji now. And another thing; was Bonnie trying to confide in Anji about her husband's infidelity? It sure felt like it. And if she were, Anji appreciated what she was trying to do, though she wished people would just talk to her, woman to woman, rather than gossip and drop hints.

"Hi Anji!" beamed Sara, popping a cup on Anji's desk as she wafted into the office. It was an occasional treat from her boss, and Anji wondered what Sara was after when she stated the obvious. "I got you a Starbucks." Sara looked like a million dollars today; full make-up, perfectly coiffed hair with every strand knowing its place, a green silky dress on which just screamed quality, and stunning red suede sandals. There was a bag to match, which Sara placed on her desk with a flourish, as if to make a point. There it was, with its signature green and red ribbon. Bingo! There were the goods, right in front of Anji's eyes. If there'd been a hope in hell that the Gucci was for her, that rumour was completely squashed now.

"Wow Sara, you look out of this world!" Anji complimented her, teeth gritted, before venturing tactfully, "Did hubby surprise you with this new handbag?"

"No, actually. I treated myself. I think I deserve it; I work very hard. I earn my own money, so why not? If you work even harder for me I'll buy myself the bigger one next time!" she said, bursting out laughing. "By the way, I have a meeting at noon, an important one. So if anyone asks for me I'm otherwise disposed, you understand?"

Oh great, thought Anji. *First she lies about the bag and now she's lying about her meeting with my husband.* The audacity! Giving the scorned wife instructions to lie about her whereabouts whilst she fucks her man. The woman is one merciless bitch.

Anji decided to use the time Sara was 'out of office' to give her mum a call, and hope that things were moving on apace with Mrs Watson. She tapped her pen impatiently, waiting for 12 o'clock to roll around, while she watched Sara touch up her make-up yet again. The Gucci bag was making her eyes hurt. An image popped into her head with no warning, showing the whites of Jeff's eyes as they rolled back in his head the look of pure intoxication as Sara rode him like a bucking bronco. Anji squeezed her eyes tight shut to banish the thought.

"Out of sight, out of mind," Anji said out aloud, not meaning to be so vocal.

"What does that mean?" enquired Sara, bemused by the sudden outburst while she pressed her lips together to blot her lipstick.

"Oh nothing, I just mean you'll be out of the office, that's the message if anyone calls asking for you." Anji covered her tracks. She jumped on her mobile once Sara had finally left. "Mum, mum – tell me what happened with Mrs Watson! I've been absolutely desperate to call you."

"Good news," revealed Jacky. "She says you have a watertight case! The photos were so explicit apparently. She said she had to print them at a self-service thing in Tesco's to avoid anybody reporting her for the pornographic content!"

"Oh God, I hadn't thought of that," Anji realised. "Sorry to put you through this mum."

"It's ok. But she said if he's clever, he can still pull a fast one somehow, especially if he gets good family lawyers. You could still be left with nothing. If you buy a house it should be in the kids' names. Try and get your own money in an account because he could freeze everything. She said it's very important to play happy families."

Anji felt completely deflated knowing that, even with all this evidence and all the risks she took, he could still screw her over. Life seemed oddly unfair. She'd still have to defend her corner, even though the evidence stacked up against him and it should be an open and shut case. A simple matter of dividing everything up fifty/fifty which she would be more than happy with.

As she left work, Anji saw the car parked at the same place as always. Only there was no Omar. Opening the door for her was a small Indian man.

"Hello! Erm, where is Omar?" she probed.

"Omar gone, Omar left," he claimed. It was just her luck that she would get a driver who couldn't speak bloody English. She knew it wasn't worth asking him again; she'd get the same answer. She tried calling Omar but his phone was off, so thinking he must be sick, she sent him a text asking him to call her. Just as she was putting her phone away to get in the car, she received a text from Lily. 'Please pop over at 8pm, I have something to tell you.' Anji replied that she hoped it was good news, but something didn't feel right. She couldn't put her finger on it, she felt uneasy.

At 8pm sharp, Anji walked round to the side door of Lily's now much larger home. The first thing she noticed was the huge television emblazoned on the wall.

"Wow," exclaimed Anji. "The house looks amazing Lily, you've done a great job. The TV looks like it belongs in outer space, it's really amazing!"

"60 inches and everything works by hand gestures," she bragged. "I wish something else round here was 60 inches!" This had them both cackling immediately. It was just what Anji needed; a good laugh.

"I'm so thrilled for you all, and I mean that from the bottom of my heart." Anji smiled, realising it had been her first genuine smile in weeks.

"Let's celebrate! Baileys on ice?" asked Lily. As she prepared the drinks, Adam walked in.

"Hi Adam, are you coming or going?" Anji asked.

"Funny you say that. I'm not done, but just popped home for a bit." He noticed Lily getting ice out of the freezer. "But I've got time for a drink!"

Anji inwardly groaned. She didn't feel like making polite conversation with him. She was tired and, with him, she always had to make the effort. She felt like making up a story so she could leave and head for the comfort of her own home. If it wasn't for Lily's excitement about the new home and talk of inviting her family over to visit, she would have made her excuses. Despite her concerns, the atmosphere was actually quite comforting, and with all the talk of family and relatives, and the kids being happy with their new bedrooms, Anji felt the tension release as she sunk into the comfy velour couch.

Without warning, Lily launched into Swedish, directing her conversation at Adam. She then galloped off up the stairs. Unsure what had just happened, Anji thought this was her perfect cue to escape. She started to get up and make her excuses when, unexpectedly, Adam started to speak to her.

"Come and sit next to me," beckoned Adam, patting the seat next to him. This threw Anji; this was weirdly out of character for Adam. Anji smiled over at him unsure of what to do next.

"To be honest, I was just about to leave. I've got to get home." She stood up and put her unfinished drink on the side table. "I just want to say I'm so happy for you both and I'm glad things are looking up for you all. You deserve it." She went to leave again.

"Well, as you know I'm a part-time husband and father. This job takes so much from me. I'm robbed of many poignant times – first step, first concert, you know…" Anji could detect straightaway the familiar vibes of emotional blackmail coming from this obviously perfectly memorised speech. He wasn't yet finished though: "I really feel it's about time I was given a promotion."

"Look, Adam, you really need to speak to Jeff about this. I have nothing to do with his work affairs." The irony of her choice of words was not lost on her. Lily came back down the stairs and Adam stood up, put his jacket on and headed towards the door.

"Didn't you just come in?" Anji quizzed.

"Yes, yes I forgot something. I have to go back to work anyway like I said." He slipped out of the door and Anji followed him closely behind him, making excuses about needing to get back for her kids.

Heading back to the villa, Anji tried calling Omar but there was still no answer. It was so strange; he always answered. She called Rita – Jeff's assistant.

"Sorry to bother you Rita especially at night, but I'm desperately worried about Omar. He didn't come in this afternoon and he isn't answering his phone."

"I'm so sorry Mrs Harris, but Omar has been dismissed." Anji's stomach lurched.

"Why? Why?" Anji demanded, incredulous. "Why

wasn't I informed?".

Rita explained that the police had been over that morning and had been sniffing around the car that Omar drove. The vehicle had been caught on a video camera outside a private house, and a figure had been seen snooping around the property. "Although the footage isn't clear, the car number plate is obvious," Rita told Anji. "The homeowner wants him put in prison, but the hotel is now involved, so he's just being deported instead."

"Oh my dear God" Anji cursed, hanging up the phone immediately without saying goodbye. Feeling winded from the blow that Omar was on his way out because of her. She hadn't calculated that far. It would be obvious that the footage didn't show Omar, if only they were clever enough to check the tapes properly. They would see that the man in the footage was actually a woman in disguise. Omar's family relied on him and his salary, and he had no hope of getting another job at his age. In his twilight years, his retirement and hopes were dashed. If Jeff saw the film, he'd recognise the snooper was wearing his own glasses and shirt. Maybe he would even recognise her. Was the game finally up? She would have to confess; she couldn't let Omar take the fall.

"Rita I don't believe it. I want to see the footage please," she typed, firing off a message.

CHAPTER 30

Anji looked at her purple eye bags in the mirror, reflecting her lack of sleep over the past 48 hours. When she had managed to sleep, her dreams were vivid and scary, making her thrash around in her sleep and waking her up. The only benefit was that Jeff had taken up residence in the spare bedroom if he did bother to come home as he couldn't face her fitful sleep. She was so scared of what the next few days had in store for her. The evidence was strong; the car was there, the driver was there. She knew she had no other choice but to admit she was the one at the scene.

Omar hadn't answered his phone because it had been confiscated as evidence. Anji wanted to own up, but somehow she couldn't. It would mean she'd get banged up in some infested jail or face instant deportation – whatever Jeff was in the mood for. Would she allow Omar, an innocent man, to be condemned? If she got away with it, she would reward him handsomely. She would make it her life goal to do so. His livelihood had been whipped out from beneath his nose, after a career spanning some thirty years with impeccable references. Even in a place like Saudi he had managed to keep his nose clean. She was sure he was only there for money to help raise his family and educate them so that one day he wouldn't have to work. He would have planned to sit back and watch all his hard work pay off, but now Anji had put an end to that. It was all her fault. She felt she had a responsibility to Omar and his family, her children, her parents and herself. She had to win hands down; she had no other choice as far as she could see. She didn't trust Jeff one bit. He was a devious, cheating arsehole and she knew, when he wanted, he could be utterly ruthless.

She checked her phone. Rita had sent a message. 'Mrs Harris, both you and Mr Harris have a meeting at 8am at the police station. Make sure your hair is covered and your abaya is closed and decent. It really isn't a place for ladies but they are insisting." Panic ripped through every cell of Anji's body. She was acutely aware of the severity of the crime and the implications. She imagined that if she saw Omar she would just fall apart and confess. Maybe she could use her eyes and sign language to let him know everything would be ok. Her mind flooded with different scenarios. What if Jeff saw the footage and realised it was her after all? He would tell them and she'd be locked up forever, never to see her home country again or her kids. Sara would take over her side of the bed and they could concentrate on being one big happy family. A message from Jeff pinged up on her phone. 'What the fuck r u doing? Why r u putting ur fucking nose in where it doesn't belong? What a bloody embarrassment. I will sort this out not u!'

Anji's eyes darted all over the message like searchlights scanning for answers. Then the penny finally dropped. Anji had indicted herself, thinking only of her involvement, but suddenly she understood. Jeff must be as scared as she was; after all, he had entered the house with his mistress, a woman who wasn't his wife, auntie or sister. Therefore, his job and reputation were at stake too. He himself had also committed a crime in the eyes of Saudi law. He was now more interested in clearing his own name, worrying that the shit was going to hit the fan and everything was going to explode. Anji certainly hadn't properly thought about the repercussions of this – if Fadi found out about Sara, there would be zero forgiveness. Sara and Jeff would end up in prison at worst, and at best deported to their home countries ruined and jobless.

Anji had visions of Omar living like an outcast. How scared he must feel, how humiliated. She needed to come clean to him, but she had no idea how to get hold of him. Would Jeff save him? She doubted it very much; he was more interested in covering in his own arse. The next few hours felt like she was sitting on death row, waiting for execution. Wondering if it was going to be slow and excruciatingly painful, or quick and painless. Finally, her phone rang and she jumped to answer it.

"Hello Mrs Harris," Rita said very matter-of-factly.

"Finally! Rita, tell me what happened," demanded Anji hurriedly.

"Omar has owned up and will be deported on the next flight to the Philippines. He is in a detention centre. Someone from HR is going now with his exit paperwork."

"No Rita, it wasn't him," Anji insisted. "I know it wasn't." She was trembling, and tears were welling up in her eyes.

"You know he has been let off lightly because of Mr Harris being so lenient with him, so it just goes to show, you don't really know anyone. You should be grateful; anyone else would have sent him straight to prison. I know I would have," Rita admitted.

Anji knew she was solely responsible for the demise of her loyal and faithful driver, and for that she hated herself. She looked in the mirror and had to look away to avoid the shame she felt from her own reflection. She knew she couldn't own up now, it was too late. But she also knew she would repay Omar as soon as she could. She would make it right.

CHAPTER 31

"Hello Doctor Hassan? I've had an episode – another anxiety attack. Can you do house calls? I can't get to the hospital; I am really not well enough. I know its nine o'clock, but could you come now?" Anji felt like she couldn't get any lower as a human being after what had happened with Omar earlier on anyway, so she threw in the towel of morality. *Fuck it. In for a penny and all that.* Feeling completely and utterly vulnerable, her self-respect in pieces after her decision not to own up and save Omar, Anji had turned to the only person, other than her parents, who made her feel like she was worth anything. If nothing else, Doctor Hassan would make her feel beautiful and worthy, and if it turned into something more, then even better. She would allow herself to be taken by the gorgeous doctor. Yes, she felt guilty and sordid, but she needed this, to be free from her emotional shackles to Jeff. He had severed his ties a long time ago, and now it was her chance to do the same. This wasn't an affair. It would just be one night to let go and be set free.

Anji knew Jeff wouldn't come home that night; the news about Omar was too hard to face and he didn't need the aggravation. Plus, if Sara knew about the video, she would probably already be putting pressure on him to make decisions. They'd already had one lucky escape today with Omar taking ownership of the crime.

Anji called the security gate. She let them know her doctor would be making a house call. Without advance notice, he stood no chance of being let in. Security was extremely tight around their compound, especially after there'd been bomb threats a few years earlier. She then went to her dresser and pulled out her best underwear. Even if he never got to see it, it made her feel good putting it on. She felt feminine and sexy; something she rarely felt these days. As she was pulling her favourite dress over her head, she heard the doorbell ring. She sprang to her feet to open the door before he rang again and woke up the kids very aware that she hadn't thought this part of her plan out properly.

It was dark inside and out. She hadn't turned on the lights; she didn't need nosy neighbours taking an interest in her already-complex life. It really was pitch black outside, but if anyone did notice a visitor and asked security, it was only a doctor on call. She opened the door to the doctor, who had clearly just come from a busy day at the hospital. He looked tired and a bit dishevelled but still gorgeous as ever. His eyes widened as he caught sight of her in her slinky dress, and she could see from his expression that the real purpose for his visit had just clicked into place in his head.

She hadn't planned it to be this way, but without a word, she pulled him gently by his waist into the house. She turned to close the door and as she turned back round, he was already leaning in to kiss her. As his lips touched hers, desire ran from her lips straight down to her inner thigh. It was instant and explosive, and her knees buckled slightly. She took his hand and led him up the stairs to the spare room – she didn't want to do this in their marital bed - but the spare room was next to the children's room, so she hesitated in the hallway. His hands cupped her breasts from behind as he kissed her neck, breathing heavily into her ear. She could felt the hardness in his trousers pressing against her and she knew she wouldn't be able to keep quiet, so she had no choice but to take him into her bedroom across the other side of the hall. As they locked the door behind them, he began to loosen her dress from her shoulders, which slipped to the floor, exposing her bra and panties. He looked at her hungrily and she was reminded of the desire in Jeff's eyes as he looked at Sara at the spring party. She pushed the image out of her mind and grabbed hold of the doctor, kissing him seductively as he rubbed his hands down her body, across her curves. He pulled away and took off his jacket, then started wrestling with his shirt buttons. She suddenly felt a bit self-conscious, not really knowing her next move. It had been years since she had ever had to think about what to do in the bedroom as she usually just let Jeff do what he liked with her. The thought of this made her angry, and the passion rose inside her, making her want the doctor even more. She grabbed him by his belt and pulled him towards her. His face contorted into ecstasy as she undid the belt buckle and unbuttoned his trousers, pulling them down over his bulging erection. He pulled her close to him tightly, kissing her passionately as he unhooked her bra and slid it down over her small breasts. She felt vulnerable and self-conscious, and her hands instinctively moved down to cover herself. Hassan grabbed her hands, taking them above her head and pinning them to the wall. Still holding her hands up, he kissed her neck and moved down her body, seductively licking her nipples. He made his way to her stomach and, releasing her hands, bent down to the softness of her inner thigh. It had been less than a minute in total and he was already down between her legs. He kissed her panties. She could feel they were already moist. "I think you're ready," he whispered, still on his knees as he tucked his fingers under the fabric and to pull them down to the floor. As he nuzzled his face closer to her pussy, she couldn't stand up any longer.

"Let's take this to the bed," she panted, as he picked her up and carried her over to the bed, placing her down gently. Anji lay naked in the dim light, watching as the doctor removed the rest of his clothing. She felt like it was her first time, nervously watching as he pulled down his underpants and kicked them away. She wasn't disappointed. She couldn't help but compare him to Jeff as his rock-hard erection glimmered from the light of the street lamp behind the compound walls.

She let down her guard. She wanted to enjoy tonight. She knew she would never see him again after this. They both had different lives. He pressed himself against her, kissing her gently. He moved down her body, teasing her with his tongue. She let out a moan – she couldn't help herself. She felt desperate for this. She grabbed his head, pulling his tongue closer into her. He thrust his finger inside her and moved rhythmically, stroking her g-spot. It was so raw, intense and delicious. She couldn't wait any longer. She pulled him up with her hands, cupping his face. He looked her in the eye as he entered her. She had to close her eyes as she felt such a deep connection with him that it unnerved her. Her orgasm was almost immediate and so powerful that she shuddered from the electricity which surged through her. Content that she was satisfied, he allowed himself to give in and climaxed powerfully.

They laid in each other's arms, both panting from the rippling effect of their orgasms. She couldn't remember the last time she'd reached orgasm, and her muscles still pulsated, delivering the most divine feelings of pleasure. She realised how she'd been denied all of this in her own marriage to Jeff and felt resentful at the years she'd lost. She could never go back now. As they lay together in her favourite position, her face in his chest as he hugged her tight, she knew that what she'd just experienced would stay with her for a lifetime. Guilt started to seep in. She had wanted this to be just sex, but it had brought about so many other feelings.

"I'm no better than my husband who is having an affair," she whispered. "I'm worse in fact." He hugged her tighter.

"I already knew about it." He admitted.

"You knew what exactly?" she asked, turning her head up towards his face.

"Your husband and your boss, right?" he spoke softly through the darkness.

"But how do you know? I haven't told anyone except my mother."

"That friend of yours, the blonde one, she told me." Anji remained silent, trying to absorb the latest betrayal.

"I should leave," he said, starting to move and gather his things. "I don't want to make your life any more complicated than it already is." He reached down to her where she lay in bed, touching her face gently. "This was my last week here. I'll be back in London from next week. When you come during the holidays, call me." He gave her a smile and kissed her on the forehead. As he dressed, he pulled a card out of his wallet and put it on the side table. "This is my new number. I'll be waiting." He winked at her which send a shudder through her body as she replayed the seduction in her mind.

Just as quickly as he had arrived, he had now disappeared, letting himself out. The amazing rush she had felt was slowly draining out of her as other thoughts were dropping into her mind. So Lily actually knew everything but she hadn't had the decency to mention it? Was she now just as bad as Jeff, using a man for her own satisfaction? How had she let him cum inside her – was she losing her bloody mind? She jumped up from the bed and rushed to the bathroom to wash herself. One thing she was absolutely sure of was that her life was a fucking mess.

CHAPTER 32

Anji's entire day was consumed by thoughts of the night before. The sex, the energy, the magnetism; despite the guilt, somehow it kept her sane knowing that someone out there wanted her. Had she really been reduced to this, so desperate and greedy for affection? Moving her attention to any man who gave her a sideways glance? But if she were honest with herself, this had been more than just sex. There was a connection, she was sure about it. All these years with Jeff she had been on a road to nowhere, trying to please him and never succeeding. But with Hassan she was on a two-way street, a kind of mutual understanding equals.

"Sara you're looking so glamorous these days. You have a glow like a woman in love." Anji overheard the comment by one of her work colleagues. *Arse licker,* she thought.

Sara grinned, unable to hide her gorgeous veneers. She was evidently pleased about something, and Anji wondered what Jeff had promised her now.

"So, Sara, Jeff and I are off to the UK next week," started Anji. "We're spending it in London looking for schools and a house. I'm looking to relocate at the end of the school year."

"Yes I know!' she declared.

"Sorry, what exactly is it you know?" Anji blabbed.

Of course she knew, but the sting was still harsh to accept nevertheless. Now she understood why Sara had a grin plastered all over her face; Jeff had promised her exclusive rights and access to their bed, along with the title deeds. The thought of Anji being out of the picture had made Sara smile. How sweet, thought Anji as the venom grew inside her heart.

"Well of course, you've mentioned it before." Sara's skin was developing a hue of salmon pink. Anji couldn't resist the temptation to have a dig at her.

"We have two rooms at the hotel, so it'll be kind of a mini honeymoon, you know? The kids are old enough to stay in the connecting room alone now, so I'm hoping Jeff and I can rekindle some of that honeymoon magic." Anji looked Sara directly in the eye without flinching.

"Is that right?" Sara said in a faux-happy tone. Her grin was fading fast as she shifted uncomfortably in her office chair.

"Well, you know, I hardly see him these days with all his *work commitments*," she said, emphasising the words. "I'm going to seduce him. Do you have any tips? You and Fadi seem to have it just right." Anji was enjoying this. Her glare was still penetrating Sara's pupils, and Anji hoped she would break into a sweat and ruin her makeup.

"No. Just don't do anything I wouldn't do," she replied without moving her eyes from Anji's. "Now, if you don't mind, I have an important call to make. Could you close the door behind you? Thanks." Sara snapped.

As Anji left her office, she smiled to herself. She felt a kind of victory. Sara was the jealous type, and the barefaced lies she'd just told must be eating her up inside. If only Sara knew that they were both after the same thing – Jeff's money! Other than that, Sara was welcome to him.

CHAPTER 33

The month of May had arrived, and London was glorious at this time of the year. The weather was fabulous, the trees were evergreen, and the hanging baskets, which lined the shop fronts, were heavy with bright colourful blooms of Fuchsia and Petunia. Jeff was busy checking them all into the friendly Kensington hotel, and was making his usual hotelier chitchat with the pretty receptionist.

Anji realised this was probably the last time she would have Jeff all to herself. For the first time she no longer yearned for his touch or approval as she always had done before. No longer the dutiful puppy that trailed by his side making him look decent and loveable. That in itself was liberating. She now found herself repulsed by his OCD and his constant checking of passports and keys; the way he repeated the same orders and commands to her and the children. It annoyed the hell out of her and his voice put her on edge. The more she saw, the more there was to dislike. She felt a freedom she'd never known. Being a yes girl all of her married life meant that she'd squashed all her own dreams and aspirations. She adored being responsible for others and her children, but Jeff was so controlling and suffocating that all that was left now was a barrel load of resentment.

Jeff had been avoiding eye contact with Anji for reasons he couldn't explain, but he had certainly noticed her more than usual. She looked incredible, better than when they got married. She was lean and toned, just how he liked his women. She was dressed in an off-the-shoulder blue dress, which, against her blonde hair and blue eyes, made her almost irresistible. Gold earrings and gold sandals completed the ensemble. She probably looked a good ten years younger than her real age. Jeff had also noticed the male and even female attention she was commanding. One Italian had shouted "bella, bella," which had pissed him off no end because he had been standing right next to her, but it also made him realise he had forgotten how beautiful she was.

What Jeff didn't know was that Anji's look had been carefully customised and tailored. Before the trip, Anji had booked in with the local department store's personal shopper. She'd asked for help with everything; from which underwear to wear with what outfit, to the perfume she was going to spray on the right places of her body each night. Anji had to seduce Jeff so she could get everything she so desperately needed. To her, this was a business trip. She was going to secure her future, whatever it took.

The first part of the trip involved a visit to a school. When they arrived, the kids started asking a million questions a minute. Why were they looking at a new school? What was wrong with their current school? Anji remained patient, explaining they were just going to look and see. It was more like an adventure at this stage. Jeff remained silent the whole way, and Anji assumed he must have been weighing up the pros and cons London or Saudi, Sara or Anji? The building reminded her of Hogwarts. The school had so much character and history when compared to their Saudi Arabian school, which was an ugly concrete monstrosity. As they walked through the doors, she hoped the children wouldn't reject the idea. Everything hinged on this. Jeff didn't know that over the last few weeks she had been upselling London to the kids. Luckily, it showed in their little excited faces. Anji kept a smile on her lips, so that every time the kids looked in her direction they would be reassured. Glen House was a fine school, with plenty of history, character and atmosphere. The walls were hung with portraits, awards and accolades. Best in sports, best academic achievements, and leadership certificate frames all crowded the walls proudly.

A spritely little man introduced himself as Mr Grindly, and straight away he was addressing the children like they were his own. He spoke to them as if they were young adults, giving them so much respect.

"We will begin with a tour of the property, and then I can answer any questions at the end," he informed Max and Georgie, directing his gaze at them.

Jeff had lots of difficult questions, but Mr Grindly answered everything politely and professionally. Jeff hadn't listened and didn't wait till the tour was complete to voice his queries; he was firing questions left, right and centre and just being damn right difficult.

"Of course, you understand," explained their host, "places at the school are limited. We would need confirmation if Max and Georgina would like to join our big family here. A deposit would be required almost immediately. If circumstances could delay your decision, you would have to go on a waiting list." They shook hands, promising to be in touch early next week.

Jeff remained silent the rest of the day, his mind no doubt in turmoil. Anji and the kids buzzed all day about how exciting and amazing their next adventure was going to be. This only made Jeff feel even more alienated. When distracted by his work at the hotel and his *extra activities* he hadn't been bothered by the huge crater which had opened up between him and his family, but here it left him feeling insecure and unloved. In truth, they validated him as a person. Without Anji and the kids, who was he?

Next stop was the town house in Kensington. They jumped into their hire car and made their way by Google Maps. It was just four minutes' drive from the school, and Anji wondered out loud if things could this be any more perfect, with the school and house in such close proximity. Anji was upselling the house before they'd even arrived, which irked Jeff. His head was full of mixed emotions, making him feel irritable.

"Can you explain how you could possibly know anything about this place when you haven't seen it?" he asked her. "Unless you've seen it and you've been lying to me?"

'No! It's the price tag!" smiled Anji convincingly. "It's so cheap for this neighbourhood. And we can do what we want with it – make it our own." She'd sensed his tension so remained upbeat and passive.

As they reached the property, Jeff excused himself: "You guys go ahead. I have an urgent call to make, I'll be with you in a few minutes."

They clambered through the entrance, with a broken gate lying fallen on the overgrown pathway leading to the front door. Weeds made their way through the cracks in the broken paving, and at first glance it was obvious the place needed some tender love and care. Anji didn't care. She was already sold on the idea, especially since the school would be a ten minute walk for them each morning. Clematis grew on the façade of the building, giving it a lived-in look, and she had to lean on the door as she pushed it open since the mail behind it had piled up and was stopping the door from opening. She looked around for Jeff but he was still engrossed in his phone call.

"Come on kids, help me push," prompted Anji, and they all giggled as they did so.

The heavy door opened to a 1970s green carpet and very retro decor. It was desperately in need of an overhaul, and the whole place smelled musty. The kids immediately dashed upstairs to vet the bedrooms, covering their noses with their hands and unimpressed with the funky smell that enveloped their nostrils. Anji envisioned them living there she couldn't help herself; she was already pulling down walls in her head and adding storage here and there in her mind's eye. She could hear the love and laughter that would echo off the walls. The home was spacious with a long garden, which had room for a summerhouse at the back. The price was around a third less than the neighbouring properties, and they could renovate and make the house feel like theirs. As in hers and the kids'.

Jeff followed ten minutes later looking frazzled and agitated. In those few minutes, Anji had fallen head of heels in love with the place.

"Look Jeff," she said, flitting excitedly from room to room. "The house is a suntrap. It has so much potential.

We can make the conservatory for you. The school is just ten minutes' walk. It's perfect!"

As she made plans in her head, she played on Jeff's ego, thanking him for being the most amazing man and being able to provide for his family. The kids hugged him in turn – unsuspecting unpaid actors in this scenario – and Anji planted a tender kiss on his lips. All afternoon Anji had played happy families, and the energy was alight. Now there wasn't even really a choice for Jeff; As much as he hated it, he knew he would have to do it for the kids.

CHAPTER 34

Georgie and Max settled down to sleep in their hotel beds that night, and spent a good twenty minutes discussing the school and the house. Max told Anji that the next football trophy the school would win would have his name on the base. Georgina was vowing to become the country's next big thing in blogging.

"What subject are you going to blog about?" Anji asked her daughter. This she wasn't sure about, so Max called her an idiot and they giggled again, kissing each other goodnight; their excitement waning as their need for sleep increased. Anji was also weary. Playing the role of the perfect wife and Mother made her brain hurt, but she was aware that she had to keep it together at least for the next few days.

"Can I ask you something?" Jeff pried as Anji entered their room after tucking the kids into bed next door. It took her aback; he hadn't spoken to her like this for as long as she could remember.

"Do you love me? I mean really love me?" This was not what Anji had expected. She remained silent for a good few moments, the shock of this question settling over her. She looked over at Jeff who had a sense of sadness in his eyes.

"Don't be ridiculous Jeff, you know the answer." Anji said with a smile on her face, but unable to look Jeff directly in the eye.

"No, you're not answering, I need a real answer," he beseeched. This time she looked him in the eye and smiled.

"More and more each day," she lied through her clenched teeth. She kissed him adoringly, reminding herself of what was at stake now. Jeff put his arms round her and it became blatantly obvious that she had aroused him. She didn't feel like having sex. She'd be prostituting herself to get what she wanted, when really all she wanted was to sleep.

Jeff searched her face as if looking for clues of love and affection; he started undressing her gently and deliberately, as if it was their first time. He was unbuttoning her dress from the back and kissing her neck. She was tense and cold, but feigned a little moan. He pulled the dress above her head and, without foreplay; he bent her over and entered her from behind. It hurt because she wasn't ready, and she realised she'd never be ready. Not for this, not ever.

She felt something wet on her back and glanced over her shoulder, expecting to see him relieving himself into the small of her back. Instead, she saw Jeff's tears falling down his face and onto her bare skin. It felt almost a silent apology, but it was far too late for any of that. She didn't feel anything. Her thoughts went back to Doctor Hassan and the intensity of her orgasm that night. It had been like nothing she'd ever experienced before; the warmth rising up into her belly and cascading her over the edge, as the wave of energy had washed over her.

As Jeff climaxed inside her, Anji felt unsatisfied and soiled. He still hadn't attempted to fuck her like he had Sara; once again she knew he had just used her to relieve himself. Old habits die hard, she mused to herself.

He lay breathless on the bed, his face turned away from his wife. Anji kissed his cheek. It was all part of the plan.

"I love you," she whispered in his ear. He took her hand and lay motionless.

She was disgusted at herself and felt like a dirty, seedy tramp. She didn't want his cum inside her. It lay there in her insides like a virus. He had fucked Sara without a condom, and the same dick had been in her. She hated it.

****

Jeff woke up at 2am. His conscience was killing him, as he lay still with his wife beside him. What a terrible mistake he had made. 129 missed calls from Sara and as many WhatsApp messages. She might be a thorough-bred in the sack, he thought to himself, but outside the sheets she was draining him. She was in his head and he was out of control, and he didn't like it one bit. She was headstrong, stubborn and ungovernable; everything that Anji wasn't. As he lay in the darkness, with the muffled sounds of night-time London filtering through the closed windows, at that very moment he knew he had to end it with Sara. He hadn't decided how, but it was on the cards. Of course, he knew she would resist. Maybe if he was clever enough he could still fuck her now and again and throw her the occasional designer bag or wedge of cash to keep her quiet.

CHAPTER 35

That morning after breakfast, after just four hours' sleep, Jeff made an appointment with his London bank manager to start the process of purchasing the house from Mr Billings. It would of course be subject to surveyor's reports – it had to be a sound investment. The house would be in the name of Georgina and Max Harris, and would become theirs when they'd both come of age. This was an idea Anji had suggested, and he liked the sound of it.

At the bank, he opened a joint account, starting with a cool £12 million balance. He contacted Glen House before noon and registered both children at the school as of September. They would have to take an entrance exam, which they would conduct in Saudi Arabia, but since they were both excellent students they didn't foresee an issue. As Anji and Jeff signed the paperwork at the bank for the joint account, the kids were fist-punching the air in anticipation of the impending move. They were so excited, working out how they could tell their friends as quickly as possible. Anji was also doing silent air punches in her head. She remained calm and reassured on the outside, making all the right moves and gestures, when inside she was jumping with joy.

"You see how much I love you? I just want to make you happy," Jeff declared when they left the bank. He took her hand. He never took her hand in public because she didn't like it but, instead of wriggling free like so many times before, she held on tight. She knew this façade would all be over in the very near future.

"Well?" Jeff asked, almost patronisingly. He was making sure she appreciated everything he had done that day. How she loathed every cell in his body. Ever the actress these days, she responded,

"Thank you darling, we love you." She said it in plural. She couldn't bring herself at that moment to say 'I love you'. She was still his partner, or she had been until a few months ago. And they were soon to be exes – fingers crossed.

Jeff was feeling oddly fresh, energised and excited. With a spring in his step, he felt good about his plans to end it with Sara and stick with his wife and children. He'd missed London and all its charms, and he noticed all the young, scantily dressed women around. The thought of that alone was making him feel like this move could work in everyone's favour. He could continue accruing his fortune while commuting to and fro. Everyone would be a winner and he liked the idea; he liked it a lot.

Anji felt quite differently. She was hoping that, by the summer, she and Jeff would no longer be an item. They would be in the divorce courts, her battling for half of everything he had. Anji was feeling stronger and more confident. No longer shedding the tears of a broken woman, she was building strength and stamina. In her previous life, she'd been a fool. Lacking judgement, gullible, and a pushover; she would have accepted almost anything. But now that version of Anji was history. She wasn't stupid; as they'd wandered around London she'd seen Jeff look at every woman or girl under the age of 40. She wouldn't have noticed before, but she was no longer the naïve, trusting woman that the narcissist had married. Now her eyes were forever wide open.

Despite everything going to plan, the thought of having to spend another evening in the hotel with Jeff was making her feel quite sick. His every move was now repulsing her; his smell, his breath and even his mannerisms revolted her. She closed her eyes and, against her better judgment, opened her legs as he helped himself yet again. *Its part of the plan*, she reminded herself, grimacing through it. She made all the right noises; moaning, heavy breathing and some sexily-whispered profanities. But she screwed her eyes shut so tears of disgust wouldn't make their way out and mark the pillow.

Once again he erupted in her. This time he had no tears, just groans of satisfaction. It was Anji's turn to cry as she laid there, dirtied by him yet again. She had years of experience by now and knew what to do. She had faked it in the past just to keep her husband's morale up, but now she was faking it to get what she wanted and needed.

"You see, I can still make you come Anji," he bragged. "You know I like to satisfy you. I love you." he crooned.

She turned to him and smiled as she got out of bed to wash his disgusting smell out of her. What a lousy selfish fool, she thought as she feverishly tried to wash away any traces of him from her insides.

Anji laid awake that night wondering what was

going on with Jeff and Sara. He'd been so attentive to her and hadn't snuck off for many long phone calls; something seemed different. Earlier the same evening she'd built up the courage to ask Jeff about the tape involving Omar. Dismissively, he'd told her that Omar had confessed and that was the end of story. Apparently Jeff had asked the owner of the house to dispose of the tape. He hadn't even gone to see it, the coward. No doubt Jeff was scared he would have been sentenced and condemned for the crime himself. He then went into a convincing conversation about how lucky Omar was not to be in prison, and how he had saved his backside. Anji made a mental note to herself that as soon as she got paid, she would send Omar all her salary to tide him over. He would live comfortably in his twilight years; that she would make sure of.

She so desperately wanted to speak to someone else – her mum, Mrs Watson – but she couldn't risk losing everything now she had got this far. She hadn't had a single moment alone, other than in the middle of the night, lying next to a sleeping Jeff. The children demanded her full attention; their excitement required all her patience and she was just managing to keep it all together. So much was happening and at a fast pace now. Like a boulder rolling downhill, every day the situation was building in momentum. And soon it would all come crashing to a stop.

CHAPTER 36

Anji settled down into her first class seat next to Jeff. Her bones ached; in fact everything did. Her skin looked slightly ashen as she sunk deeper into the leather recliner. Her insides were in chaos, like a jumbled puzzle that she couldn't complete because she didn't know what the finished picture should look like. She pinched her shoulders slowly to ease the tension she was feeling; her head weighing heavily on her neck.

Moving her chair back into a more comfortable position, she rested her head on the pillow. Anji looked out at the clouds, letting her stressful thoughts drift away with the peaceful view. Jeff was engrossed in a hotel magazine he'd picked up in Duty Free, and had been in such a good mood when they'd boarded the plane, she decided to ask him about Adam. Was a promotion on the cards anytime soon?

"Not this again!" he snapped. "I'm on vacation! My God Anji, do you fancy him or something? Why the hell are you so obsessed by him?" he growled at her, going from harmonious to hostile in a matter of seconds.

"Of course not! I'm just making conversation that's all," she took a deep breath, immediately regretting bringing up the subject.

He glared at her accusingly. His face was full of disgust at the question she'd dared to ask. Suddenly Anji's insides felt like curdling milk. The nausea clawed at her throat and she heaved as stomach acid rose towards her mouth. She swallowed it back down immediately, but the stench of vomit hit her nostrils. She put her hand over her mouth to hide any odour and, when she felt it was safe, swigged water from the bottle that was placed in the pocket in front of her, courtesy of first class.

"Stop crossing the line. I work for the hotel. You don't. Ok? Don't think I haven't noticed. This isn't the first time you've taken an interest in him," Jeff warned threateningly. She felt a little guilty; her conscience wasn't totally clean, as she'd been naughty between the sheets and wasn't as innocent as he believed. Anji's cheeks prickled as she blushed; she realised that she also held the title of an adulteress. She'd been so busy acting like the perfect wife that she was losing sight of fact and fiction.

It had all gone so well up until now. Anji had Jeff exactly where she wanted him. She didn't want to make the situation any worse, so she decided it would be best to turn her head and pretend to sleep. Maybe then it would just go away. Once a cheater, always a cheater; how could Jeff trust anyone when he couldn't even trust himself? He was probably a sex addict, a chronic cheater. Anji tried to comfort herself with the fact she was in a whole different bracket of cheater as a one-night-stander. In reality, she closed her eyes, disgusted at herself for sleeping with another man while she was still married. She should have waited until after she and Jeff had split. But it was too late for regrets now. With her eyes closed, she reminisced about her evening with Doctor Hassan; him standing there in all his glory, his dark silhouette outlined by the light from the street lamp. The experience had awakened something inside her, something that had been dormant for an extremely long time.

What if Anji hadn't heard Karen that day? What if she was still her old self? She shuddered at the thought. She was beginning to like the new person she was maturing into. It was the first time she felt like a whole person instead of the daughter of, the wife of, the mother of... She would always continue to be the best mother she could possibly be, but now she was going to discover who she really was and what she wanted. She would rely on herself more and learn about her own strengths and passions. No doubt it would be an uphill challenge, but she was ready for it. She still needed to recover, that was sure. But maybe all this emotional pain was a gift to help her move on to a much better place? And, after all, life without feelings would be lifeless.

CHAPTER 37

The children were so excited to get back to school after their holiday. They had fresh news to tell their friends and teachers: they were moving! It would be the first time they'd lived in the UK since they were just babies, and Georgie described her new school in careful detail to her friends while they listened intently. Max was not so enthusiastic, but for him it was just another move. They saw people come and go all the time, so it was a normal part of their lives as expatriate children. Third culture kids like them were generally a lot more resilient than others.

Anji didn't know if she could muster up the courage to go into work. Could she keep up the pretence? Well she had to, she told herself, as arduous as that was. Each day was as difficult as the last; living this lie of being happily married. But it was absolutely necessary to secure the outcome she so desperately required.

Sara pranced into the office like a recurring nightmare. Full make-up and smelling like the Chelsea Flower Show. It was kind of overpowering and Anji wondered if Sara was spraying scent everywhere in anticipation of her afternoon intimate sex sess with none other than Jeff, Anji's soon-to-be-ex husband.

"Tell me," pried Sara, "So is it definite, your move? You should let me know immediately because I have to replace your position here," she sang. A chord of happiness rang in her voice, like she already knew the answer.

"Yep, leaving for sure. We have everything signed. It'll just be the children and me; Jeff will continue here and commute when he can that is." Anji was almost singing back, keeping up the fakery. "The house should be ready by August. We're all so excited."

"The house in Kensington, right?" Sarah confirmed, almost toying with her.

"That's the one!" Anji replied refusing to bite.

"I am so happy for you really I am," Sara lied through her perfect white veneers.

"Here is my written resignation, I will work this week and then I will leave." Relief spread instantly across Anji's face as she placed an envelope on Sara's desk.

"Oh Anji, I will be so sad to see you go. So how do you feel about Jeff staying here and commuting?" she asked

"Good question!" smiled Anji. "Well this week was enlightening... We rekindled something that we hadn't felt in a decade. We will miss each other, but needs must. We were at it like teenagers," she added as an aside. The lies were now as smooth as honey dripping from her lips.

Sara's face turned fifty shades of green and she held her head in her hands for a brief moment, trying to recover from the blow that had just been delivered. She obviously thought that being on the phone twenty times a day to Jeff while he was in the UK would be more than enough to keep him away from his wife of fifteen years. The truth was that Jeff had a sickness for women. Sara was going to have a hell of a job keeping him in check. Good luck to her if she was that deluded, Anji concluded. For the first time she believed that they most definitely deserved one another..

"I'm tired Anji, I've been working so hard. I'm just going to slip out for a few minutes, take a breath of fresh air, you understand." Of course Anji understood. It made her wildly happy that Jeff was in for it as soon as she stepped out of the office. Oh how that fucker deserved everything he was going to get in just a few moments. Anji watched from the window, giggling to herself silently. Sara's arms gesticulated wildly as she shouted down the phone to her lover.

That evening, Jeff arrived home very early. He was attentive to Anji's every need, being in the doghouse with his mistress probably made home feel like a haven.

Jeff opened a bottle of red wine, trying to rescue himself from the mess his life was becoming. He rarely drank at home on a normal day, so it must be a very special occasion. He must want to get her in a good mood, Anji calculated. She went to prepare some cheese and crackers for them to enjoy with the wine. Looking out from the kitchen, she saw her husband pawing at her mobile phone. He was going through it, but she didn't give a damn. She had nothing to hide – she'd made sure of that by being extremely clever and careful. Jeff wouldn't ever let anyone near his phone, blaming work. But here he was, looking for clues and evidence. She hated him a little bit more.

As she bought out their modest feast, Jeff threw her phone down, annoyed that he hadn't noticed her creep up on him and been caught in the act.

"Babe, what are you looking for on my phone?" She never called him babe; that was new and she didn't know why she'd done it today. Maybe her acting skills were getting the better of her. She would have to tone it down a peg or two.

"Oh I heard it going off, so I just wondered if it was important," he fed her a rubbish attempt at a lie. It felt good to have the upper hand, and with a glass of wine in her she felt on top of the world. It had been a good day.

Anji nodded and smiled at him. She held out the platter she had prepared.

"Cheese?

CHAPTER 38

"Are you ok in there?" Anji was knocking on the bathroom door, listening with one ear pressed as close as she could. It was very easy to hear that Sara wasn't ok in there as she spewed up her guts in the toilet. Sara eventually opened the door. The stench of gone-off clam chowder wafted through, making Anji retch as it hit her nostrils. She held her hand over her mouth and coughed, trying to cover her reaction from Sara.

"I'm fine, normal symptoms of pregnancy. I was the same with both my boys. Vomiting for the first five months," she declared.

"Pregnant?!" Anji asked, totally gobsmacked. Her eyebrows had shot up and she was taking a few steps back.

"Yes, pregnant. And you can't catch it, you know," snapped Sara as she watched Anji move slowly away from her.

"Wow…I didn't know. Congratulations. So, there's going to be a nine-year gap between this one and your youngest son?" Anji stuttered in disbelief, her busy brain already calculating the age difference. "Does Fadi know about this?"

"Of course he does!" bellowed a furious Sara. "Why wouldn't he?" She was now irritated and Anji was smart enough to know when to stop asking questions.

"For your information – although it is none of your

business – we always wanted a little girl. It was now or never," Sara stated in a monotone voice, delivering the message clearly and precisely as they walked back through to the office.

A fog formed, a thick mist in Anji's brain, leaving her feeling confused and disorientated yet again. She felt completely lost but in a familiar place; it was the only way she could explain it. A child wasn't something she had considered in this train-wreck of a love triangle. Now there was going to be a step brother or sister. That bastard had sex without protection, the selfish prick, and she was fucking him without contraception. She must have planned this. Anji pressed her head back into her desk chair, waiting for the sky to open and drop the next big idea or plan, because, quite honestly, she had nothing left.

Anji tried to think, but the past few weeks had taken their toll on her brain. What had once seemed like the perfect plan hatched out of nothing now seemed irreversibly fucked. She prayed a silent prayer, hoping for an answer. It was her only hope, praying to whoever might be listening. She needed guidance but didn't want to worry her mum; she had brought enough heartbreak to her recently. She worried incessantly about Omar, and about her children and their future. The interlude with Doctor Hassan also hung over her head.

Out of nowhere thoughts of ending it all came crashing through Anji's mind. A feeling of absolute hopelessness was sinking into the pit of her stomach, and an invisible agony was eating away at her soul. Maybe everyone would be better off if I wasn't in the picture? She could feel the anxiety rising up within her. *Breathe, you are strong*, she reminded herself. With each steady breath the spiralling negative thoughts began to ease. She imagined her loved one's faces if she were gone; Georgie and Max crying for her, her own mother – usually so strong – broken with tears. Anji would go on for them, but the feelings of utter despair weighed heavily on her shoulders. Why, she asked herself constantly, why her? She had never broken the law. Always followed the right path. Never hurt or destroyed anything or anyone...not until now anyway. She thought of poor, innocent Omar. She had already sent him money; all her salary from the month before. She had emailed him and his son had answered, giving her all the details of his address and who to send the Western Union transfers to.

She had to get out of Saudi. The cage was sending her crazy and she didn't want to watch that home wrecker's belly grow with her husband's love child. Anji prayed for the baby to go away and cried because she knew she must be an awful person to want those prayers to be answered. Was she possessed, wishing harm on someone? On a child? She quickly said a silent prayer for the child to be born full-term, beautiful, healthy and loved, and asked whoever was listening to forgive her under the current circumstances. These thoughts were going to drive her insane. She took another deep breath.

There was no way Jeff could possibly want another child. A few years after having Max she had begged Jeff for another baby and he had made it clear that he needed a wife, not just a mother for his children. Why did this child have to be a pawn in this already complicated saga? She had no doubt that Georgie would love a younger sister, and Max too, but they both detested Sara. Her maternal instincts weren't her strongest point. Georgie had noticed her trout pout, and often pointed out Sara's fish-like lips. Sara had met the children many times, but she'd never even spoken to them. Why bother if they couldn't provide her with anything that she could possibly want? Plus, she didn't do small talk. Anji was grateful for this – the less the kids knew Sara, the better. She just hoped the unborn kid was a boy if there had to be a child, because a mini version of Sara would be downright harrowing. There was only enough room in the world for one.

CHAPTER 39

Georgie came in from school crying and screaming for her mum. The run from the bus had left her breathless and sweaty. The girl was beside herself and, as Anji let her cries run dry, she looked into her daughter's eyes and saw her face was flushed and poker red. Her hair stuck to her face from sweat and tears.

"What is it honey?" Her tone was soft and comforting as she took Georgie's little face in her hands. Inside, Anji felt anxious. This country was getting to her and everything felt like it was coming to a head. She secretly hoped that they hadn't heard about their future brother or sister, although she knew in her heart the reasons behind this upset had to be related to the situation somehow. Georgie was deaf to her mother's soothing words, and a trip to the bathroom to wash her face ended with a full-fledged tantrum. Georgie threw the towel on the floor, then began pummelling and hitting her mum. Anji stood there trying to prevent the blows from landing on her, holding space for her daughter's frustration, when Max walked in.

"Mum, its Lydia," he explained. "She said she can't play with Georgie anymore because we're a bad family. 'Your mum is no good' – that's what she said." His head hung low as he focused on the floor, tears streaming down his cheeks now too.

"Ok you two," said Anji, falling to her knees so she

could look into her children's eyes. "I need to tell you something. I didn't want to bother you with it, but it seems I have no choice now. I am getting the blame for someone else's behaviour. It's unjust, but I can't tell people who the real tattletale is. Everything will happen at the right time," she explained.

"But that's not fair!" wailed Max.

"Lydia sits next to me on the bus," screeched Georgie, letting off more steam and tears.

"Well tomorrow I'll take you to school and explain to the teacher. Don't worry, we have a few more weeks and the truth will come out sooner or later. What matters now is that we love each other and we stay strong. That's all that counts, you hear me?"

Neither of them said anything. Max blew his nose into a tissue, following up with, "What's for lunch?" Anji wished she could be nine or eleven too, and get over things that quickly.

The very next day, the children's teacher, Mrs Gravesend proved to be very supportive. "Of course I understand, and we'd like you to know Georgie is a wonderful student," she explained. "We often know when a parent is very involved in their child's life from their habits and manners. These days the maids are running the house, and they often turn up at parent teacher meetings, would you believe? We see a lot of that here, I can tell you. But I can see how involved you are in your children's lives, and how much this is worrying you. I'll keep an eye on things to make sure there is no bullying going on. Both Georgie and Max are a pleasure to have at the school. They will certainly be missed when they leave us here and go to the UK."

Anji wanted to tell her to expect their half sibling

soon. It was too early to know if it would be a girl or boy, but one thing she did know was that it would be one of those kids who would be raised by the housemaid.

As Anji made her way back to the car through the grounds of the school, her head was burning from the sun. At 8.30am it was already a punishing 42 degrees; this alone was enough to make her want to leave Saudi Arabia for good. It was miserable and she hoped the children were able to stay inside for their breaks. She wondered how so many of the expat ladies were able to make the most of this weather by lying by the pool, day in day out. They looked more like crocodile handbags at the end of their husband's contracts than women with perfectly fabulous tans.

"Work," she requested, and motioned with a flick of her hand to the driver that she'd not even tried to get to know. He was a small Indian man who dressed smartly in a navy blue suit. He was very quiet and polite. *Poor guy*, Anji thought as she started to feel guilty. He didn't deserve to be treated with such a lack of respect. But there was no way she was she even going to try to get to know him; she might just ruin his life like she had Omar's, and no one deserved that. She realised if she had to point this guy out in a line up, she wouldn't even recognise him. Maybe it was because she only ever saw the back of his head. By this stage she'd forgotten his name too, but she didn't bother asking him for it again. She was better off not knowing, as was he.

She looked out of the window on the journey to the office, hoping for inspiration and wondering whether all these life lessons she was receiving would all come to an end soon. All she saw was sand, endless sand, the barren world of the dry desert, with harsh rays beating down mercilessly. Dabbing at the sweat, which beaded on her top lip, she rolled her eyes in exasperation, let out a sigh and stepped out of the car.

Right on cue, Anji's phone started ringing as she began her morning break. It was Jeff; a rare call from her soon-to-be-ex-husband. The man was furious, absolutely seething, as he told her about a letter he'd just received from the compound management office.

"Listen to this and explain yourself!" he snapped. "Listen! 'We hereby give Mrs Harris formal warning to remove her belongings from the compound premises within five days'. What the fuck have you been up to now? Can't I leave you alone for five minutes? I don't need this Anji, I've got enough on my plate as it is! And now this!"

Anji's bony fingers pressed into her temples as she leaned into the wall by the water cooler. Her head was swimming. Jeff explained that thirty female residents had signed a petition to evict her from the compound. He ranted on and on, saying he couldn't understand why. The pressure of the anger that had been brewing up in Anji's head for weeks was about to explode. Behind her stony expression, a volcano of rage was smouldering, but she managed to compose herself, not wanting to leave a lava trail of regret.

"If you would allow me to talk for a second..." she butted in. "Look these people will just have to suffer me for the next few weeks. I know you want an explanation, and you will get one. But not right now. Explain to the management that I'll be leaving by the end of June. If anyone can butter them up, you can," she suggested.

The old Anji would have been devastated by the latest news, but the new Anji didn't have the energy. She relished the way she had handled the phone call with Jeff for a moment before dialling Lily's number to see what she knew.

"Hi Lily, did you know about my impending eviction from the compound?" Anji asked.

"Oh, I thought you might call," Lily said. "I didn't know how to tell you, but since you asked there's quite an uprising going on. I was checking my post box and I had a letter." Anji was waiting for the bombshell to drop. What was it this time? "The usual suspects were asking people to sign an eviction petition," Lily admitted.

Anji remained silent, doubting how much her friend really knew, and if she was being told the full story.

"I thought it wouldn't matter so much anyway now as you're moving back to the UK. And did you know Karen is selling all her stuff from the house? The new girlfriend wants a fresh start – new furniture, new car, everything!" Lily reeled out the news of her impending eviction alongside her gossip about Karen as if they were the same thing to her. Anji's heart sank as she ended the call and thought about Karen's pain and what she must be going through. She had to talk to Karen soon, she needed to have closure and was no longer the coward she used to be. She decided she would knock on Karen's door tomorrow morning, right after she dropped the kids off at the bus. Her legs turned to jelly at the thought, but she needed to prove to herself she could do it.

She couldn't deny that everyone wanting her

evicted from the compound hurt like hell. She was feeling more and more suffocated with every day that passed. The walls of the compound seemed to be closing in on her, but she wouldn't let it. Anji was ready to scream and punch her way out, counting down the days until her freedom from this life.

CHAPTER 40

Anji stood on Karen's front door step, rehearsing the speech she had prepared the night before. She had tried to dig out all the profound statements that had crossed her mind and the heart-wrenching words that would make Karen believe her this time. She wanted to, needed to make things right between them before she left. She rang the bell, holding her breath in anticipation. After some wait, the door eased opened to reveal a dishevelled and blank-faced Karen. Her usually stunning tresses were all over the place, halfway between an untamed lion's mane and a scarecrow. Her lips lacked the usual flash of red, which enhanced the big black bags hanging heavy under her squinty eyes. Without the red lipstick she looked like the moon, all waxy and pale.

Anji gasped, shocked at seeing Karen looking so wrecked. She couldn't have imagined that things could have turned so bad for her in such a short space of time. Anji didn't know where to look for a few moments, it was hard to see such an eyesore in front of her, plus there was an offensive smell, which she couldn't pinpoint. Was it cigarettes, wine or even the faint stench of urine? She couldn't be sure. But one thing she knew for definite was that this woman needed a friend.

"What the hell do you want? I've got nothing to say to you, nothing!" Karen's speech slurred.

"Look, I'm not here to clear my name as you are well

aware I've already tried to do that," said Anji warmly, making her way into the house. "I really just want to thank you for everything, for all your friendship and warmth. You'll always have a place in my heart. I could tell you a million truths, but would any of it help? So I just want to tell you that it wasn't me. That's all."

"Well if it wasn't you, who was it? They told me you would be round here, protesting your innocence," she scoffed.

"Look Karen, I do know the actual culprit but telling you won't help. You'd just end up hating someone else, and they'd have an eviction notice on their doorstep," she explained.

"Pure selfishness, that's what it is," she snapped. "I don't believe anything you say." She walked into the house and lowered herself carefully onto a chair at the breakfast bar, her head swinging down towards her knees, the weight of her sadness and anger seemed hard for her to bear. Anji cautiously followed her.

"Well I've written my address and phone number here if you want it," offered Anji, pressing a square of notepaper into her friend's palm. "The kids and I are moving to the UK as soon as school is over."

They both looked into each other's eyes. Karen was searching for the familiar clues of a broken woman, discarded by her man. Why else would Anji be leaving? She softened just a little, folding the paper carefully. Anji had so many questions. She wanted to compare situations and take notes, but neither woman said anything, not wanting to burden each other more than was necessary. At that moment, there was a spark of mutual understanding, and a silent truce was declared. Anji smiled a meek smile as she stood up to leave, closing the door gently behind her.

****

Karen watched Anji from the kitchen window, waiting until she was completely out of view. She fell to the floor, unable to bear the pain any longer. Her body ached for her old life, the one with Steve. There was no one in the house, no maid to hide her tears from, because that maid was now sharing new memories and smiles with Karen's husband. She had always acted so strong, so capable, but she couldn't go on like that now. Inside she was lost and afraid, with the loneliness in her heart causing constant pain. She'd never felt so helpless, so isolated and deserted.

These days, Karen could hardly drag herself from her bed. There were days she didn't even try. She had no direction without Steve, no reason to wake up in the morning. She hadn't showered in weeks and she could even smell herself. It was awful but she didn't care. In fact, the smell matched how she felt – just disgusting. Steve would barely recognise her now. Her hair was tatty, her breath foul from drinking whatever she could get her hands on. She'd had to try and tidy herself up a little when she'd been called into school – twice – as Alex had been beating up a poor boy that was two years his junior. Karen had been forced to divulge a little about their current crisis at home, leading to a mini breakdown in front of the teacher.

She could feel herself losing sight of everything. She had no plan and no ideas. Her mother had kindly offered to take them in, to live in her two-up, two-down house back in the UK. It wasn't a perfect situation, but it was on offer nonetheless. She hadn't even contacted schools back home, and her imminently-ex-husband was too loved up fucking Martha the maid to partake any parental responsibilities. Apparently, Martha had a huge sexual appetite and he had been bragging about the two of them spending all day in bed. She was making up for lost time after a long dry spell it would seem.

Karen crawled to the kitchen on all fours. Hauling herself up to a chair, she reached for what was left of the gin, swigging it straight from the bottle. She winced at the taste, but was sobering up and didn't like the feeling. Her head was pounding and the cure was to drink more. She'd stay here until the kids came home, greeting them with bleary eyes and incomprehensible babbling. She'd drifted off for what seemed like a few minutes but had actually been hours as she was awoken by the sound of the kids coming in through the door. She tried to get up to make them a sandwich but when she rose, she fell head first onto the marble floor, just as the children were entering into the room. Allie screamed when she saw blood coming from her mum's nose and mouth, and Reggie ran to get help from next door.

Their neighbour, Bonnie, came running through in a panic, helping Karen up to her feet. She managed to get her up the stairs somehow dragging the dead weight, sitting Karen on the floor in the shower cubicle fully dressed, to let the water rinse over her. Bonnie knew she should call a doctor, especially given all the blood that was draining down the plughole, but no doctor out here would do a house call for a drunkard. Trying her best to sober Karen up, Bonnie switched the shower to cold, eliciting a tiny whimper from her sodden friend. With Alex's help, she managed to lay Karen on the bed, before sending the kids to her house. They didn't need to see any more than they already had been subjected too, and they were already blaming themselves for something that was way beyond their control. Men can make or break a woman thought Bonnie, but her heart bled for the kids. They were innocent and in as much pain as their mother. Their lives had also been turned upside down.

Bonnie took the liberty of calling Anji – not knowing whom else to call – and explained the situation. She asked if she would sit with Karen to monitor her, while she took care of the kids. Anji left her kids with Lani and rushed over. She sat quietly next to Karen, who was either unconscious or asleep but was definitely still breathing, and held onto her clammy hand. She said a prayer for her and wondered what else could possibly happen in this cursed cage.

CHAPTER 41

Anji had stayed up with Karen all night, and today she was paying the price for it. She stifled a yawn as she sat at her desk staring blankly at the computer screen. The sound of her phone vibrating jolted her out of her numbness. She picked up her phone and saw an incoming call from an app she'd never used. Lily had encouraged her to download it as 'no-one just calls each other now, it's all about the messages and video calls.' She'd downloaded it to please Lily, but was quite happy just using her phone to call and text as usual; not that she'd had many people to call or text over the last few months.

A picture of Lily and her family filled her screen and a green phone icon prompted Anji to answer the video call.

"Hello Lily" she said, clicking on the green icon. She quickly pulled the phone away from her ear as a loud crackling noise came through piercing her eardrum. After a few seconds she pressed the phone back to her ear.

"Hi, Lily?" she attempted again, before realising the phone must be in Lily's bag as the screen was black. She must have called in error. She was just about to put the phone down when she heard the familiar sound of Lily's voice, faintly.

'Leave you fucking idiot; get the fuck out of this

house!' Anji's eyebrows shot up as she shifted uncomfortably in her office chair, glancing round to check that no one else had heard or was listening. 'This is my house! I asked for it and I got it. Which begs the question, what the fuck are you good for? I'll tell you. Nothing! You are one useless excuse of a man, if you can even call yourself a man. I don't need you; I don't even know why I married you, my parents were right about you! I've always been the one to do everything. Where is my lousy promotion? Maybe if I strap on a pair of balls I'll walk in and get it. I married a goddamn pussy!'

Anji listened in on the call even though she knew she shouldn't, but Lily's tone of voice kept her glued to the open line. The sound made Anji's blood run cold. It was mean and bitter, not like the Lily she knew. This Lily was nothing more than a bully, using her husband Adam as an emotional punch bag and making herself feel superior. The little threads of doubt which she had pulled from her friend over the past few months were weaving together in her mind; although she didn't want to admit it to herself, part of her had always known that, deep down, Lily was like this. She had so desperately wanted to see the best in Lily, to think that she had a true, loyal friend here in this lonely pit. Suddenly Anji felt great sympathy for Adam; this guy who worked double shifts, usually seven days a week. Adam reminded Anji of who she'd been before – a stupid victim. She understood clearly how he felt at that very moment. If only he could be strong enough to stand up to her, he might stop all of this; but since all he did was run straight back to work, nothing was ever going to change. Not a damn thing. Anji imagined Lily's face, distorted, sneering and frothing. She sounded so aggressive that even Anji felt a little frightened with chills running down her spine.

'I told you, there is no promotion,' she heard Adam say pathetically.

'Bullshit!' she screamed. 'Bullshit! Are you telling me you know more than me? That's rich!'

'Speak to Anji like you did last time, work your magic,' he subtly sneered.

'I told you already that she's leaving. Anyway, she's not taking the bait anymore. Don't think I haven't tried already,' she retaliated. "I will have to go to the source I will have to speak to Jeff", she continued.

"Is something wrong, Anji?" asked Sara, walking up to Anji's desk and breaking her trance. Anji turned to look at Sara, her mind still on what she'd heard.

'No, no its just a friend calling I just thought this might be an emergency, but it wasn't. I'll call her back later." She was half glad for the interruption or she may have been listening in for hours; she didn't know if she had the strength take any more betrayal. Anji had never felt so deceived, double-crossed; not only did Lily know about the affair and hadn't told her, but she was exploiting the situation to further her husband's career. She'd spent the past few months – years, maybe – manipulating Anji, who had fallen straight into her trap. Anji had never felt so stupid as she did right now. She didn't know what felt worse; the betrayal and loss of her best friend, or the humiliation and stupidity she felt towards herself. Her head was rotating, spinning; she had to get some fresh air. She stood up to walk towards the door but before she could even take a step, she felt herself beginning to black out and her legs suddenly gave way.

"Anji, are you ok?" Anji could hear Sara's muffled voice and blinked to see her blurred face staring down at her. She blinked a few times and Sara's face came into focus. "I'm the one who's pregnant, not you!" she teased, unsympathetically.

"Oh gosh, I…. I'm sorry," Anji's arm and head were throbbing and she was disorientated. She wasn't sorry at all, although she did feel queasy and ghastly. "I forgot to eat breakfast this morning." Anji peeled herself up from the floor and pulled herself up into her chair. The other ladies in the office were staring down at her, but no one said anything. Sara was dusting herself off, one hand on her growing bump. She didn't offer Anji any water, so she carefully got up and moved her way around the furniture to the water cooler. Sara watched her as she took a few mouthfuls.

"There you go,

"How are you doing with the pregnancy?" she asked, in an attempt to divert attention away from herself.

"Oh brilliant. No side effects at all, I'm feeling on top of the world," she boasted.

"Do you know when you're due?"

"It's going to be a February baby," Sara beamed.

Oh my God, thought Anji, Jeff is a February baby – how lucky they were. They could celebrate the baby's birth with his own birthday. She grimaced. Anji started covertly doing the maths on her fingers, working out when the baby had been conceived. It would have been the month of May. But May was when they'd been in London; so there could be a slim chance that the baby could possibly not be Jeff's. She thought this would be a relief, but it seemed to complicate things more in her mind. She looked up at Sara and suddenly began realising what Jeff liked in her, those big luscious lips, that thick blonde mane that cascaded down her back and that fabulous figure that would soon be transformed by pregnancy. Jeff wouldn't like it when her arse dropped south, followed swiftly by her breasts. Today Sara looked smoking in a teal coloured top that brought out her vivacious eyes. Would the baby girl that Sara had wanted so badly inherit Jeff's perfectly formed nose and almond eyes with Sara's colouring? She would be fabulously good-looking – another heartbreaker.

"Enough," Anji said out loud, trying to erase the image of the perfect child in her mind.

"Enough what?" asked a surprised Sara.

"Enough sitting, more work," she responded quickly and convincingly. "I have to finish everything before tomorrow. It is my last day, after all."

CHAPTER 42

Jeff was crushed. The news of his mistress carrying his child – if it even was his child he certainly had doubts and reservations – made him feel helpless and out of control something he hated. He shouldn't have believed her when she said she had an IUD. He didn't have the first clue about contraception. Anji had been in charge of that, that was most certainly her department. They had decided to have a child; they got a child. The next time, it happened in the exact same way. Anji must have been exceptionally fertile; there was no waiting around, no disappointment; just a pregnant woman bearing a child that they both wanted. How had she managed her fertility afterwards was her problem, because she hated the dry, clinical feeling of condoms. Sara had said the same thing; he chose her precisely because she already had a husband and two kids; well, that and her amazing body and sexual promiscuity. Had she done it on purpose to poach him? She wouldn't be the first to try but she would be the cleverest to make him sign up for another child. When Anji had begged him for a third kid he had deprived her of sex for months just ordering her to give him blow jobs, until she agreed never to spring any pregnancy news on him ever again.

He didn't like being out of control. In fact he hated it. His frown lines were deepening day by day as it was and he had a permanent headache, ensnared in this perpetual nightmare. Sara had known he was a married man and now she had him trapped. When Jeff had demanded a DNA test, Sara had threatened to call Anji. It was like an atomic bomb had been dropped on his life. If he chose to accept this child, how would he break the news to his kids? The kids that he had planned and wanted not this one that he had no real plans to raise as his own. He didn't like being cornered or being given orders, but now he had a new baby to think about. He wasn't ready for this.

In a few short weeks, his family would be in the UK and he would be with Sara alone. Their relationship didn't seem so exciting anymore, no more thrill of the chase. The reality was that he was going off her – he didn't want her, or her ghastly boys. He'd promised to take them all in, but he couldn't imagine life with her or them. Those boys were spoilt and impolite on the very rare occasions he had met them at school or in the compound. He had no room or love for those kind of kids.

He decided to call Anji; sweet Anji who he so loved and would always love. He loved her more than ever now. She was blissfully unaware of his betrayal, so he still had the sanctuary of his marriage to fall back on. He would work on his recovery; try to stop his wandering eye and infidelities.

"Anji darling," he greeted her. "Dinner tonight? I want to spend time with you before you leave me. Eight o'clock at Alabama's, and you can get dressed up – it's in the compound, so no Abaya inside. Ok darling?" Anji couldn't see him, but he was sweating. He desperately needed a shower. All this stress and angst was causing him to sweat more than usual, so he decided to pass by the spa to have a shower and freshen up. He let the water wash over him for a good 15 minutes, feeling the stress of Sara's news ease a little with the warmth of the power shower. His head was still a mess though that wasn't going to change instantly; as his mind ran through questions he had no answers to. How had he got himself into this mess?

Half an hour later, he was back in his office but he didn't look any happier. Rita, his PA, looked even more agitated.   '

"What is it?" he demanded, as tetchy as she was.

"A covered lady pushed her way into your office," Rita explained. "Said she knows you. I told her it's not allowed and she isn't in your diary, but she pushed her way past and that's where she is now. She's been there for fifteen minutes. I'm so sorry…"

"Well it's too late to be sorry," he scolded her. "I will have to sort it out."

Feeling flustered and annoyed, he had an inkling it would be Sara. The tight feeling gripping his throat was back and he was sweating yet again. The shower had been in vain. If she was there to demand sex again, he was going to tell her where to go to get on her bike. It was the only weapon she had, and she was using it to her full capabilities. As soon as he walked in, she rushed to the door and locked it, just as Jeff had done the time before. As she turned, her Abaya had already fallen to the ground, revealing a lacy red pair of crotch less knickers.

"Look I can't," he glared at her. "You've already annoyed Rita, and I've just had a shower." Sara looked at him seductively as if she'd heard nothing he's said.

"I need you, your magic, inside me," she purred as she put one foot up on his desk chair, spreading her legs to reveal black stockings and suspenders. The panties revealed just a hint of her lips, and the matching bra cupped her full, pregnant breasts. He felt a rush, the familiar feeling of arousal, and covered his erection with his hand. But Sara had already noticed it and was signalling for him to remove his trousers. He didn't move, not knowing what he should do next, but she was already unzipping him. She knelt down and gripped his member, making it slick with her saliva, and he knew right there was no going back. After a couple of minutes, she stood and perched herself on the side of his desk, lifting her foot back onto the chair and opening herself up for him. He entered her quickly, taking her foot off his seat – he didn't want it marking the leather – and, as he ground into her, the feelings of ecstasy returned, against his better judgment. She had managed to awaken his desire so effortlessly. The build-up and intensity was fast, like shaking a bottle of champagne, as his semen burst inside her. He reached over and took a tissue to wipe himself off, before passing her the tissue box, expecting her to do the same.

"Listen," he said as she was covering herself up, keeping his eyes low to avoid her gaze. "Tonight I'm going to tell Anji everything. So don't expect me this evening. It's best you go so I can get myself ready. Don't call me, I will call you when I'm done." It was so unlike the last time they had made love in his office. There were no sensual kisses and no words of adoration. It reminded him of the sex he had with his wife and he felt a pang of guilt in his stomach, and a desire to be with her instead.

"I love you so much," she gushed. "You're the best. I will always make you happy, I promise. This baby and me! Call me straight after please, I'll be waiting."

'Leave tonight or live and die this way'. The words of the song suddenly played like a broken record in Jeff's head, lying heavily on his chest, unrelenting and intrusive. He shook his head, trying to unhear them.

"What about you and Fadi? What's your plan there? And the boys?" He asked without actually caring what the answer would be.

"Let's cross that bridge after you tell Anji. I don't think Fadi will let me take them, but you never know. Either way, we have the baby to think about now. Our baby!" She smiled shyly.

Good he thought. That would buy him some time, and the truth was he didn't want her to leave her husband. Not now, not ever. Well, not for him anyway. He had fucked lots of women in the past and now he was paying the price for a married woman with her own kids. Karma was certainly a bitch! Panic rose inside him as he realised he was out of his depth and sinking fast.

CHAPTER 43

Anji had carefully chosen her outfit for the evening, opting for a black off-the-shoulder jumpsuit. It was elegant and tailored, the tapered trousers elongating her silhouette. Her natural blonde hair fell across her shoulders and her golden brown freckles were in full bloom across the bridge of her nose. They appeared every summer, and were set off perfectly by the minimal gold jewellery she had chosen. She looked fabulous – even the children said so, which was enough for her. The fine lines around her eyes creased as she smiled, kissing them goodbye.

The Indian driver was standing with the car door open and Anji was painfully aware that she still hadn't even bothered to try and remembered his name. She smiled at him courteously as she climbed into the backseat, the leather cool against her skin on this hot evening. He gently slammed and closed the door behind her, returning a beaming grin in her direction. As soon as she arrived at the restaurant, she removed her Abaya and suddenly felt overdressed and self-conscious. It had been a long time since she had been this dressed up in Saudi, and everyone else appeared to have gone casual.

"Oh my God, is that you Anji?" asked one of the school mums who had recognised her. "You look absolutely amazing!"

"Date night," she replied, smiling in the woman's

direction. She was very grateful for the compliment but could feel her skin flushing as all eyes were on her. She looked around for Jeff but didn't notice him instantly because he had sat at very back of the restaurant and until he stood up and motioned for her to join him. She wondered why he'd chosen the furthest table because usually he loved to be seen to be the centre of the universe. She deliberately pushed her hair to one side, pulled her shoulders back, and strutted over to the table with false confidence. It had worked, and Jeff had noticed that every man had taken a second look at his gorgeous wife. Sitting down, she had hoped for a compliment, but all she sensed was an uncomfortable, perturbed atmosphere. It was impossible to ignore.

"Anji," he began, taking a huge gulp from his glass of water. "We need to talk." He held the glass, staring at its contents while he carried on: "What I'm about to tell you isn't easy for me, but I don't want secrets between us," he admitted. Anji's muscles went tense and a shiver ran through her. What was he about to say? Surely he wouldn't do anything rash in such a public place. She waited for him to talk, looking straight at him. He paused for a brief second and took a deep breath.

"I've been having sex with someone else. I'm so sorry; I lost sight of the kids and us. I want you, I mean I need you to know it was just sex and its over now". He tried to block out his sexual encounter from the same afternoon in his office. "If I could turn back the clock I would, I swear." He'd blurted it all out in one breath, and took her hands in his in a show of unity.

The Indian waiter passed just as Jeff had finished saying what he had to say, asking if they were ready to order.

"No, we'll let you know when we're ready," snapped Anji, pulling her hands away from Jeff's and placing them well under the table.

Even though she knew everything already, she couldn't understand why it felt like she was hearing it for the first time. Maybe, because her husband was the one fessing up everything. She hadn't expected it. Anji bit her lip; she couldn't gather her thoughts quickly enough to retaliate, to show that she was indeed the heartbroken wife. The hurt and betrayal were stabbing away at her.

"It was short, it's over and it was a stupid mistake." Jeff pleaded, as he broke into tears. She had never seen him like this. A few months ago, she may have found it endearing, but now he just seemed over dramatic and rather pathetic. "Will you forgive me? Tell me you'll forgive me," he begged, holding out his hand and waiting for her to take it.

"You really expect an answer now? With me being the one looking after the family, keeping the home fires burning, while you're out chasing women? I don't believe this," she glared at him.

"You don't understand, I can't live without you or the kids" He sounded desperate, as more tears cascaded down his face.

"First of all, who is it? Do I know her?" Anji probed, wanting to hear the truth coming from his mouth for once.

"No, I'm not that stupid. It was a few times, and I don't love her – it was just sex. How many times do I have to repeat myself? It was just sex!" He blew his nose violently into a tissue.

The waiter turned up to the table again. That was

Anji's cue to leave, and she told him she wouldn't be ordering any food. She was suddenly aware that she hadn't shed a tear; it was Jeff doing all the crying. She had shed enough tears that he didn't have one clue about. Being that he was spouting a load of half-truths, she didn't buy his tear-jerking performance. Anji walked away; relieved she was over the worst. He hadn't even bothered to mention the new baby in his mistress's womb. He was nothing but a coward. Anji would enjoy acting the victim for a while, and then make him pay the price until her final exit from the Kingdom. Maybe him not mentioning the pregnancy was a good thing; it would only complicate an already arduous labyrinth of lies and deceit.

Jeff didn't bother to go home and face the music, just as Anji had expected. She found herself lying once again in the fetal position, her back curved, head bowed, her limbs bent and drawn up to her torso. Sleeping on an empty stomach, and knowing that she some-how had the upper hand, seemed to keep her awake for longer. The gnawing emptiness in the pit of her stom-ach made her think of the crushing desolation of being yet another cheated-on wife in the Middle East. Her UK friends had been right – it really was the marriage graveyard; the place where relationships came to die.

CHAPTER 44

Sara's face contorted into every emotion as Jeff told her about the events of last night; how he'd explained to Anji he was leaving her, and how he didn't love her anymore. In his version, Anji had been completely devastated, beside herself begging for another chance of course. Sara bought every line of his fabricated story, relishing the fact that Jeff was almost hers.

"So you didn't tell her who it was?" Sara pried. "Why not? I was expecting her not to turn up to work tomorrow. You know how tough it is to see her every day," she admitted.

"Look, she would have gone straight to Fadi. Do you need or want that right now? Let's wait," Jeff advised. "Am I right?" For the first time, Sara realised she'd have to tell Fadi and the boys. That would most definitely leave her ostracised from her immediate family and extended family. Fadi would certainly take the boys from her and she would lose them for sure, but with the money from Jeff she could lavish them with gifts that Fadi couldn't afford. That would win their love and affection. She could see her boys' faces now in her minds eye as she gave them the latest iPhones, laptops and designer goods. They would understand the sacrifice in the end.

"Ok, ok," she agreed. "We will reveal all when Anji moves back to the UK, then I can move straight in with you." She was talking like it was already a done deal.

Meanwhile, Anji was home alone and couldn't help but dream of her impending freedom as she congratulated herself on how in control she'd remained. Looking back, Jeff had always been a narcissist. He'd never allowed her to make any decisions and dictated her every move. He always caught her at the first hurdle, which she'd initially adored about him as it made her feel comfortable, protected and safe.

Now, without knowing it, he had dropped her from a very high height and she was discovering that she was actually capable of surviving, having to fend for herself and face all her insecurities, fears and demons. She was surprised at her very own strength and even more amazed by her capabilities. How happy she had been to play the pretty little housewife as he manipulated and bullied her, verbally keeping her in check. He'd managed to isolate from her friends, mocking her for wanting to go for a girls' night out and shaming her into turning down invitations. Crazily, and without argument, she had accepted his views. "I can't save you from unnecessary situations," he had warned. She had, without question, believed him. She felt like she had been brainwashed for the past decade and the spell was finally being lifted. Now all she really wanted was a good night out with the girls; a chance to laugh, cry and tell them all about her arsehole of a husband. She vowed to make regular girls' nights out part of her new life. She couldn't wait to get started. On reflection, she began to realise that, within their marriage, she'd always been the more likeable one. People were automatically drawn to her, and Jeff must've been jealous of that since he was always putting her down. On so many occasions he had warned her not to be so friendly, reminding her that people knew how to take advantage of weakness. Now it was clear to her that he'd been taking the piss out of her. How many times had he interrupted her or kicked her under the table to keep her in check? How often had he had scolded her in the car about things she had said, or people she had spoken to? He'd even commented on her clothing, giving her the green or red light depending on whether her outfit met his approval.

It was all so obvious now. She was the one who had won his bosses over and he knew it; they were always asking him about his lovely wife. There was also their bedtime routine, on the occasions he actually came home. He'd never asked anything of her other than the usual missionary position. Once she had gone to Agent Provocateur and bought a beautiful embroidered bra set. She had looked incredible in it, yet Jeff had taken one look and shot her down. "You look more like a prostitute than my wife," he'd said. She had never felt so cheap and ashamed in her life. It wasn't something she would ever repeat, and the expensive lingerie went straight in the trash.

Now she realised this was all part of his manipulation; he was keeping her less sexy, keeping her sexual appetite low and her confidence down. Because he wasn't loyal, he couldn't believe anyone else could be, so bullying was his way to keep his home life in order. Anji thought back to Sara, with her crotch less undies and her gorgeous snake-like moves as she'd straddled her Jeff. He clearly couldn't get enough of her and obviously loved what he saw. It must have been awfully hard for him that night to turn Anji down in her slinky knickers and smelling of Chanel No 5, but he had to remind her that she was his wife.

Anji re-lived her interlude with the Doctor. It had been more sensual than any sex she'd ever had with her husband. Only once she had tried initiating sex with Jeff. Fixated on the Fifty Shades trilogy, which she'd finished in the space of one week, had given her food for thought. After reading it in bed one evening, Jeff had climbed in beside her. Inspired by the chapter she'd just finished, it took Anji all her guts to pluck up the courage to instigate something with her husband. But he had turned to her and said: "I'm not a machine! The bored housewife is such a cliché." Anji never tried anything like it again. And now he was living every sex scene from the trilogy with her boss would you believe.

At the time of the book's release, Anji and Jeff had been living in Bangkok, the sex capital of the world, and perhaps he was already fulfilling his needs with whoever was available there. She'd never even been suspicious of him until Karen had voiced her accusations. The thought that he could cheat had simply never crossed her mind stupidly.

Anji shook her head, trying to get Jeff out of her mind. Sex with the Doctor had been something else. Although it was a one-time event, for the first time ever she'd been able to let all her guards down. With no inhibitions, she hadn't worried about her technique or if her thighs were jiggling, or whether or not he was going to enjoy it. She'd been concentrating on how he felt inside her, and because of that the orgasm had been shuddering, earth-shatteringly good. She'd allowed the Doctor's tongue to pleasure her until she almost came. Jeff would have gagged; performing oral on a woman was, in his words, a sick act. When the Doctor had entered her moments later whilst kissing her, the pleasure was insurmountable and she came in just a few seconds. She closed her eyes and waited for the tingling sensation to pass while she reminisced about her stolen night of passion.

CHAPTER 45

The ladies on the compound had arranged an emergency meeting with Karen. They were discussing details about her leaving party, which would be held at the end of the school year, just before the mass exodus of all the families for their summer vacation. Karen didn't give a damn about the farewell, but agreed for the sake of her children. A few of the women were debating whether or not to invite Anji. One said they were kind enough to allow her to stay until the end of the school year on the compound, even though they had agreed to evict her. Another said the children would suffer and asked if that was fair. Quite a few arguments were sparking off over what to do about Anji.

Amal was feeling particularly ashamed, keeping very quiet at the back of the group. She knew it was her fault and that she was the whole reason behind the campaign against Anji. She pursed her lips, stopping the words from escaping, but she was so desperate to tell the truth. The guilt felt like ice in her gut; it may have been one hundred degrees outside, but inside her body felt frozen. Was it too late to be honest and come clean? She was holding a silent argument with herself when all of sudden she heard Karen holler.

"No! I insist that she comes. I have no hard feelings and she's leaving too. It makes sense to have a joint party."

Beatrice, a short woman with the attitude of a little Rottweiler retorted in her South African accent: "Well you girls might not have feelings, but I do. If she goes, I will not be going," she confirmed. Some of the ladies gathered around made their approval known by applauding her. Bonnie chirped in, her ruddy cheeks turning crimson.

"Bravo Karen, I take my hat off to you, it takes a better woman to forgive. Whoever started that rumour did you a favour. You may not like hearing that he is a horrible arse but that's the truth." There were gasps from the crowd, but the heated debate had been completely defused by Bonnie; they would be having a joint party. Amal stood behind, relieved at the outcome and burst out with a sigh of relief at the minor victory. She decided that the truth would have to be buried and she was caught between a huge sense of relief and a knowing feeling about being a coward yet again and missing her chance to do the right thing.

Karen was still very much in crisis. Waking up in the mornings was torture. Her days and nights were spent drinking. She was out of control. She knew she needed to crawl out of this perpetual gutter, especially as her mum was coming to help her soon with her impending move, and she knew her kids were suffering which ate her up even more, sending her even more deeply into despair. The fatigue was beginning to wear on her once-smiling face, leaving hollowness, an empty shell of whom she once was. The sadness flowed through her veins and was killing her generous, vivacious spirit. She knew it, but there wasn't a thing she could do about it.

Karen knew people had affairs – she wasn't stupid,

she had helped close friends who had been in the same situation. So she couldn't understand why she was being so weak, but she didn't seem to be able to stop herself. The feelings of abandonment made her ache. She had followed him to Saudi Arabia for a brighter future, to strengthen their marriage. Now, she was just dead to him. He didn't give one damn about her. That alone made her cry herself to sleep every night, but the endless pain was still there when she woke up in the morning. She yearned for Steve. She loved him, she would forgive him and she still wanted him back. Sadly Steve had no plans to return. He was happier than he had ever been.

When the crowd of vultures had left the compound meeting, Karen decided she wanted to tell Anji herself about the party. She could ask her ideas about what she and the children would like.

"Hello Karen," Anji answered, trepidation in her voice. "Hello?" she repeated, worried it would be a repeat of the last call, when she'd discovered the news about Jeff. That all seemed like such a long time ago now. All she heard was weeping at the other end of the line. Anji instinctively knew it was a cry for help – she knew because she was in the exact same boat.

"Look, I'm coming over. Hang up and I'll be there in a few minutes," said Anji, as she headed to the outhouse for her bike, and pedalled across the playground to the other side of the compound. When she arrived, she immediately took Karen in her arms. The stench of alcohol on Karen's breath bit Anji's nose and her pores oozed a cocktail of scents that were equally dreadful. She didn't care, hugging her friend as hard as she could. She felt so incredibly sorry for her. Steve had taken his housemaid and Jeff had taken his wife's boss. The two women didn't need to exchange words, since there was nothing to say anyway.

"You know Karen," Anji began. "You're a survivor. I know you'll get through this. Come on; let me take you to the shower. Let's clean you up. Tomorrow is a brand new day." Anji led her to the bathroom, sitting her on the side of the bathtub. Holding her with one hand, she reached to turn the tap on. Anji felt a tug on her arm as Karen lost her balance and fell back onto the bath edge. She heard a heavy thud as Karen's head collided with the edge of the bathtub.

"Oh my god, Karen. Karen! Karen can you hear me?" Karen was lying unconscious, slumped on the floor. Leaving the bathwater still running she ran to get her phone, struggling to keep her own balance as the room span around her. *This isn't happening, this can't be happening.* She ran back into the bathroom, finding Doctor Hassan's number in her phone book. She couldn't call the emergency services, as Karen was intoxicated; he was the only other person she could call for help. She called his number and, with the phone held between her ear and her shoulder, she checked Karen's pulse and was relieved to see she was still breathing. She turned the tap off and almost dropped the phone into the bath.

"Shit!"

"Anji? Is that you?" The call had connected just as Anji had managed to save the phone from landing in the bath. She put it back to her ear.

"Doctor Hassan? Thank God." She explained to him hurriedly what had happened. "Please come quickly, it's Villa 23 Street 5."

"I'll be five minutes," responded the Doctor. "Put her onto her side and check her tongue doesn't roll back and block her airways. She may vomit – be prepared." Doctor Hassan was calm and in charge, but Anji's brain felt shredded. She waited with Karen, holding her hand with her quivering hands. The doorbell rang after what seemed like an absolute. She ran three stairs at a time to open the door, almost breaking her own neck. Doctor Hassan ran up the stairs, his bag hitting the wall and knocking off a big chunk of plaster as he did so.

"Give me water, pass me the shower head, quickly," the Doctor ordered, as he sprayed her face. It must have worked as Karen stirred, coughing and choking. Her hands reached for her neck and her eyes bulged with fear. He quickly turned her onto her side to prevent her choking on the contents of her stomach which spewed out - probably a couple of bottles of whatever she had downed earlier. The smell was indescribable, like it had been stewing for days. It was everywhere – in the bath, in her hair, her face and even clinging to her eyebrows.

"She is intoxicated. We will have to get her to the hospital, but through the back door. If she's drunk they won't help her," he informed Anji.

"Oh my God, I am so sorry to put you in this position, I really am."

Anji grabbed two of Karen's Abayas, and Hassan rinsed her down before carrying her bloated body to the car. Anji watched in adoration as he took the lead, with no questions asked. Anji arrived at the hospital reception desk and passed them Bonnie's number, asking them to call her, as she was Karen's neighbour the closest to her next of kin.

"No, we call husband, we call husband. What husband number?" demanded the Indian receptionist.

"No, husband not here, you call neighbour," said Anji

Once they were in a side room with Karen safely transferred to a bed, Anji found herself alone with the Doctor – other than a sleeping Karen – for the first time since their encounter.

"I know this looks bad," admitted Anji "I was trying to help her out. I know you don't know me – really know me I mean..." she trailed off, embarrassed to remember their sexual interlude.

"Don't worry, I'm a good judge of character," he interjected, checking Karen's heartbeat with his stethoscope as she slept. "There's no need to explain." Anji felt relieved; she was mentally and physically exhausted and the last thing she needed right now was to explain herself.

"I'm so glad you hadn't gone to London yet. I don't know what I would have done."

"I'm glad I got to see you again before I left. I haven't stopped thinking about you." Anji's stomach flipped at the Doctor's words. She gave him a hint of a smile.

"So, why are you moving to London anyway?" Anji asked inquisitively.

"I needed a fresh start," said the Doctor, bluntly.

"After your divorce?" asked Anji, immediately regretting bringing this up.

"Ah ha, you remembered. Well, I had what you would call a kind of arranged marriage. At the time we both hoped we would learn to love each other, like the older generations. We tried to make it work but we couldn't in the end. It's bitter sweet really; she's a lovely person, but we just weren't in love."

"I'm sorry to pry," Anji said apologetically. "It's not my business."

"I know it's not," he grinned, "but I want to tell you anyway."

Doctor Hassan suggested that Anji might want to go home and get some rest. "The good news is that her intoxication actually helped at the time of the fall as her body was relaxed. She only has swelling and a little bruising – nothing serious. She'll feel like she has a very bad hangover, that's all. We just need to watch her tonight. I'll keep an eye on her for you, it's my job," he offered.

Anji was pleased that it was nothing more than a bump. She gladly took his advice and walked home across the waste ground that separated the compound and the hospital. The 47-degree heat was unbearable, especially when draped in a nylon Abaya, but at least she could put the scarf over her head to avoid burning her scalp.

She walked towards the prison walls of the compound. She used to cherish those walls; inside there was some freedom from Saudi's strict rules, no Abaya, no compromises. Now she saw the compound as a place that made people go crazy and do stupid things.

Alone with her thoughts, Anji decided she'd look for the paper that the Doctor had given her with his UK details on once she got home. She'd be sure to keep it in a safe place. She may never contact him. Or she may call him just to say thank you for helping her. She wasn't exactly sure.

By the time Anji reached her villa the kids were beside themselves. "Where have you been?" asked Georgie. "We were calling. No one knew where you were! We called Lily who said she'd look for you."

"There was an emergency with Karen. Everything's fine," revealed Anji. "I'm sorry, what is it that's so important?"

"We heard about the joint leaving party – Alex told us. We want a pool one like them, and a water slide, maybe a magician – you know, the one with rabbits and stuff." The children spoke over each other, giggling. Anji was delighted. Their smiles were the best thing she'd seen in days. But she hadn't even thought about the party. Who would come? Everyone hated her for God's sake, and the thought dragged her mood down. She reminded herself to breathe and faked a beaming smile for the kids. They deserved to be happy and needed to experience as much of it as possible before the bomb dropped and would be changing their lives forever.

CHAPTER 46

Anji had finally finished up at work, leaving her with more time to get things packed at home. She had moved countries a few times before and she didn't want to take much to clutter up her new home. She only really wanted the keepsakes from their travels and personal belongings. Anji had to think twice about the family pictures, which were scattered around the front room. Each one had been positioned just so, to remind her of her perfect family; an illusion which had now was shattered eternally.

Anji began wrapping the silver frames carefully in bubble wrap, placing each one side by side, remembering each moment. She was trying to recapture her old emotions, but nothing was coming. There was a sense of déjà vu, of a past life, a fleeting feeling of familiarity. But that was all that remained. She grabbed a picture of her and Jeff on the beach of Saint Thomas during their Caribbean honeymoon. Smiling happily, her long blonde hair dancing in the wind, her sun-kissed skin glowing smooth caramel, bringing out the blue of her eyes. How she wished she were still in her twenties. How she wished she'd known then what she knew now. She didn't understand then that Jeff's love was all about possession. His treasured wife was just a pretty girl on his arm a trophy. Regret washed over her like the long slow waves on that beach. She longed to go back and take a different path, but then she wouldn't have had Georgie and Max. They were her everything. Her mind elsewhere, she accidentally dropped the photo frame on the marble floor and it shattered. Glass skittered everywhere, and she looked down at the mess of the fractured frame, reflecting on how its brokenness matched her broken insides. Reminding herself that her feelings were only temporary – this awful time in her life wouldn't last forever – she hoped that one day she may even look back with a kind of nostalgia to see the role this turbulent period played in shaping the person she should have been all along.

Anji wondered why Jeff was still trying to play the happy husband. He was being more attentive than he'd ever been before – calling her incessantly, wanting to know her every move, declaring his love for her and needing constant reassurance over her love for him. His neediness was sucking her energy reserves. In the beginning his possessiveness had made her feel special and wanted, but now it was just downright suffocating. Why wasn't he directing all of his attention to Sara? By now she had a cute baby bump and glowing skin. Pregnancy suited her. But on Anji's last day in the office, she'd thought slyly about how Jeff would be massively turned off by how much weight Sara had gained. She'd look huge now as she rode Jeff, looking more like a slippery dolphin. And the cellulite would set like cement since Sara was forty now. She'd probably end up resorting to liposuction as soon as the baby was born, and Jeff would turn his nose up before starting to look for his next victim. He'd hardly touched Anji when she was pregnant – stretch marks, veins and weight gain were all he saw, rather than his beautiful wife growing life inside her.

Being at home and off work gave Anji time to think, and as she packed her belongings, she thought of Karen. Her friend was still drinking and had no recollection of the day Anji and Doctor Hassan took her into hospital. Everything had been a blur apparently. Anji had picked her up from the hospital the next day, with Karen nursing a blinding headache, just as the Doctor had predicted. Anji had asked the nurse if he was around, but no one seemed to know if he was on duty or not, so she left it. She didn't bother to call him since she'd exploited his generosity one too many times. As soon as they got home, Karen opened the gin, swigging it neat from the bottle.

"Anji, I'm not like you, I'm not strong. You thought you were the weak one, do you remember?" she'd asked, her words all over the place.

"Come on, the kids need you Karen. Do it for them." This had only reduced her to more tears. To stop her from crying, Anji thanked her friend for telling her about Jeff. "I didn't believe it in the beginning, I can tell you. But you planted the seed."

"But I didn't tell you, did I?" Karen looked confused. "I swear I didn't."

Anji ignored her pleas of innocence, reminding Karen: "Jeff doesn't even know I know so..." But there was no point in warning Karen to keep quiet; the gin was already doing its job.

Martha the once employed housemaid of Karen, who was now the girlfriend of her husband and maybe soon-to-be-mum if she wanted to land herself a deal of a lifetime, had collected the children. Luckily Karen had sedated herself with booze and didn't hear her arrive.

"Martha, Karen isn't in a fit state today so please have them sleep at yours tonight," Anji asked politely. She actually wanted to say 'why couldn't you just ask for a pay rise – you didn't have to steal someone else's husband', but she didn't because Martha would tell Steve and it would cause more domestic havoc. Anji had had enough of that for a lifetime.

As well as packing and looking after Karen, the leaving party was taking up a big chunk of Anji's time, which she was grateful for. Jeff was calling at every opportunity, wanting to know all the details. He took a particular interest in the guest list. When Anji had mentioned that Sara and her family were invited, he had asked if those vile boys of hers needed to be there. Anji had told him they had already sent their RSVP, so it was too late now.

It wasn't enough that she had Jeff on her back, but Anji also had to deal with Lily, who was trying to take over. Insistent that no one should organise their own leaving party, she was meddling in everything, which of course gave her every opportunity to mention Adam and his non-existent apparently impending promotion. In the end Anji had to warn her away, reminding her that the party was for Karen and the kids. It had already turned into a bigger beast than she could handle, with 200 invitations being sent out and people in the habit of bringing along extended family members and housemaids. Anji secretly hoped that people would decline the invitation, due to her current status as home wrecker.

Max and Georgie had invited their entire class, their friends' parents, plus all their friends on the compound. Karen had left it to her friends, who were all once Anji's friends as well, to work on the guest list. That meant that the final number was unknown, which scared Anji more than a little. The food had been ordered and would be provided by the compound restaurant and a bouncy castle and inflatable slide had been booked, plus party bags for a hundred children already purchased and packed. Alcohol had been sourced through the embassy at normal prices, and Jeff had insisted on covering the cost of everything in a bid to show everyone what a perfect husband and father he was.

"I want your farewell to be magnificent. You and our children deserve the best," Jeff had declared. "I think paying for everything for Karen as well will give people a chance to forgive you for gossiping about her in the first place. Your way of saying you're sorry," he smirked.

"But –" Anji began to correct him, but she sighed and kept quiet. It wasn't worth the argument at this late stage and she was just glad Karen and the kids would have a great send off too.

Expats looked forward to any kind of function in Saudi Arabia, and towards the end of the school year there would usually be a flurry of them. Temperatures were scorching in the mid-forties, so a pool party would be most certainly welcomed by all. Anji imagined Sara there with her bump, Jeff's sperm germinating into something beautiful. The thought about Karen's husband Steve turning up with his girlfriend; her with her fake Louis Vuitton handbag, trying to fit in, going from housemaid to madam and trying far too hard. It takes all sorts, thought Anji.

CHAPTER 47

"I should be feeling happy about this baby," Sara howled down the phone to Jeff, interrupting the flow of his workday once again. "I should be with you. I can't wait for her to leave!"

"How many times do I have to repeat myself?" he asked yet again, gripping his phone more tightly in his rage gritting his teeth. "In a week they'll be gone, then I'm all yours." Jeff was feeling gagged, bound and tied – a virtual prisoner of Sara. She was suffocating him with her constant demands and needs for approval; her jealousy was almost strangling the life out of him. Life as a hotelier did not support an over-emotional, needy not to mention jealous woman. He felt cornered like a fox, no way out and nowhere to run.

The situation had got well out of hand, with Jeff feeling claustrophobic, controlled and patronised. It seemed he had met his match. Why the hell hadn't he used a condom? The shackles were heavy on his ankles and he had no idea how to free himself. He wanted out, and he certainly didn't want those two awful brats coming to live with him. The only thing he could think of would involve money and bribery. He knew he had to leave Saudi; that was a certainty. She would bleed him dry if he didn't get away and, what's more, his job would suffer. He needed to leave work on a high. He also needed Anji and, with her in London, if he stayed in the Middle East, he wouldn't be able keep her on a tight leash. He had already made up his mind.

"You know I love you," he lied through his teeth. He was going to put an end to this shit. Who the hell did she think she was, pressuring him? She was just a fuck, and now he was finished with that. Jeff and Sara were too alike for a relationship to ever work. Their conversations always started with the letter 'I'; there wasn't enough room in the world for the two of them, let alone both of them in the same vicinity. If one of them were unhappy the whole fucking universe would have to know. They were both jealous, fearing rejection, and they both had to have the last word.

Jeff knew that he and Sara were toxic for one another, and he was fast realising what a horrendous mistake he had committed. He couldn't even please her sexually anymore as she had become even more insatiable with the pregnancy. She was insanely horny; wanting to swing from chandeliers and give him blowjobs if they were anywhere he could drop his pants. But her being pregnant did nothing to arouse him he hated that kid growing inside her and he hated her for conning him in into this relationship. Anji had been his perfect cover, the loyal little wife raising his two gorgeous kids. His perfect missionary girl in bed, grateful for anything she got. He needed the stability of her love, and he wasn't going to give that up for Sara not now not ever.

CHAPTER 48

Party day had arrived. Everything was in place and it all seemed to be going according to plan. Anji considered this phase to be the calm before the storm. Jeff was still being the perfect loving, adoring husband, and she wondered how he'd react when she introduced the idea of divorce to him as soon as Mrs Watson gave her the green light. She presumed he'd be understandably shocked – after all Anji was playing the role of the perfectly happy wife. If he knew what was going on in her head, he would deny her the right to leave and would sell their new Kensington home straightaway.

Anji was in the restaurant organising the balloons. Karen's friends were doing their thing, looking very busy. A children's entertainer was getting her tricks ready for a special show after lunch. Giggles and laughter filled the room; the children were all hyperactive, fired up for a day of fun and action. It was music to Anji's ears and she loved being surrounded by such excitement and positivity.

Anji had been living out of a suitcase for two days. Her furniture and belongings had been picked up by the removal company to begin their long journey back to the UK. She had to warn the kids not to get dirty as they only had enough clothes for the next day.

Outside the sun was already a ferocious 47 degrees. "Drink plenty of water," she advised them. "We can't afford to get sick before we leave."

The chairs were lined up in the shade and, because Riyadh was so arid, there was little humidity. Thankfully, sitting outside but keeping out of the sun was manageable even in these extreme temperatures. Anji had asked the security guards to take care to keep everyone safe in the heat, especially since there were so many coming and plenty of them would end up having fun in the pool. She tried so very hard to avoid all of the other ladies, so busied herself with getting everything ready, although she could sense tongues wagging all around her. Anji had to remind herself that in just a few hours she would be on a plane out of there. There was relief and sadness. She was grateful for her time in Saudi; she'd had some amazing times and it had been an amazing experience for the kids, but recent dramas made her desperate to get away and the truth was it was time. With a new stepchild on the way and the kids soon to be getting a new stepmother, it was time to flee.

Karen charged into the room, obviously under the influence of a gin or two. Her mother hadn't arrived suprisingly, as her Visa hadn't been granted for some reason. Maybe Steve hadn't even bothered trying to get one, knowing the state his wife was in. He didn't need the disapproval of his soon-to-be-ex-mother in law.

Karen looked bloated, not the head-turner she once was. Her crowning glory that once hung so perfectly around her face looked matted to her scalp, like a doll that'd been over played with. Her signature red lipstick was way above her lip line, making her look more like the Batman's Joker. Anji wanted to tell her, but also didn't want to cause any hard feelings, so kept her mouth shut.

"Where are your kids?" enquired Lily, looking concerned.

"Outside," slurred Karen.

Anji was worried for them, and turned to try and spot them from the window. It was their day and they deserved to enjoy it. The children were both checking out the water slide, looking excited like the rest of their friends. Anji looked at her watch and caught herself thinking six more hours, six long hours and it'll all be over. This day would mark the end of an era; the end of Anji's marriage, the end of having to uproot her family to move every few years, the end of her life, as she had known it for so very long.

The guests began arriving, laden with gifts. Anji had forgotten about the bloody gifts. How was she going to get them back with her to the UK? It would be impossible. She would ask the children to give them to the workers' children; they would be happy and it would solve the problem.

The booze was already freely flowing from the hidden store. There was more than enough to go around and people were esctatic, looking far more relaxed now than when they'd first walked in. Mums were making polite chit-chat about their summer plans, talking about heading off to their home countries while their husbands stayed behind to fend for themselves and keep working.

"So Anji, why are you leaving?" she was asked maybe a million times. Exhausted by that single, constant question, she had prepared an answer a long time ago and it tripped off her tongue easily.

"The kids need some stability so we're off to London which is home for us. It'll be a great base. We had a good run, but now it's time to go back." She'd rather have said: 'well, you may or may not know this, but my husband is a lying, cheating bastard. So I'd better get home to file for divorce so I have a bloody chance of getting something. Oh and he's having a love child with my boss of three years', but she stuck to answer number one, realising it would make things a lot less complicated.

The buffet was opening at two o'clock, which couldn't come soon enough since it would absorb some of the alcohol that people were guzzling. Anji was sure everyone would be ravenous by then. The echoes of laughter from the children on the water slide and bouncy castle filled the air, and the atmosphere was buzzing. She was thrilled that the going-away party was a success, full of fun, people and chatter, just as it should be. But she was also stressed, worrying about how much Karen was drinking, and concerned she'd make a show of herself. Lily was in her ear constantly asking about Adam's promotion, which annoyed Anji no end, especially since she was also juggling watching the kids on the inflatable slide. It looked like an accident waiting to happen. Karen's good-for-nothing friends were nowhere to be seen, so the responsibility all rested on her shoulders.

"Please Lily," Anji begged, "tell everyone to help themselves to food. I can't leave the slide until all the children are off." As the last of the children slid down, Anji ushered them to the buffet. The carefully laid-out food – burgers, chicken strips, French fries and fruit kebabs – made the little ones squeal with delight. She was relieved to close the slide for a short period, as the entertainer would start her show shortly. As soon she looked at the spread, she realised Karen could probably do with getting some food down her. It may help her to sober up, or at least prevent her from drinking, as her mouth would be busy chewing. Anji wished Karen would pull herself together for the sake of her kids. She looked worse for wear in front of all the guests and they had definitely noticed her, their heads turning with second looks and glances.

"Karen, can you please eat something?" Anji pleaded, filling a plate up for Karen like she was a small child. "Here, try this."

"What the fuck do you care?" she rambled, hardly coherent. "Look at you, your husband is doing the deed with someone else and you keep your shit together. Like Mrs Friggin' perfect. I'm not you – I'm not perfect!" she carried on, looking like death warmed up, with her waxy skin and red-rimmed eyes. Anji looked around; glad no one seemed to have heard the foul-mouthed words.

"For God's sake Karen, keep it together," Anji encouraged her friend. "Don't lose it now, not in front of your kids."

With that, Karen stood up abruptly; drink in hand, to launch into an unrehearsed speech, which caught everyone's attention. Heads began to turn as Karen started slurring loudly.

"I wanna say cheers to everyone for coming to see me and my kids, to watch us get kicked out of Saudi. Extra thanks to my husband for causing it, by fucking our maid, the old slut!" Karen was teetering on her feet, her head drooping, her belly poking out of her too-tight clothes, and eyeliner running down her cheeks. "Fuck you all," came the final word from Karen, before Juliette, an irritating American lady who wouldn't hurt a fly, came running with a bottle of water, trying to steer Karen away from the rest of the crowd. The room fell silent; all the guests open mouthed trying to digest what she had told them and their innocent children.

"Come on Karen, let's have a little sleep, you'll feel better," said Juliette as she tried to bundle Karen out of the room. Out of nowhere, Karen took a swipe at Juliette, her fist meeting Juliette's face haphazardly causing blood to pour from her nose. Juliette screeched in shock, crashing to her knees with both hands covering her face. She was trying to stop the blood from gushing all over the floor so the children wouldn't be scared and start to panic. Two men came to the rescue to chaperone Karen to the kids' playroom, which was currently vacant. Squaring up alongside her and grabbing an arm each, they carried Karen away, her legs dragging way behind her.

Anji looked for Jeff. After a few minutes of searching for him, she spotted him in a shady courtyard, deep in conversation with Sara. Fadi was away by the pool watching the boys. Sara was pointing to her swollen belly, and Anji had a bad feeling; it seemed like something was simmering, maybe taking a turn for the worse. The temperature outside was rising, matching the mood of the crowd, which was simmering away after Karen's outburst. Anji watched from a distance as Jeff turned to storm off, with Sara in hot pursuit. Anji tried to call him but he was already out of hearing range.

"Sara, where is Jeff going?" Anji urged.

She spun around in shock, unaware that Anji was right behind her. Losing her balance on her too-high heels, Sara went crashing hard to the floor, automatically grabbed Anji's ankle in desperation.

"Oh my God, my baby! Is my baby ok?" Sara shouted as she cupped her hands around her belly in a panic. Anji looked around her and clocked one of the ladies.

"Stella!" Anji called out. "Call an ambulance please, quickly!" Sara was writhing around in agony, as if someone had reached in and pulled out her guts with their bare hands. A niggle in Anji's mind told her that Sara was probably putting on an act so she wouldn't have to explain herself, and so she could win Jeff back through emotional baby blackmail. She brushed the thought aside, ashamed at herself.

An ambulance had been called and was on its way. Anji felt absolutely frazzled, her nerves frayed. This party would be the final straw for her, and although it was a joint one, she felt like she was the only one who gave a damn about Karen leaving. Kneeling down to support a sobbing Sara, Anji phoned Jeff. She thought he should know about Sara and their unborn child, plus she didn't want to be the person standing by Sara's side supporting her through this.

"Where are you?" she said, as he picked up the phone. "Sara had a fall, she is going to A and E, and she's very worried about the baby." Jeff appeared almost instantly on the other side of the courtyard, as if he may have been hiding in a bush the whole time, trying to avoid getting involved. He obviously wanted to say something, but he had an obvious audience. Anji looked at him, keeping silent, like a secret agent who had sworn an oath not to reveal anything. No one had even thought about letting Fadi know, as Jeff ran to Sara to check out his goods. He cradled her without hesitation.

He didn't realise most of the ladies were watching; so this was the mistress they had all been wondering about. Suddenly everything fell into place and added up perfectly.

Raised eyebrows rippled through the crowd and, just like that, everyone knew everything. The ladies were all excited; the freshness of the news igniting the wires in their brains as WhatsApp messages began pinging from phone to phone with the newfound knowledge. The secret was out. Some were even snapping photos of Jeff, Sara and the bump. Anji was so glad she was leaving the very next day. The impulse to just run was stronger than ever, and the thought of making polite conversation with people who didn't give a rat's arse about her made her stomach turn.

When the ambulance arrived, the paramedics wouldn't allow Fadi to ride with Sara because he was in swimming shorts and topless. He agreed to take the boys home, get dressed, and drive back to the hospital. Anji said a prayer under her breath as the vehicle pulled away. "Please let the child be born full-term and healthy. Please, I promise to be a much better person," she begged, watching Jeff as he looked on helplessly, his brow sweating and his face vacant. He was helpless and in despair because he couldn't be with Sara or their unborn child. He was trapped between two women and had to choose to either abandon one, or wait till one of them broke. The mess felt endless. He was way out of his depth.

Luckily the children had already moved on. The younger ones were in the room waiting for the entertainer to begin, and the older ones were busy at the pool. Anji was relieved – the water slide had been chaos earlier, and she had been worried about the younger kids hurting themselves. She clutched at her neck as she tried to release the tension, when suddenly the spine-chilling scream of a child echoed around the complex. The terror resounded like a siren; the screams went on and on, bouncing off every whitewashed wall and paved surface.

Anji stood up, trying to sense where the screams were coming from. She scanned the bouncy castle, the water slide – anywhere there was unmanned equipment. The screams were getting louder, more ear piercing. She ran to the side of the pool where the commotion was coming from and there it was, right in front of her. She knew immediately it was Karen even though she couldn't see her face and she fell to her knees.

Masses of black hair were floating in the pool; a listless, fully clothed body drifting on top, with arms outstretched and legs dangling deeper into the water. One of the children's dads didn't hesitate, springing into action to launch himself into the pool. Another dad-followed suit and they both made their way to the body, dragging it to the side and, with the help of other men they heaved the limp shape out of the water and onto the hot paving around the edge of the pool. A group of mums and housemaids were busy ushering any remaining children out of sight, away from the tragedy that was unfolding right before their eyes.

"Get the first aid box, quick!" screamed Greg, the man who had been the first to reach the body. With shaking hands, he slapped at Karen's face, trying to rouse her, before bending down to begin chest compressions and mouth to mouth. The blood had drained from

Anji's face. When had she last seen Karen? How long ago had it been? She glanced at her watch thoughtlessly; realising two hours must have passed since Karen's speech, which is when she'd last seen her. If Karen had been in the pool for two hours, any attempts at resuscitation would be useless. Greg continued to pump her chest relentlessly and, with each pump, water spouted from Karen's mouth. But she didn't gag. Her staring eyes stayed transfixed to the sky. Again and again he tried, with no one telling him to stop. He wasn't giving up on her, but it was already too late. She was dead.

A large crowd had gathered, with most of them holding their hands over their mouths in pure shock. They were frozen and rooted to their places, their eyes not flinching, waiting for Karen to breathe, to choke, to show signs of life. Anything. Greg's wife approached him slowly, cupping his face and looking him in the eye. There were no words spoken between them, just eye contact telling him 'enough now'. Greg closed Karen's eyes gently with his fingers and began weeping. His wife Shona took him in her arms and rocked him. They placed a towel over Karen's body and called Steve, who had just arrived with Martha. Before anyone could stop them, the kids ran towards their mother, wailing, and had to be torn away from her lifeless body. This would scar them for the rest of their fragile lives, and it was torture for Anji to see Martha pull at their little limbs as they resisted her. The memory would haunt Anji for a lifetime.

CHAPTER 49

As all the guests filed out of the party, distraught, some crying and hugging each other, Anji stood alone, holding her own grief. She wanted to join them in sharing their shock but knew she wouldn't be welcome. An ambulance had arrived to take Karen's body away the second one of the day. No one went with her; she was just packed away and gone – just like that. Anji's whole body shook. She had no one to hug, not even Lily who was with the other group. She didn't want to show her own desolation, having looked over at Lily who'd caught her eye twice but quickly looked away again. Lily no longer had any use for Anji. She'd be leaving tomorrow, so it was better for her if she stayed friendly with the other lot.

A flash of white died blonde hair passed by Anji, and she realised through her tears that it was Magenta, a Polish woman who wasn't one to be messed with.

"I hope you know you're responsible for this, the death of this beautiful woman. Can you live with that?" she snarled in Anji's face.

Anji ignored her, turning away and looking for her handbag hurriedly, keeping herself busy. Losing Karen felt like one of her limbs had been severed. She couldn't deal with any more hurt.

"I'm talking to you, stupid bitch," she goaded.

Against her better judgment, Anji wanted to say

her peace before she left forever. It was a now or never moment.

"Look," she said, taking a deep breath. "I never meant to hurt anyone and I will take the blame, no problem. I have to live with this forever. I won't point the finger at anyone."

Suddenly a voice piped up. "It was me, it was me," Amal confessed. "If you want someone to blame, blame me and Lily! Lily told me, and I told Karen, so blame us ," she said, pouting sadly.

Lily stood by Amal, clutching at her arm and pursing her lips in a bid to stop her making any more accusations. But she carried on, nonetheless. "It wasn't Anji – not at all, it was me! I'm the devil, a shaitan." Amal was reverting to Arabic amidst her wailing.

Anji stood there dumbfounded, her mouth wide open. All the lies of the previous months had been swept away by this truthful confession, and she imagined the chains that had bound her falling to the ground with a thud. But it was too little, too late. No words would ever bring Karen back, and seeing her lifeless body had made Anji realise that her days of compromising, of making do, were over. She wanted Jeff out of her life and out of her head. She wanted to enjoy the rest of her life with her kids. Every day was going to count. Every day from now was going to be a better day than the last.

Karen's friends had nothing to say. They stood together, speechless and silent. There wasn't a thing they could do about Karen's death, but Amal's admission certainly changed things. Karen's suffering was at an end; her short existence over way too early. It wasn't Steve who had killed her, although he did have a hand in her demise. And now he would have to release his wife's body as her sponsor in Saudi Arabia, and organise its removal or disposal. Every night he would have to return home to Martha, who would resume her duties once again – looking after Karen's children, cleaning the house, and cooking the meals. Only this time she'd be legitimately sharing Steve's bed.

Anji knew that, from this day onward, nothing would ever be the same for her. She didn't hang around for any apologies, although they didn't seem forthcoming anyway. Anji would fight on in the name of Karen. Her death gave Anji an inner strength, making her realise how lucky she was. She had so much to go on for and, unlike Karen, she was going to watch her children grow up and reach every milestone in their lives, for as long as she was fortunate enough to do so.

Leaving the party without needing to say another word, she held her innocent head high and looked each one of her ex 'friends' in the eye, before giving them a knowing smile. She didn't need their approval or their apology. She wiped a tear from her eye, turned on her heel, and rushed home to her kids. Max and Georgie were in the front room with all their gifts, unwrapping everything in a frenzy. She took them in her arms, scooping them up and drinking in the cuddles as she sat and cried a thousand tears.

CHAPTER 50

Arriving in the UK meant a fresh start for Anji, Max and Georgie, but there was a heaviness that weighed down Anji's heart. The sinking feeling extended to her limbs and, as she tried to keep her head above water, she had to remind herself that she could do anything if she really wanted to.

Her grief had not run its course. There was no more crying now; her tears had all dried up. Anji had spent nights sobbing noisily, with snot running down her face. Now that stage she had finished, she was onto phase two, which was anger. She had suffered so many horrendous incidents in the last few months. She remembered the ladies' faces as they'd tried to apologise the day after Karen's death. Amal and Lily hadn't even tried to get in touch. All the others turned up at Anji's villa to catch her before she left, trying their best to be forgiven. It was of course not enough, but she had the chance to ask the group to excuse both Amal and Lily for Karen's sake. She knew it would be difficult, maybe even impossible, but she wanted to leave knowing she had at least tried to make things better.

She had contacted Omar and was sending him small sums of money to tide him over. She had explained her situation to him in great detail and he was more than thankful, but it didn't make things right in her eyes. Not yet, anyway. It was the best she could do right now. Anji had made sure she had spoken to each member of Omar's family, his two sons, his daughter, and his wife. She made sure they knew his record was untarnished and that he was indeed a good man.

Starting her new life in London, Anji frequently thought back to her old self. You never truly know anyone until they're in hot water, she reminisced. She knew the old Anji was dead and buried, and she never wanted to be that weak ever again. What's more, she was a little bit in love with the new version of herself. And why not? If Karen's death had taught her anything, it was that life was too short, and loving yourself was so important. Sure, Anji still had low days and was very raw at times. Sometimes the pain of Jeff's cheating throbbed like an open wound. But some days she barely felt it at all. In her bad patches, Anji remembered Doctor Hassan's advice, breathing slowly and holding still until it all passed. Every now and then a new wound opened, leaving a little scar in its place. But it was nothing she couldn't live with.

Her lawyer was busy pulling her case together. Thanks to all of this, Anji had acquired knowledge, experience and a wealth of patience. Because she'd been able to gather vital evidence, the case was rock solid in Mrs Watson's eyes, but she advised her client not to be over-confident. Always expect the unexpected, she'd said, maybe even a blood bath in court.

Anji only wanted justice, not revenge. She wanted everyone to be happy; after all, Jeff was still the father of her kids and they loved him. Her efforts had paid off and she had given him no reason to expect anything, other than his loving family waiting for him back home. When the ball did drop eventually, though, she knew he wouldn't give her up easily and she had to be ready for a fight.

"It's time to go after him Anji," declared Mrs Watson at their first appointment after Anji had moved to London. It was the news she had been waiting for, the green light to forge ahead. To move forward, be brave and quit the charade that she'd kept up for so long.

"Ok, let's do it! I'm ready," Anji said, feeling equally excited and terrified. It was good timing, as Anji was at breaking point trying to play happy families for the sake of the children. Jeff was still trying to control everything from thousands of miles away and she needed closure, not from him as the children's dad, but from him as her husband. She knew he would remain in their lives somehow, but he had to understand that she was no longer his property.

"He will try and manipulate you; stay strong. He will beg for forgiveness; stay strong. He is a manipulator, and he will use everything in his power to get his way – even using the kids. Stay strong," advised Mrs Watson who by now had asked Anji to call her Eleanor.

"The woman is your lawyer, not your best friend," Anji's mum had reminded her afterwards. "Don't confuse the two." But it was too late. Anji felt a strong connection with Eleanor, who at this stage seemed to be more than her lawyer.

Anji didn't hate Jeff, although she didn't like him much either. She even had a few things to thank him for. She had two wonderful children, who were the best things in her life. She and Jeff had travelled the world together, and she would never be the same woman who'd left Brighton fifteen years before. She reminisced about all the people she had met, friends she would keep for a lifetime and how her experiences had made life much more colourful. From zip-lining in the rainforest to sitting on the glorious beach of Koh Samui, she had hundreds of images stored in albums, as mobile phone photographs and as memories in her mind. They would stay with her for a lifetime.

Since leaving Saudi Arabia, she didn't miss Jeff, but she somehow feared him. She didn't miss the comfort of his touch or their sex life – that had never been great anyway. She'd discovered how good that could be much later on in life, in her own marital bed with the gorgeous Doctor. Those recent memories had given her some mouth-wateringly good bits to fantasise about. She remembered that delicious feeling of his tongue between her legs, and the thrust of him grinding inside her. It left her wondering if she would ever in her lifetime experience such ecstasy again. If not, she was grateful that at least she'd had it once in her life.

In the few weeks since their arrival in Kensington, Max and Georgie were expanding and spreading their wings, flourishing in their new surroundings. They both loved school for completely different reasons. Max for the sports – he had been picked to play for both the rugby and football teams – and Georgie for her new-found friends. "Mum they're so sophisticated! Rose has an Instagram page and her mum was a famous model!" she'd said, shoving her phone in her mum's face. Anji was subjected to constant chatter about famous bloggers like Alfie and Zoella, who lived in Brighton: "Do you think we can pass by their house next time we visit Granny?" she pleaded, her independence blossoming day by day.

Anji was so pleased that moving away from Saudi

and leaving their father behind hadn't seemed to unsettle the children. Life was busy, not like the life of an expat where you had too much spare time so watched everyone else's every move. They enjoyed walking to school down the busy Kensington High Street, wandering through parks, riding their bikes – the simple pleasures of life.

Anji had been honest with them from the beginning, trying to be as truthful as she could but leaving out the fact that he was a narcissist and a cheat. She told them that mummy and daddy had simply fallen out of love. Of course they had cried and bombarded her with questions, which she had answered from the heart. Because they moved so often and were used to being thrown into new lives, meeting new people and going to new schools, Max and Georgie had amazing coping mechanisms. They took it in their stride with as much maturity as any adult she knew. She'd even heard Max secretly giving his father some advice: "Just give her time Dad and some space, she'll come around." Similarly, Georgie had a very matter-of-fact view, saying one day: "Mum, its ok you know – half of the kids at our school have divorced parents. It's no big deal." Anji's children gave her so much to be proud of.

CHAPTER 51

"Mum," whispered Max at the dinner table as they settled down for their evening meal. Things were getting into a routine and Anji liked it, and because Jeff had never been a part of their ordinary everyday habits, they didn't really notice him not being there.

"Yes Max, what is it?" asked Anji. "Is everything ok kiddo?"

Looking down at the plate in front of him, he pushed his food around with his fork. Murmuring quietly, his question knocking Anji sideways. "Dad said this is all your fault. Why do you want to break up our family?" He hung his head to his chest in shame. It must have been weighing heavily, too much to bear at his tender age; his little spirit battered by his own father.

Just as Mrs Watson had predicted, saying: "The saddest thing about betrayal is that it always comes from loved ones and hardly ever from enemies." It was sad how Jeff was beginning to believe his own stories and lies to make himself feel and look better. And now it would seem that his emotional blackmail had begun with of course the children. They were Anji's weak point, and she knew it was low and conniving of him to use them as his pawns in a game of family roulette. Jeff was abusing the kids mentally, yet another way to control Anji. It was working.

Eleanor had anticipated nothing less, and had said

as much. "Don't think he won't try and manipulate the system, the judges, friends and family," she'd said. "He will be doing his utmost, everything in his power to make you look like the gold digger, the harlot and the home wrecker, believe me. He'll even use the children." What pressure for such young shoulders. Anji's heart ached as she took Max in her arms.

"Listen Max, I want you to know that this isn't and will never be your fault. This is between your father and I. We are no different from millions of other families, because divorce happens every minute of every day. Just remember that you two are both amazing. I'm so proud of you and Georgie, and how you adapt to your situations. There are no limits to what you can do and achieve. Your dad and I love you very much; that will never change, no matter what." She was very careful not to scream obscenities about Jeff, although she was holding the insults back. She had to keep sucking her cheeks in so she didn't call him a no-good bastard like he deserved.

Anji realised she had to treat the children with double the kindness and understanding now, because she was on a one-way street battling traffic coming in the opposite direction. Thanks to Eleanor's previous warnings she had rehearsed a dummy speech in her head. The original one had been a lot longer, but she knew the kids just needed words of comfort and support so decided to keep it short and sweet.

Max blew his nose. His eyes red from crying, but the hurt which had built up was fading away slowly. "It's ok to cry Max, strong people cry," she comforted her son. "It's your heart speaking when your lips can't explain. You can come to me anytime, understand? You'll never be alone." He hugged in tight to Anji, who squeezed him back.

The Jeff who Anji knew, who had always been her protector, her everything, was now just an empty, pointless arsehole with money. The biggest crushing blow came when the children informed her that daddy was moving back home. "He has quit his job and is moving back here to be with us!" they announced. When Anji had called Eleanor with this news, she hadn't been fazed by it. "Of course he has," she replied sarcastically. "He has to control the divorce and he can't do that from Saudi now, can he?"

Anji knew Jeff too well, and had a grip on the depths he was willing to stoop to, but she was totally unsure of any of his next moves. He was now totally unpredictable and behaving erratically, not to mention his moods. She wondered what Sara would be thinking right now. A baby on the way and this fucker was leaving her back in Saudi, unless he was moving her and the kids with him. Anji didn't have the first clue. Maybe he felt like he could conquer the world with her? Perhaps they completed each other, or some shit? The only person he could really fall in love with was the one who stared back at him in the mirror everyday. Everybody else was just a toy to him, a plaything to fill his extra time.

Whatever he was up to, Anji knew Jeff was on his way back to London. He would be in her life now, whether she liked it or not.

Once the kids were safely in bed that night, and Max had dried his eyes and calmed down, Anji nestled into her feather duvet, her head under the covers trying to hide from the world. The nights were drawing in now, and autumn was in the air. She loved the smell of the changing season as the leaves on the trees began to turn; growing old gracefully as they wilted from the tree outside her house. The season reflected her need to hibernate and weather the storm. She could hardly wait for the spring to reveal its green shoots.

Anji slipped into her nightly meditation, although it wasn't strictly a meditation, more of a remembrance, and an excellent way of getting to sleep. She imagined his hand reaching for hers as they kissed tenderly, before he passionately pulled her nightie up over her head. His hands were touching her skin, then his lips followed to leave a trail of electricity that managed to cover every inch of her body. Their naked torsos pressed together and goose bumps lined her skin, as she ached for him to enter her so she could feel him deep inside. She imagined the bed creaking as he pushed himself deeper, her legs resting on his arms ever so gently. His honey eyes boring into hers, his soft lips saying 'I love you' before kissing her mouth sweetly while he shuddered, letting out a deep groan of pleasure.

Anji had imagined this scenario many times now. She didn't feel guilty about having erotic dreams featuring Doctor Hassan; after all, they were only in her imagination, and they were more effective than the sleeping pills the Doctor had prescribed during her short stay in the Saudi hospital.

CHAPTER 52

"Look, I don't give a shit about you or your baby," Jeff admitted, finally owning up to the feelings he'd been having for weeks now. "I care about the kids I have with my wife, and that bitch is filing for divorce. On what grounds, I have no idea."

"It's not my baby, it's ours," Sara retorted. "And if you remember, I have a hell of a lot more to lose than you. All these promises you made and you ain't done shit. No wonder she's leaving you!" she screamed.

Jeff swung a punch that landed on the side of her face. Sara hadn't bargained for that and it caught her off guard, not to mention it hurt like hell.

"I'm calling the police, you son of a bitch. No one touches me – do you understand? Are you trying to kill this baby, putting me under this much stress?" she bellowed.

Jeff began to crack up and howl. "Don't make me laugh! Who would believe you at the police station? They'd send you to jail immediately. And by the way, who the hell asked you to have more kids? That was your choice. I've got two already and I didn't want any more. Those two boys of yours," he said, rolling his eyes, "you couldn't give them away for free! They're a menace to society."

"Didn't your promise mean anything?" pleaded Sara, realising everything Jeff said was right and she didn't have a leg to stand on. She had to get back in his good books before she lost him forever.

"No, not now. I'm losing my family and she will take me to the cleaners – who will want me then?" he asked her. "You sure as hell don't want a penniless man who can't wipe his own arse." That he was absolutely sure about.

The thought of Jeff being broke did not appeal to Sara one bit. The money and the title was what had enticed her in the first place. There was no way that bitch was going to get a penny from him. It was his money. The money gave him power and he was nothing without it.

Frown lines were etched in his face, forming crevices around his sunken eyes. He was drinking more and more, which gave him the imagination to cook up crazy ideas of how to win back Anji and get back to his old idyllic life. She had been his perfect little trophy wife; the idea of anyone else having her was completely out of the question. He would never allow it. She belonged to him and he had the marriage certificate to prove it. She was nothing without him anyway. Absolutely nothing. She couldn't tie her own shoelaces without his say so, and she'd soon be begging to come back. God knew she would have to pay the price first. It had been the hardest decision for Jeff to give in his resignation, after everything he'd put into this job. But Anji had left him no choice; it would be virtually impossible to be in control of the divorce from Riyadh. Sara had made the decision that much easier with her constant nagging and ultimatums.

The day after their row, he called her to arrange a meet-up. "I've got something for you," he promised. He was ready to pay-up – it was deal or no deal.

"I want you and this kid out of my life," he pointed at her swollen belly as they stood facing each other in a compound car park while he took a quick break from work. There was no need for secrecy now that everyone knew about their affair. "How much do you need to raise it? The deal is though I don't want any updates, I don't want to know it, and I don't want you contacting me. One thing I will do is pay for my mistake." He was blunt and to the point, but Sara didn't seem to mind. This was exactly what she wanted to hear. She didn't want him now – he was an emotional mess who couldn't keep it together. She'd seen his true colours; in reality he was one arrogant arsehole. She wasn't ready to gamble anymore, she wanted to play it safe and stay with Fadi, a steady, decent man. So in the end she would get exactly what she wanted from Jeff – his cash.

"Oh, Jeff how could you do this to me? To us?" She looked down and stroked her bump, playing the game. "How can you leave me now with your child growing inside me? Do you have no feelings for me, or for this innocent child at least? I love you," she lied disgracefully.

Thankfully he kept his head down. His dishevelled hair and five o'clock shadow were disgusting her. The slight whiff of booze made her stomach lurch, her senses heightened due to the pregnancy. He reached into his suit pocket and pulled out a piece of paper.

"Here's a cheque," he said, stretching his hand out towards her. "It's a million dollars."

She stared at the cheque in disbelief. She couldn't believe her luck. She had contemplated asking for a mere 150 grand, and she was ready to leave his life for good for that paltry amount. But here he was offering her one million dollars. Of course she was going to accept that; she'd spent the last eleven years in Saudi barely surviving with all her family's demands back home. It was hard enough raising two children, let alone a new addition. She also had the pressures of paying for her parents' apartment and medical bills. This cheque was more than heaven sent. And it would be all hers. Fadi didn't have a clue, living in ignorant bliss and thinking the child was his. He would never know either way, about the money or the baby's father. Tears pricked Sara's eyes with happiness. Everything was falling perfectly into place.

"How can you be so cruel, buying off your own flesh and blood?" Using the tears of happiness to her advantage, she reached out for the cheque. As she went to grab it, he pulled it back slightly. Her adrenaline shot through the roof; she had dreamed of holding that kind of money in her hand, proving that money can buy you happiness.

"I'm warning you now," he said, glaring. "If you ever contact me again, I will ruin your life. You know I can do it. I know a lot of people here and they can make your life miserable." She nodded her head in agreement and he finally placed the cheque in her quivering hand.

"I have one request before I'm out of your life forever," she told him. "I can't possibly place a cheque for this amount in my account here in Saudi Arabia. I need a wire transfer to my bank in Lebanon. I don't need Fadi to know about this; I couldn't begin to explain it to him and after all, he has to believe this child is his now, right? From where I'm standing, I have no other choice. I'm going to keep this cheque in my possession until the money has been transferred, and then I will dispose of it. Is that a deal? If yes I promise to never cross your doorstep again," she said.

Jeff stood up, agreeing to her last and final demand. He was quite relieved that it had been just a simple case of money and was delighted at the transaction she had accepted so graciously. He really was a true business-man through and through. Mentally he congratulated himself.

Sara walked away, the biggest smile spreading across her face. This deal bought her a kind of freedom that she could have never imagined, not in her wild-est dreams. After he confirmed the transfer she would jump on the next flight out to Lebanon to bank the cheque that she'd so graciously accepted. She hoped that he trusted her enough not to cancel the cheque so she could bank it, leaving her with two million dollars. In her eyes she deserved it anyway. Even if he cancelled the cheque, she still couldn't wait to see the money sit-ting in her account with her own eyes. All those extra zeros seemed impossible to imagine. She could envision it there already. She folded the cheque carefully, tucking it into her bra, and keeping the dirty secret close to her heart.

CHAPTER 53

Now that Jeff was back in the UK he had nothing to do, so to fill his time he dedicated most of it to the pending court case. He grew angrier each day, especially since all his calls were left unanswered by his wayward wife. And, just as Mrs Watson had predicted, he had contacted the most prestigious divorce lawyers in London.

Hardays were the best and most expensive around. A 'Mr Parker' would be representing Jeff, who was apparently well known in the industry as being absolutely ruthless. When Eleanor had told her this, Anji's heart sank. She knew what Jeff was capable of. He was a brilliant liar and also incredibly insecure. Together it was a lethal combination, and with the guidance of a similarly moral-free legal team, Anji felt like her situation was doomed. Even with a solid case, she wasn't going to let her guard down for a second.

"Don't be weak now Anji. You've got this far." Eleanor was so encouraging. "You will gain strength and confidence, you'll look fear in the face," she added, as Anji imagined all rubbish he was feeding his fancy lawyers.

"I know, but he's so toxic and he'll try and manipulate the people around him, spreading lies about me. I feel like he's stripping the meat from my bones." It was the only way she could describe it.

"Don't rise to the bait, the truth will prevail. That's the best and only advice I can give you."

Anji thought about everyone who was relying on her and all the people she needed to be strong for – Omar, Karen, Max, Georgie, her mum and dad. That was enough to give her the strength to push forward. Anji's mum Jacky was an absolute blessing; solid and reliable, always available, always there. Anji tried not to tell her everything, but some days she couldn't help herself. When it all felt too much everything would tumble out to her mother.

"You know Jeff called," Jacky told Anji down the phone one day. "He wasn't very nice Anji, in actual fact he was quite awful. He blamed you for everything. I just put the phone down and he didn't call back. Luckily your Dad wasn't here. He would have threatened to kill him!"

"Oh Mum," Anji sighed. "It's to be expected. He could be taping the calls, so don't say anything. Just let him rant. I wouldn't put anything past him at this stage. He's going completely nuts, I swear."

Suddenly, Jacky's tone of voice changed, as she said, "We didn't want to tell you Anji, we've been holding out, but your Dad isn't well. He would kill me for telling you, but you're my daughter and we tell each other everything. I don't want that to change."

"What is it, what do you mean unwell?" Anji asked, fearfully.

"Prostate cancer." As she uttered the word cancer, everything in Anji's life seemed to change. The emotional rollercoaster she was on began spiralling out of control, threatening to come off the rails. With so much on her plate, Anji hadn't wondered how it had affected her parents. Guilt, sadness and hopelessness stabbed at her; not tiny pricks of a needle but more like big slices from a professional butcher's knife.

Dad snatched the receiver and butted in. "Look it's very common! Don't worry girl, I'm going to beat this, just like you're going to beat this arsehole Jeff. If you can do it, so can I." They both waited for the other to talk, but Anji couldn't think of anything to say to make light of this grave situation. She was stifling her sobs down the phone, covering her mouth with her arm.

'It grows slowly," her dad continued. "In my case Anji it's been detected early. We had to tell you." She had been so wrapped up in her own problems that she'd forgotten about her parents advancing age and what her situation might be doing to them. Anji feared she had brought this on them with the worry of the impending court case. She wondered if she could put her divorce on the backburner, but knew that was out of the question. She imagined her poor dad being told he had the dreaded C word and her shoulders shook with tears.

Anji planned to go and see them the very next weekend. A visit was long overdue, and it was her weekend to take the kids. When Max and Georgie learned of the fresh plans they were absolutely thrilled. She told them their granddad was under the weather, and as concerned as they were, they didn't feel the absolute emptiness that Anji felt. She remembered Doctor Hassan's words in that moment, and took a few laboured deep breaths.

CHAPTER 54

Boarding the train at London Victoria, Anji and her kids took their seats near a young family. The mother looked exhausted and frayed at the edges. Anji gazed at the boy, who was no more than four years old, and remembered the days when she was in that exact same position with two young kids in tow. She smiled at the boy and he smiled back, but that soon changed when he realised he didn't have a red pen to colour the red fire truck in his book and he threw a loud tantrum. Other passengers started to glare and tut, and Anji watched the boy's mum turn crimson with embarrassment.

On many occasions she had been in the exact same position as that poor mum. She recalled when Max had been around three years old, and spent a large part of a flight to the UK kicking the chair in front of him. Anji had tried everything to stop him, from giving him cookies to letting him play with her phone. Nothing had worked. Finally the man in front had had enough and began screaming at them. Max immediately wet himself and Anji had screamed back, "Get yourself a first class ticket next time then! That's why we're sitting in economy, so we sit with other families, not the toffee-nosed idiots who travel alone!" The man hadn't bargained on getting a response, let alone a woman shouting back in his face, and he had kept his mouth shut for the rest of the flight.

"Here little guy," said Max, handing the boy on the train his yellow pen. "You know, I lived in Saudi Arabia, and the fire trucks are yellow there." The boy calmed down instantly while the mum mouthed a very grateful 'thank you' at Max. Why couldn't people be more understanding, more concerned? People took themselves far too seriously, thought Anji, and couldn't see further than their own silly messed-up worlds. Anji felt so proud of Max in that moment.

Despite her empathy with the other mother, she wasn't in the mood to listen to a child screaming all the way to Brighton either, so she closed her eyes for the rest of the journey and focused on her breathing. Thoughts flickered through her mind and she relived the events of the last few months as if an old black and white movie was playing on the inside of her eyelids. Somehow everything had come out ok, up until now with her dad becoming sick. Would he honestly be unwell if she hadn't brought her worries on them? She worried incessantly about that. "We'll fight this," her dad had said. She was going to keep her end of the bargain.

Anji and the children jumped out of the taxi to run up the path, and Granny and Granddad threw their arms around the kids. She could see the absolute joy in their faces – all four of them. They talked for hours, laughing and giggling, firing questions at one another. Both of the children were sharing stories of their not-so-new school, with funny tales about friends and teachers. They had fun imitating the British accents they heard at school. "Everyone talks like the Queen," giggled Georgie, pushing her nose up with her finger and sending her grandparents into fits of laughter. A feeling of wellbeing hit Anji as she enjoyed the roar of happiness. She was sure it must be a little medicine for her dad too, even though no one dared mention his illness. Anji desperately wanted him to say it had all been a scare and the doctors had got it wrong. Looking at him, he looked the same – a fit man, full of life. The dad she had always known. She'd obviously done her Google homework and, just like her dad had told her, it was common and usually grew ever so slowly. He also had a better chance of successful treatment because it had been detected and caught early. It didn't stop her worrying though, as much as she tried not to.

Anji had told Jeff that she was at her parents this weekend. She was following instructions from Eleanor to keep him in the loop. He would take the children next weekend; he had the same parental rights as she did, and saw them every other weekend up until now. It killed her, having to message him to let him know their whereabouts, especially as she was now petrified of him. He was unpredictable and unstable. He had been using the kids for weeks, trying to destroy the little self-esteem she had left. His mind games were making her feel like she was letting everyone down. How she had ever given him the power to fuck her up, she would never know. She realised crazy people always think they're absolutely sane, and that was the scary part – Jeff thought everybody else was off their bloody trolley. *He might want to try looking in a mirror,* thought Anji.

Jeff had really let himself go, drinking heavily probably every evening. In his drunken stupor, he was planning and plotting how to get Anji back, or at least how to get rid of her for good. She was a bitch and he would never trust another woman again – in his eyes, they were all bitches. How he had laughed to himself when the other bitch, the real bitch, Sara had banked the million dollars, plus the million he had stupidly transferred to her bank in Lebanon. He couldn't understand the missing million, so after one call to the bank he realised how stupid and gullible he'd been. How bloody clever of her, he scowled, she thinks she's smarter than me, well let's see. He had called her to threaten her.

"If I don't get that money back by the end of this week, I will call that pathetic husband of yours and tell him everything. That way you'll be nothing but a homeless, worthless whore," he promised as he tried to extort his money back.

"Oh really?" She had an answer for everything. "Well, I'll be a homeless whore with your child and two million in the bank. Either way, I win. I will call Anji and tell her everything, then she can take that to the divorce courts, can't she?" Sara retaliated, with an answer she had obviously already prepared. She knew he wouldn't be thrilled about her banking the extra million. "I'm sorry but you seem to have mistaken me for Anji, someone who would take your shit! That's not me!" she snapped, hanging up the phone.

He didn't have a leg to stand on. He'd certainly met his match, with neither of them backing down. Both of them were as stubborn and as demented as each other. He slammed the phone down, pissed off that she had the upper hand this time. He certainly didn't need any hiccups in his way, not before the divorce was concluded anyway. He would break her afterwards. He would make sure of that. He planned to make her life a living hell, baby or no baby. Maybe he would organise someone to plant drugs on her, or go and visit Fadi himself to tell him what a little slut his wife really was. He wasn't sure of his plans yet, but he was going to make her pay. But for now he had bigger issues.

He was calling his lawyers continuously, and they were pestering Eleanor, trying to wear her and Anji down. Just as Anji had expected, he was also spreading venom amongst their friends, who in reality were his friends, since she'd never been allowed to let anyone get that close to her. He portrayed himself as the victim and at this stage they were all behind him, although they'd always known he was an egocentric, bigheaded twat. All these people had believed Jeff when he told them it was Anji having the affair. He probably drove her to it; after all, who could put up with him? But they also felt sorry for him. She had made him quit his job and they could all see he was quickly losing his mind.

Jeff had all his friends call her, trying to trap her. But she was one step ahead of the game, with a little insider knowledge about surveillance, thanks to her own experience in Saudi following Jeff.

"So it is true!" squealed Francesca, one of Jeff's old school friends. "Come on, tell me all the juicy details," she pressed, calling Anji out of the blue. "I want to know all about your dirty little affair." But Francesca was out of luck. She was a flaming red head who'd a fling with Jeff back in university; according to him she was a nice girl but way too intense. She had been too clingy, talking about wedding bells on the first date. And when she'd told him she loved him on the second date, Jeff knew it was time to say goodbye. They had remained friends for some strange reason, with Jeff saying he felt sorry for her.

Anji brushed her off immediately, fully aware of what she was up to. "Francesca, I hope you and your husband are doing great," she said, keeping everything above board. "I really can't speak to you right now, but you can believe what you want. Jeff and I have children together, and you should know better than asking stupid questions." Anji slammed down the phone, furious that Jeff would stop at nothing to win. Whilst her anger was stewing, an idea came into her head. Could she persuade Sara to come and take a paternity test, to prove the baby was his? It would raise the bar to a new level. It wouldn't be easy to get her onside, and Anji didn't know the deal Sara had worked out with Jeff, but she had to try.

"So what did she say? Come on, quick – tell me," Jeff was cozied up on the sofa next to Francesca, eagerly awaiting her response. "I need stone cold evidence or I will lose everything – the money and the kids. I'd rather die," he said, dramatically. "The lawyers are doing some digging but I've kept her nose so clean that they can't find anything on her. I have only myself to blame for that," he admitted convincingly to himself.

He really believed it had been him who had protected her so much that her slate was clean as a whislte. Her Facebook was full of loving family pictures, as was her Instagram. The deeper they dug, the cleaner Anji was. He would have to plant something false, fabricate some evidence. It was the only way he could sway the divorce case and settlement. He wanted to prove that she was the one having a full-blown affair. The more he thought about it, the more he liked the idea of paying an actor to own up in court. He was sure he'd find someone willing to take the money and play pretend...

Right now, though, he had other things to think about, as Francesca was already unzipping his Gucci pants, getting him ready to give him oral. He sat back on the settee with his arms spread out across the back of the sofa and his legs apart. He stared at the wall wondering how he was going to find a willing thespian as Fran worked some magic down below. He barely gave her a second thought as he took her hair in his fist and pushed her head up and down at the rhythm that worked well for him. She was in pain as his grip tightened, but she didn't say a word; for one, her mouth was full, and secondly she wanted so badly to please him. He couldn't care less about Fran as she gagged, trying desperately to win his affection with a mind-blowing blowjob, but he was too consumed by taking Anji down.

As Fran rinsed her mouth out, Jeff was already calling Ben, her other half. Ben was a human rights lawyer, and Jeff thought he could use that to his advantage.

"Hey Ben, I need a favour. Anji has a lawyer helping her, and I need to know if there's any evidence against me. Can you help me mate? Do you know how I can get a meeting with this Watson woman?"

"Are you bloody nuts?" Ben responded, incredulous. "I wouldn't put a foot there. I can't help you. This is your fight; I'm not going to break the law for you or anyone. In case you've forgotten, I'm a human rights lawyer!" Ben wasn't about to do a favour for a man he couldn't stand. Francesca was always glued to Jeff anytime they met up, hanging on to his every word, and Ben knew it. Fran may have fallen into his trap, but Ben knew he didn't owe the arsehole a bean.

Who did this Ben prick think he was, talking to

him like that? Jeff would make him pay for that one day. He'd add his name to the list, right underneath Sara's, who was currently living off the interest of her unscrupulously-gained two million, with her husband none the wiser, awaiting the birth of 'their' little girl. In his drunken stupor, Jeff only wanted revenge and that would have to wait until after he had won in the divorce courts.

The seed of an idea had planted in his mind. He would break into Anji's lawyer's office, and steal the evidence. He had always been so careful not to get caught while having some extramarital fun, but he knew Anji wouldn't be this confident if she didn't have some good hard evidence. She must be doing him for adultery, he reasoned. If no one else was going to help him, he would have to help himself.

CHAPTER 55

"Hi Sara, I've been trying to get hold of you. How are you?" Anji had eventually called the office directly, having had no joy calling Sara's mobile number that seemed to be disconnected.

'Hi habibti, what a surprise its nice to hear your voice we miss you around here," Sara said, mournfully. "It's lonely without you. I had a crank caller so I had to change my number."

Sure, Anji thought, rolling her eyes. Twenty seconds into the call and Sara was already lying – the crank caller would no doubt be Jeff.

"I'm going to get straight to the point," Anji began. "I need to ask you a favour. In February my divorce should finally be finalised. I need you to bring Jeff's baby to London and testify it's yours. We'll need a DNA test to prove it." Sara was silent on the other end of the line. "Look" said Anji "please don't deny it. We all know I have undeniable evidence – rock solid in fact'.

Sara had been so relaxed since Jeff had left; she was so busy playing happy families that she had almost forgotten about her big love affair. It had been so easy to just wipe the slate clean, but here was Anji raising the its ugly head again.

"Look," Sara declared, "I'm sorry about your divorce, but this has nothing to do with me. Please don't call me again." Suddenly worried she'd end up having to pay back the two million if she ended up back in Jeff's life somehow again. Anji would just have to lump it.

"You don't have a choice," responded Anji, confidently. "I will call Fadi – I don't like to resort to such lengths, but Jeff is out of control. He's making my life unbearable. Do it for my kids and your kids. I will protect you, I promise," Anji assured her.

"I am so sorry Anji, I can't do it. I just can't. I don't think I'm strong enough to face him again," Sara argued.

"Did he make you sign anything, like any documentation?" enquired Anji.

"No, but I received a settlement and he told me to never contact him again which I agreed to," she admitted.

"Sara, listen to me. You won't be in direct contact with him. You'll only be dealing with me. You're not breaking your agreement. While you're in the hospital, after the baby's born, just ask for a DNA test. Tell them you want to put it in your file. Then you can come here for a few days. Think of it as a free holiday. I promise you one thing – Jeff will continue paying for his baby. I'll demand it in court," she confirmed.

Sara's ears pricked up at that statement. She had two million that was true, but if there was more and she was due it, then she would gratefully take it. She had always wanted to visit England anyway, and if Jeff saw the baby she knew he would forgive her about taking the money. "I'll have to see how the delivery goes really, but if there is a way I will try my best. I will be in touch after my baby girl is born."

Up until that moment, Anji had pictured the baby as a faceless, genderless entity. Now she knew it was a much-wanted baby girl, would she be able to tell Max and Georgie that they were having a baby sister? She very much doubted it.

"Right then," Anji declared. "I'll wait to hear from you." She paused. "I just want to do what's right." Anji knew that if everything went to plan, Sara would fly out to show off her baby as quickly as she could, especially with the possibility of more money involved. Anji wondered how much she had already got but she would ask about that later.

No goodbyes were exchanged as Sara had already ended the call. Anji had been clever and called Sara from a public phone box just around the corner from the school before picking the kids up. She had now become suspicious of being followed, and was sure Jeff would be doing everything in his power to prove she was a home-wrecking, selfish, money-grabbing adulteress. She dialled her mum's number and to say a quick hi and goodbye, in case someone was clever enough to go in after her and discover that the last dialled number was in Saudi. She always had to stay one step ahead of the game.

Jeff had hired a private detective but hadn't found a thing on her.

"She's cleaner than Mother Teresa," he had said. "I can't take your money; I can't even find an unpaid parking ticket," admitted the private eye. "She is squeaky clean."

"Do you know anyone who can plant something? If you get something on her I will pay good money." Jeff was now desperate.

"I can ask around. I'll let you know what I can do," he said, making a mental note that Jeff was on the 'avoid' list, and knowing he would block his number straight after the call.

CHAPTER 56

Anji's jaw was clenched as she sat on the phone talking to Mrs Watson. It made her face ache, her body ache and even her heartache. Having to be perfect all the time was having an impact on her mental health. Perfection was definitely overrated, and Anji was keen to let off some steam and be crazy for a bit. She was finding this perfect solo-parenting lark punishingly exhausting; not once had she raised her voice to the kids, just in case they told Jeff. She was overly patient with everything; it was torturous. As soon as this was over, she would take her dad to a private doctor, and then she would have Omar and his family over for a well-deserved vacation.

"Anji this should all go through straight after the New Year. Don't give Jeff any more time to drag any stuff up from your past. That team of his is ruthless," Mrs Watson advised.

"Eleanor," Anji said wearily, "we have to wait until the end of January or beginning of February when his child is born. Sara promised to come – it will be the final nail in the coffin, please hold on till then."

Christmas was fast approaching and the thought of the upcoming festivities lifted Anji's spirits. It would be the first time they would celebrate as a separated family, but Anji was thrilled because she had the kids for Christmas and Jeff would be having them for New Year. Anji's mum and dad would be spending the day with them too, which she was more than happy about. It had been years since they'd celebrated with her parents. Christmas was always high season in the hotel, so it had been an absolute necessity that Jeff and his family stayed around to show that they weren't off enjoying the holidays when the rest of the staff were working their hardest.

Anji had booked herself and the kids into the Grand Hotel in Brighton, with Jacky and Andrew joining them for the lavish Christmas brunch. Anji was super excited because her dad had responded exceptionally well to treatment, which alone was a reason to celebrate. She had promised them a holiday when the course of treatment was over. A small thank you for everything they had endured, and her way of saying a big fat sorry to them both.

Jeff was on the verge of a major meltdown. He spent hours sitting alone in his beautiful apartment in Chelsea overlooking the harbour. For the first time in his life he was useless and jobless. He was losing all sight of reality, delusional in his attempt to salvage his marriage. He contemplated jumping off the balcony, but then he imagined himself ending up like a cabbage. That would leave Anji free to do and be whatever she wanted, and he wasn't going to allow that. He was angry, and swore that once the divorce case was over, she'd be the one spending her Christmases alone.

He spent Christmas Eve in his scrupulously neat home, cooking up a plan. He plotted how he was going to oversee Anji's demise. She would see in the end that she was absolutely nothing without him. He knew of their plan to have Christmas with her parents down in

Brighton. Max had told him. He mooched off to bed, but couldn't sleep a wink. As he lay there in the dark, insomnia hitting hard, an ingenious idea came to his head. He would drive to Brighton and surprise them. They could always add another seat – after all, Christmas was the time for forgiving. Maybe Anji would take him back because he'd been so kind and thoughtful. It was fool proof – how could she resist him?

He was half-cut when he'd concocted the plan, but as he hit the motorway at midday he was feeling more sober than he had in months. He imagined their faces filled with precious delight. He was going to make everything all right again. The New Year was going to be perfect; life would be back on track and better than ever before.

Jeff imagined Anji back in his control and the children in their house. Everyone would be just where they all belonged. He would keep the flat in Chelsea, just in case Francesca felt like giving him a blowjob now and again. Then he could think about finding another job, maybe taking them all out of the UK again and starting somewhere afresh. He would never take another woman; Anji was all he needed now. How had he not seen it before? He could pay for extra services if or when he felt the urge, but Anji was the one he wanted to spend the rest of his life with. After all this time, he was at last sure about it. She had been so supportive and trusting all these years. Even the private detective had said she must be one hell of a person. Jeff had even told the lawyers about her anxiety attack, and he had contacted the hospital and discovered that the doctor who had treated her was now on Harley Street. That had all worked in his favour, showing how much he cared.

As he drove into the lovely town of Brighton, he remembered with nostalgia the early days of courting Anji. His in-laws had loved him at the start. Would they still love him the same way?

Pulling up to the hotel, Jeff was about to find out. It was two o'clock now and he was sure lunch had started. He headed straight for the toilet – in his haste he had forgotten to check his appearance. He washed his face and used some water to push the hair off his forehead. He cursed himself in the toilet mirror for not taking more pride in himself; this was Christmas, which was all about appearances and keeping smart. Splashing himself with the free cologne, he headed out of the door towards the restaurant, congratulating himself for his impromptu exceptional idea.

At the table, the children were beaming at the new iPhones they'd received from their mum. They couldn't wait to get back to their room to set them up and call their friends. Anji had given her mum and dad travel vouchers so they could fly to wherever they wanted after Andrew's radiotherapy. The joy in their faces said it all. Anji had insisted there should be no gifts for her, since her gift was having everyone there to celebrate Christmas together.

Georgie craned her neck; sure she could hear a voice she recognised. The maître d' was insisting the booking was for five, but Jeff won her over, telling her he was a General Manager and he knew how easy it would be to add one more chair to a table of five. As the hostess followed him with an extra chair through the crowded restaurant, Georgie clocked him.

"Daddy! Daddy! Daddy's here," she called, pointing towards the entrance of the restaurant. They all turned to look and saw a very pleased Jeff smiling from ear to ear. Anji turned to look at her mum and dad in horror. Confused, she had no chance to react as he was greeting and kissing the whole family. He looked like a shadow of the man he was just a few months before. His clothes hung off him and his hair was wet and messy. His beard growth was verging on unkempt. As he held out his arms to embrace his mother and father in law, he welcomed everyone to sit back down at the table chatting away like nothing had happened and the issues between them had been non existent.

"I'm so sorry I only had time to buy these gifts," he said, handing a small box to each child. "Yours will follow don't worry," he promised, glancing around the table and suddenly feeling embarrassed that he hadn't bought anyone else anything. Max and Georgie behaved ever so well when they saw it was the latest iPhone, the same gift their mum had bought them.

Anji realised they were playing the same game, trying to keep everyone happy. They didn't say anything, as they were almost too scared to see his face crumble. They should have said something as kids of that age do. She didn't want them to grow up a coward just like her; she wanted them to speak up.

"Where are your parents this Christmas Jeff?" Anji hissed. She wanted a nice pleasant lunch without him.

"Well Anji, to tell you the truth, they won't have anything to do with me," he replied. She couldn't tell if he was lying or telling the truth. "They say it's my fault, this whole situation. They were so happy when I settled down with you Anji. They love you, Max and Georgie." He looked at her, pleadingly. "My parents want me to fix this Anji. Please, I beg you. It is Christmas Anji, please."

All Anji could think was how pathetic he looked.

"Mum please, it would be the best Christmas gift for us," pleaded Max and Georgie, feeling very sorry for their father.

It was true, Jeff's parents had been so relieved when he'd met and married Anji. He had been such a playboy before and they were exasperated by his constant exploits with women. He hadn't managed to keep a girlfriend – a decent one anyway – for longer than a month.

His mother, Cecilia, had been enraged when she'd found out what had happened. "You haven't changed one bit have you?" she'd spat down the phone. "How can you let these kids go? Go get them back. Who is the boss – you or her? What a failure you are." Anji had never seen eye to eye with Cecilia. She was emotionless and cold. She showed no tenderness towards them or the children. She never cooked at home; the kitchen just wasn't her thing. Jeff had told her that, growing up, he would often eat bread for breakfast, lunch and dinner, which he'd had had to prepare himself. There had hardly ever been a hearty dinner to come home to.

"Can I have a private word Jeff, just for a minute?" Anji turned to her family and excused herself. "Give us two minutes, ok?" she asked sweetly. As Anji walked to the lobby, she was wondering what she was going to tell him. The kids were pleading with them to get back together, and she was mad that he'd turned up unexpectedly. Especially given the state he was in.

"Jeff," she began, standing in the lobby.

"No, you listen first Anji." He fell to the floor on his knees. "Please let's get married again, renew our vows. I've been thinking about it, I love you and I can't let you go." Anji had never seen such a pitiful performance. Just looking at him now, a hollow man, a shell of his former self – if there was ever a time when she would forgive him, that would have been the moment. But unfortunately things were way too far down the road to ever turn back now. She knew she would have to keep moving forward.

"Get up now," she said, embarrassed. "I'll allow you to have lunch with us for the sake of everyone else, but I can't Jeff. I know you had an affair, and I know whom it was with. For God's sake Jeff, I worked with the woman. What were you thinking? How can I go back to being with you, knowing what I know?" She didn't mention the baby; he might try something with Sara and she didn't need him calling her and scaring her off since she had promised the DNA test.

"Anji, please, I've changed, I've realised what I've lost," he continued. "You made it so easy for me because you allowed me so much freedom." *Wait*, Anji thought. *Is he blaming me for his own affairs?* "People make mistakes, you know? But I swear it's over, I'm a new man. Just think about it, please. How did you find out? Can I ask you?" He pleaded.

"Someone on the compound told me. Said they'd seen you together," she lied.

"I promise it wasn't sex Anji, we were just friends," he vowed. "I swear, I swear on my life, I swear on your life."

At that moment she realised he was beyond saving. He was still lying to save his own arse. "Ok, ok," she said. Mostly to just shut him up. "Let's go back in and have a nice lunch. I promise to think about it. Don't mention anything to the children or I will change my mind." She lied to buy herself some time, just so he could pull himself together. She gritted her teeth and took a deep breath, trying to be the bigger person.

As they sat back down at the table, Jeff was excited: "Kids, your mum has promised to reconsider. Let's celebrate," he said, raising his glass towards the middle of the table, waiting for everyone to join him in a toast.

"Champagne please, champagne," he said, motioning to the waitress. "Your best bottle. We are getting married again and you're all invited!"

Anji's heart sunk. Jeff's behaviour was unpredictable and he was still manipulating her as much as he could. He'd been doing it since the day they met; him preying on her naivety and vulnerability. It now made her fume. Using the kids was the lowest form of exploitation and, when the children realised it was all fabricated, their hopes would be dashed and they would blame their mum yet again. His actions were despicable but there was nothing she could do about it. All the same, everything he did that afternoon made Anji more determined to get out as quickly as she could.

Jeff drank and drank until Anji, her parents and the kids were exchanging worried glances across the table. What was he going to do next? For Anji, Christmas was ruined. It was beyond salvaging, but she kept up a happy front in her bid to ensure everyone else enjoyed the holidays. Anger boiled deep inside her; she'd never felt so mad. She was desperate to erupt, but knew she couldn't spoil Christmas dad. She realised that she'd have to help this man to get his life together; otherwise he was going to be intolerable. It was the best idea she'd come up with since news of the affair had surfaced, and it dawned on her that, by helping him out of his mess, she could turn the tables and become the manipulator.

Her anger began to dissipate and she felt calmer than ever before. She was going to get him back on his feet so he wouldn't be under hers. He was the bane of her life, and if this were how things were going to be she would never be free of him. She had to think how she was going to help him, without him being aware.

She said a silent prayer asking for answers while she fake-smiled to everyone around the table, pushing back her urges to jump across the table, smash a wine glass over his head and pound her fists at his chest.

By the end of the lunch, Jeff was so plastered he couldn't even stand up. Anji said her goodbyes to her mum and dad, promising them a Boxing Day visit. Jeff was in no fit state to go anywhere and, since the hotel was fully booked, she had no choice but to put him in her room. She would sleep in the kids' adjoining room. She put Jeff on her bed, covering him over with blankets. As she did so, Jeff pushed the covers back and took Anji in his arms. Anji didn't do anything. She just lay there dumbstruck.

"Tell me you love me, tell me now," he uttered.

"No Jeff, you're taking the piss now," she whispered, desperately trying to be quiet so the kids wouldn't hear.

"You what, bitch?" He clambered out of bed, keeping hold of Anji's arms the whole time. "You bitch," he snarled, as he pinned her against the wall. He was bigger and stronger than her, and held one of her arms across her chest as he raised his fist above her head. He pressed it against her skull and dragged his knuckles down to her cheek before resting it on her cheekbone. His knuckles had made an imprint all the way down.

"Jeff, Jeff," she implored. "It's Christmas." She felt her eyeball being squeezed from its socket under the pressure of his hand.

"You know in Saudi I could've had you killed for 100 Riyals... but no, I kept you around, I mean what for? So you can fuck me over. Who do you think you are?" His nails were now embedded into the skin of her cheek.

"Dad, dad," came Max's howling voice. "Leave mum alone, please dad." He grabbed his dad from behind, while Georgie looked on crying, her little face ashen from fear.

Jeff was struggling to keep his balance and, on hearing the kids, the floor began rocking beneath him and he plunged to the bed, defeated. He laid his head down, pressing his face into the pillow, and cried himself into a stupor. *The self-indulgent pig*, thought Anji, *feeling sorry for himself after what he's just put her and the kids through.*

Anji grabbed their belongings and threw them in a suitcase. Taking the children's hands, she strode out of the hotel, leaving the bedroom door wide open, and walked to the hotel next door. The kids didn't say a word, but seemed to understand. Anji managed to get the last double room, and they fell into the room and snuggled up in the bed together, reliving the day's events. Anji explained to the kids why she couldn't get back with their dad. She'd changed, she explained, and Dad wouldn't like her any more. More to the point, she wasn't prepared to change back.

After the craziness of Christmas Day, Anji was glad that the New Year was peaceful and seemed to go without a hitch. She'd been a little concerned about leaving the kids with Jeff; she thought he needed professional help, given that he said he'd contemplated having her killed. But having the children over New Year gave him something positive to focus on, and they seemed to have a good time. Having a few days to herself gave Anji time to think, and make some plans to fix Jeff up.

She needed to find someone who could fill the void in Jeff's life. Sara was out of the question – she was settled with her husband and wouldn't want the new baby having a dad like Jeff, whether they were biologically linked or not. Jeff needed a tough woman; someone who could keep him in check. It wouldn't be easy, but the fact he had a ton of money certainly helped. She picked up the phone, making a call to an old friend.

"Happy New Year Steph! How are you? I know it's the holidays but I have a favour to ask please. Could you possibly go and see Jeff after the festivities have died down? I think he's losing it, and I think maybe you could speak some sense into him. You're smarter than me – I can't seem to get through to him."

"Oh, anything for you Anji. And happy New Year! I'm sure your first Christmas apart must've been tough?" Steph asked.

"Well, actually he turned up. So we spent it all together."

"Oh," Steph paused, the penny dropping. "I see. Well, I'll go and see him, and let you know how I get on." Steph said she would visit him in a few days' time.

"I'm truly grateful, I know it's a lot to ask," Anji replied, as honestly as she could.

Steph had been an acquaintance of Anji's since they'd met through Jeff. They'd been in each other's lives since Anji and Jeff got married, meeting now and then at social engagements. Steph was a prize catch; a real head-turner, but she'd never been fortunate when it came to keeping a man. She was always on the prowl for a wealthy guy – anything for an easier life. Anji knew Jeff wouldn't risk sex without taking precautions after his last mistake; so Steph would be perfect – she'd never been married and had no children, so there'd be no emotional baggage to bother him with. His life was already complicated enough. If Anji's hunch were right, Steph would at least help fill the emptiness Jeff felt at being single. Jeff was a social animal more than most, he needed gatherings and to be kept busy. Otherwise he could turn into his own worst enemy, as well as Anji's.

Anji cracked on; she had other calls to make and messages to send. 'Sara, you will be happy to hear the court case is set,' Anji typed. 'I have booked your seat for Friday's flight. Please send details of the baby's passport and yours. I hope you have your Visas."

Sara opened her phone and saw the message. She'd been so relaxed since Jeff left, enjoying the rest of the pregnancy in peace. Other than keeping the identity of the baby's father quiet, there had been no more lies. Fadi was blissfully unaware. The money had changed her; Sara felt more motherly for the first time in her life. She was going to enjoy this baby more than ever. Having such a large sum in the bank helped her sleep better at night. She could rest easy, knowing life's little luxuries were covered and she didn't have to worry about the future.

It would be easy to explain to Fadi that she needed a break. She'd just say she was going to visit Anji, and that would be the end of it. She didn't need to ask him to pay for the trip of course, which made things easier.

When Sara and baby Mia flew into Heathrow Sanjeev, a lovely driver, met them. Anji had arranged everything, from the pick up to the boutique hotel booking. She wanted to make sure Jeff couldn't find out Sara was in town.

Anji was waiting for Sara and Mia in the small and friendly hotel lobby. When Anji clocked her she was gobsmacked; baby Mia was a copy of Jeff, but so full of innocence. With the baby's beautiful, perfect features, Anji couldn't keep the tears from falling. She didn't want to subject this wonderful creature to any court case or DNA test, and felt sad that the bastard Jeff didn't want anything to do with his own child. Like any new mum, Sara was proud to show off her gorgeous offspring. Mia was lucky she had Sara and Fadi; they would look after her, even if she did have Jeff's eyes and nose. Fadi must be as blind as a bat, Anji thought to herself more than once. Or maybe he was only as blind as he wanted to be.

The events of the last few months were building to a head. Anji had imagined she would detest baby Mia, but she was smitten at the first glance. It was so hard to look Sara in the eye in the beginning, so Anji concentrated on the baby, even though Sara hadn't noticed or given it a second thought. She was basking in her joy, the money and her new baby girl. In actual fact, the situation had enhanced her relationship with Fadi; she was now living her dream. Sara was totally oblivious, just like the child in her arms, and she hadn't even considered Anji's pain or hurt. Once baby Mia was asleep, Anji had a window of opportunity to talk Sara through the next stage, what she should expect and worst-case scenarios.

"If it means anything to you," said Sara after Anji had finished her explanations, "I am sorry but I have to admit, I wouldn't change a thing. I know you may be hurt, but look what I gained. To me she is the world." Sara was still thinking only of herself as usual, and Anji realised that Sara still had no feelings, let alone any morals. At least she was happy with the new addition, and Mia would be well cared for. Anji knew that nothing Sara could say would make time go backwards. Jeff was still a cheating arsehole and Karen was still gone.

"I have to go ok," said Anji, getting up to leave. "Please stay in the hotel until the court hearing. Let's not jeopardise anything. Jeff isn't good; he's drinking too much. It's important you keep a low profile. If you need anything, the concierge will arrange it. This is Sanjeev's number, in case there is anything urgent." They had got this far, and she really didn't need Sara screwing things up now. Anji also explained to Sara that she could be followed, so if any strangers asked her questions then she should pretend to be someone else. Sara had no concerns about this; she was a good liar and could twist the truth in a fraction of a second. Anji knew only too well, having been at the brunt of it for so long. She just hoped she could play the game on Anji's behalf.

CHAPTER 57

The last few days had been intense. Anji was feeling over emotional and sensitive. Too much was at stake now, and the realisation had hit Anji over the head like a baseball bat. The looming court case brought only dread and fear, so much so that her whole body shook. She was rattled, constantly fearing that he may pull a fast one and somehow win custody of the children. Endorse her as completely incapable and leave her with out a bean to her name.

Eleanor was preparing the case and had lots of last-minute questions, prepping Anji for all the worst-case scenarios. Anji had told her about the Christmas incident and baby Mia's arrival. Eleanor arranged another DNA test, advising that the one Mia had had at the Saudi hospital may have been doctored and would not stand up in court. Anji already knew the result – that face of hers was undeniably Jeff's.

"Eleanor, I don't want Sara and Mia under the microscope for too long. I don't want Sara traumatised; she has a baby to look after," Anji appealed.

"Please Anji, we'll do what it takes. I wish all people thought like you. She messed with your life and you're still sticking up for her. Just let me do my job, that's what you're paying me for," Eleanor implored, trying to make Anji understand that one wrong move could change everything.

"Well, without Sara I would still be the old person I once was – naive and pathetic. I would have never discovered my true self and for that I owe her something, surely?" Anji challenged.

"The answer is no, you don't owe her anything." Eleanor raised her eyebrows, amused by what she'd just heard and dismissing it instantly.

Anji's mind went back to Karen's funeral and how distraught she had felt while watching Karen's parents, deep in grief. Emptiness had engulfed her that day like never before; a heavy feeling. It was like the weight of the world was resting on her head, and there was nothing she could do to get away from it.

The funeral had been held in the town of Stratford in Lincolnshire, where Karen's parents resided. It had been a sunny day and she was laid to rest in such a beautiful place. Anji had travelled up the night before and checked into the Crown Hotel, in the heart of the historical town. Her mum and dad were looking after the kids, which she was grateful for; one less thing to worry about. She didn't really want to go alone, but she owed it to Karen. Anji had terrible nerves as she was still learning to walk on her own, but the funeral would be a good test. She'd had a huge battle in her head over whether to go or not; after all, it would have been so easy just to send flowers and stay in her comfort zone. As much as she would've preferred to do the latter, something was pushing Anji to attend. She had no choice but to follow the voice in her head. She wanted to say goodbye, and she needed the farewell in order to move on.

After checking into the hotel, Anji asked the concierge to book her a table for one so she could get something to eat. She wasn't in the mood to traipse around looking for somewhere, and really her nerves had left her feeling nauseous and frayed. She dumped her luggage in the small, cosy room and washed her face. The reflection staring back at her looked tired and worn. The last few months in Riyadh had really taken their toll, but she had got through it. She was in the UK now, and her new life was just starting.

Not bothering to change, she snatched her handbag up from the bed and left for dinner. A British pub, it was casual and busy with a warm atmosphere, just as the concierge had described. As she reached the doorway though, Anji suddenly felt self-conscious. She hadn't entered a restaurant alone since heading on her 'date' with Jeff, back in Saudi where he spilled the beans about his affair. Right now, she felt sick and sensed everyone's eyes boring into her. Her shoulders froze and anxiety rose in her belly as people turned around to look at the loner in the waiting area. She panicked, having second thoughts and decided to leave. She could just order room service. But as she stood up to make a fast exit, Anji was sure she could hear her name being called.

"Anji Harris, Anji – yoo hooo!" called a voice.

Anji looked around to see a woman with her hands whirling above her head, determined to catch her attention. Anji waved back sheepishly and the woman beckoned her to come and join them at their table. There were two ladies there, neither of whom Anji could quite place at first, then realising they were Lottie and Abigail, two familiar faces from the compound. Anji took a seat at their invitation, realising as she sat down that they'd been the first two to sign the eviction petition to have her removed from the compound; it was too late to get up and leave now though.

"Wine, you want wine?" asked Abigail, already motioning to the waiter to bring another bottle.

Anji certainly wasn't going to say no. She needed as much Dutch courage as she could get right now. Once the waiter had filled Anji's large glass, Lottie made a short toast. "To new beginnings, ladies. Let's raise our glasses."

"I really want to apologise Anji. I just wanted to protect Karen. I am so sorry. You can't imagine how many sleepless nights I've had since." Lottie said, sincerely.

Abigail butted in. "And we heard about you and Jeff. He told us, but we want to say we are with you. We always thought he was arrogant and you were too good for him. He's nothing but an ass wipe." Anji burst out with a fit of nervous laughter; it was just the break she needed. She had been so stressed and wired, she was pleased she had bumped into these two after all.

"No hard feelings. Whatever was said, we can't bring Karen back. Just promise me you'll think before you judge the next victim. I can tell you from personal experience that it's no fun," she said, gazing at the contents of her wine glass as she swilled the liquid around.

They began reminiscing about life at the compound. They joked about Jeff and his pig-headed ways; Anji hadn't realised he was so unlikeable. She had loved him so much she hadn't seen anything untoward; love really was blind. Abigail asked what had really happened with Jeff. "We want to hear if from the horse's mouth," she prodded.

"It was a simple case of a man having an affair," explained Anji, sighing. "Sorry it's not racier than that, but that's the simple truth. He's still in Saudi Arabia working, so we won't say any more. Honestly, we are trying our best and working through it," she lied.

"You mean he is finished with the woman? I think she was your boss, right?" Lottie probed. "We saw at the leaving party he was a little too attentive to her when she fell over."

Anji knew the information would be circulated as soon as she left the table, so it was best to keep it short and sweet: "Well, people do stupid stuff sometimes. He did – big time. But it's all forgotten now."

Abigail looked down at her drink. She was a sweet looking lady with tiny eyes and ears, a bit like a kitten. She looked embarrassed but Anji didn't care what she was thinking. Anji raised her glass again. "To Karen!"

"Yes, to Karen," they all said in unison.

The next day Anji had woken up feeling strangely glad that she had bumped into Lottie and Abigail. She was patching up old broken bridges, and opening the way for new ones. She also knew that if they were apologising, everyone at the funeral would be thinking about doing the same. It made the awful day a little easier for her knowing that everyone wasn't blaming her and pointing the finger.

Although the ladies had invited Anji to share their taxi, she had declined. She just wanted to say her farewells to Karen and leave; not have to make small talk. As she reached the graveyard, she was pleased that Karen would be laid to rest there. The lawns were covered with thousands of pretty daisies, and majestic trees lined the pathway. A medieval church with stained glass windows stood at the side of the grounds. Anji had looked through the crowd during the service, searching for Lily or Amal. She thought they may have had the decency to turn up, but Anji couldn't spot them. She probably didn't want to be faced with the truth. Karen's son Alex had spoken a few lines from the Bible, which had choked Anji up even more. "There is a time for everything. A time to be born and a time to die, a time to weep and a time to laugh, a time to mourn and a time to dance." She wondered if Alex even understood what he had said, and certainly hoped that Karen was dancing, wherever she was now.

Those words had opened old wounds for Anji and, as the feelings she'd tried so hard to damp down came flooding back, she had a realisation. Whatever words she wrote on her blank pages were now hers to choose. She was in charge of her life from now on, and responsible for every outcome.

Outside, as Karen's coffin was lowered into the ground, the vicar recited the committal and threw some dirt on to her wooden casket. Her parents and the children each followed. There was a pile of floral tributes nearby, and Anji kneeled down to place yellow roses to symbolise friendship and hope.

Anji left quietly, moving away before everyone else; she had no polite conversation left. She didn't say anything to Karen's husband Steve – she hadn't even greeted him as he stood hand in hand with Martha. She had only held the hands of Karen's parents, as they seemed the only ones who were truly suffering.

Life was moving on without Karen, and soon she would just be a memory. There was a message in there somewhere for Anji. In the taxi on the way back to the hotel, she remembered the promises she'd made when Karen had died, to be true to herself and to make each day better. When Jeff had turned up at Christmas, when he'd fallen to his knees begging for forgiveness, for a moment there she could've given him another chance. But if it hadn't been for Karen, Anji may have still been in the perpetual cycle of pleasing everyone but herself. And when she'd looked into Jeff's eyes that day, she swore she saw Karen reflected back, screaming at Anji to remember her worth.

CHAPTER 58

The weekend before the divorce hearing, Sara and Mia had spent the Saturday together with Anji. They had decided to avoid public places, and Sara wasn't the type to traipse around zoos or anywhere that might be full of kids, so Anji suggested a trip to a designer outlet near Wembley.

"Oh my God, really?" Sara had squealed excitedly, getting into the car with her eight-inch heeled boots. "That would be wonderful. We would love that! Wouldn't we Mia?" Sara of course was beautifully turned out, with her flawless make-up and hair. You'd never have guessed she'd only recently given birth. She smelled like a summer bouquet in the midst of winter and it lifted the mood. Mia cooed like the perfect adorable child she was.

The shopping centre was a safe bet. Jeff had the kids this weekend and they both knew that Max abhorred shopping while Jeff wouldn't be seen dead at an outlet. Anji was keen to ensure Sara was as calm and as happy as possible, ready for Monday mornings meet with the lawyers. Not once had Sara asked any questions about her or her children; not once did she mention the affair. Sara was in her element as she tried bags, jewellery and make-up on oblivious to the real reason she was actually visiting the UK.

A leisurely lunch gave Anji time to broach the sub-

ject of the impending case and the results of the DNA
test, which proved there was a ninety nine perchant
likelihood that Mia was actually Jeff's. Even without the
test, the child's blue eyes showed without a shadow of
a doubt that he was indeed her father. "Sara," enquired
Anji, "I will not judge you, we all have our reasons for
everything. But everyday you'll look at this girl and
know she isn't Fadi's. How can you do it, how can you
live with that fact?"

"Look, you don't know anything about me," sighed
Sara condescendingly. "I come from a different culture
and background to you. Jeff didn't want me after you
left God only knows why? I'm not so stupid but I know I
love this girl more than anything. I think I love my husband so it will be easy for me, very easy. The alternative
is, if they knew the truth, my family and friends would
make me an outcast. I'm scared Jeff will tell Fadi, but I
thought about it already. I have the money that Jeff gave
me," she admitted.

"Can I ask how much money?" Anji pressed.

"A million dollars. He gave it to me and wrote us
both off. He doesn't want anything to do with us. I am
ok with that, but it's not the money, it's my reputation.
If that is ruined, my whole family is tarnished, including my mum and dad. I am here because you left me
no choice. You blackmailed me, I had no choice, you
understand. I am here it because you forced me by my
arm." Sara lied effortlessly; knowing she'd in fact received double what she'd actually told Anji. And with
the divorce case, she was still hoping for a monthly
settlement as a little extra boost.

"You looked at me every day in the office, knowing
you were at it almost every night with my husband. I

have kids, just like you…"

"Look!" she almost shouted, grabbing Anji's attention. "This wasn't the first time and you would be stupid to think it will be the last. If you care to know my opinion, once a cheater always a cheater. As I see it, you should be sitting there thanking me. I saved you from yourself. Another beautiful girl is in the world, and she will be loved, whatever happens. I saved you, believe me." Sara stared into Anji's eyes, as if trying to make her see things from a cheater's standpoint. "I never loved him. It was sex, some excitement. I live in Saudi Arabia not through choice, but for the money. We earn more money there than we ever could in Lebanon. You won't understand this, but it's a dream come true for me and Fadi," she admitted. "We could never be friends Anji, maybe business friends at best. I say it like it is."

The truth hurt, but Sara was right. When Anji dropped her back at the hotel in the early evening with her bags of designer wear, she realised how different people could be. She didn't dwell on it, but was grateful that Sara was here for the court on Monday. It couldn't come soon enough.

Sunday dawned, and as the day dragged on it turned into a painfully slow wait until Monday. Anji's stomach was churning like the inside of a washing machine. She couldn't eat a morsel of food. The kids were with their dad thankfully, and Anji wondered how the hell he was handling it. Hopefully he was sober and not relying on the bottle. Although Anji had wanted to open a bottle of wine herself, she thought better of it; it wouldn't work well on an empty stomach. She hadn't slept a wink all night, her mind running through every scenario of what may or may not happen. Eleanor had called earlier, telling her to keep her head clear and to expect the unexpected. "He has the best team behind him," she warned.

"Well, I have the best team behind me too, right?" Anji replied. But she believed Eleanor and to be prepared. Jeff was unpredictable and seemed to be capable of anything. That thought didn't help to steady her nerves. She decided to call Sara one last time before tomorrow's hearing, asking her to stay in the hotel room for the day and keep a low profile.

"I have everything I need Anji, please don't worry," Sara reassured. "I want to say good luck for tomorrow. We'll be waiting for you downstairs in the morning," she confirmed.

After hanging up the call, Anji paced the room. The walls were drawing in so, before anxiety took hold, she decided to take a walk in the neighbourhood. She layered up in a hat and scarf, bracing herself for the crisp London weather. She loved London. The wet streets were laced with the remnants of multi-coloured leaves scattered under her feet. The restaurants brimmed with all kinds of people of all different cultures. Being just one person in a big, busy place helped to calm her down a little. What was the worst that could happen tomorrow? Maybe he had paid someone to lie about her. He had already poisoned his friends, saying that she was the one who'd had the affair. Expect the worst, Mrs Watson had warned. Maybe Jeff would confess to the judge that he was possessed by the devil to excuse his appalling behaviour. Wishful thinking, she thought as she sighed to herself for the hundredth time that day.

The fresh air was clearing Anji's head. She now understood that her life with Jeff had been a total lie. It had been an almost perfect lie, until Jeff had lost control of his other life and got one of his women pregnant. Anji had been a good wife and mother, forfeiting her career and making huge sacrifices to be with him, and now she was going through a nasty divorce, dealing with a disgruntled spouse who was blaming her for his wandering eye.

Anji arrived home from her walk around Kensington just before the children were supposed to be back. They arrived home and both were happier than normal. Apparently Jeff had taken them to London Dungeons and had been in an above-average mood, singing Anji's praises.

"Dad kept saying what a brilliant mum you are," giggled Max. "He was so funny today, we had such a great time."

Something didn't smell quite right, thought Anji. She smiled sweetly as she unpacked their overnight cases; pondering what game he was up to now. Probably building her up in the kids' eyes, making her think she was doing a great job, so he could crush her tomorrow before taking over custody. She'd be the one begging to see her children. The thought of it scared the living daylights out of her, and the small hairs on the back of her neck prickled with an uncomfortable sensation.

How quick her love had turned to hate. She'd tried so hard to stay neutral, but he had taken the best years of her life. If he took the kids too, her life would have no meaning left. Now she was going to rebuild her life, get over her train wreck of a marriage, and start to build trust again. Being sad had taught her one thing; how valuable happiness is, in the same way that being weak makes you know what it is to be strong. Tomorrow would reveal what the future held, even if it tested her faith in humanity.

CHAPTER 59

Anji's alarm barked at her, the shrill tone bursting through the calmness of her tastefully decorated bedroom. She hadn't slept and had been looking at the clock on and off all night, running through the order of the day and worrying about how things would go. Despite the fact she'd been awake for hours, waiting for the alarm to go, the sound of it still shocked her.

Heading downstairs, she busied herself with the kids, getting their breakfast and lunch boxes ready, wondering if everything might be completely changed by the time they were due to come home in the afternoon. She'd decided not to tell them about today and since Jeff hadn't mentioned it to them either, she decided it would be best to break it to them gently afterwards, whatever the outcome. If things went in her favour, it would be easy to deliver the verdict to the kids, but if it went against her she would be laying on the cold floor of some doorway in Marble Arch probably, begging for change. She let the immediate silence after that thought swallow her whole and, for the twentieth time that morning, went to wash her face with cold water.

The hearing was set for ten o'clock. Anji had everything organised, and was hoping to get there early to get some encouragement from Eleanor. She walked the kids to school and hugged them extra tight. She took a good, deep breath of them both and watched them walk into school, the sweetness of childhood tingling in her nose. As soon as she got home, Anji got changed into a high-necked blouse with ruffles, a pale grey skirt that stopped at the knee, a matching jacket and simple court shoes. Anji couldn't look plainer if she tried. Her hair was pulled off her face and she decided she wasn't going to wear a dash of makeup in court. She considered the potential for meltdown and the chances of her mascara rolling down her sodden cheeks.

Anji looked more than a little dowdy, like the down-trodden wife she was supposed to portray. Today, more than other days, she certainly felt it too. She was sure that family courts were absolute miserable places and she certainly matched that mood perfectly. Being careful to be conscious of London traffic, Anji rushed to pick up Sara and Mia before meeting Eleanor and her team on time. Since Jeff wouldn't settle anything privately and had contested the divorce, it was up to him to adjudicate the dispute and terminate their marriage. All Anji wanted was the children and half of the money. The house was in the kids' names anyway and Jeff would have the children every other weekend as usual. She would ask the judge to award baby Mia a settlement for her upkeep, after all she was an innocent in all of this. Jeff had to pay for his mistake, if you could call that beautiful little creature a mistake.

The building was just as Anji had imagined; very clinical, not family-orientated at all. It was more like a police station. All around she saw sullen-faced, smart-suited men walking in and out while wheeling carry cases. She imagined the cases loaded with documents, probably all coded with shit on Anji. The sound of people coming and going, their footsteps on the scuffed parquet flooring, reminded Anji of sitting in a hospital waiting room, waiting for someone to deliver the news, either good or bad.

Eleanor looked composed as she explained that the evidence would operate on a 'card face-up' basis, which meant everything should be shown to the court and there should be no surprise ambushes. Anji was escorted into the hearing room, while Sara and Mia had to sit outside for now. Anji wondered if Jeff would go past them as he arrived, and thought about what his reaction would be like when he found them there. Jeff was late – five minutes late – which was fantastic for Anji as it meant he wouldn't have time to see the evidence Eleanor was presenting. Only his lawyer, Mr Parker, would see it. Mr Parker looked nothing like she had imagined. He was an ageing nerd with mouse-like features, whereas she had pictured someone more debonair, more dramatic and far more handsome. All the same, he looked articulate and well educated, and Anji wondered if Mr Parker would be able to see through the tissue of lies she was sure his client had cooked up.

Eleanor opened her briefcase and lined up all the paperwork, videos and tapes, representing months of hard work and preparation. Anji sat completely still, with her hands and feet feeling completely frozen. Her teeth started chattering quietly in her mouth, thanks to a lack of food due to her unkempt nerves. She hadn't eaten properly since lunch at the outlet with Sara on Saturday. She asked for some water, and a plastic cup was pushed in her direction. Drinking it greedily, Anji began to have flashbacks of Omar losing his job, she wanted, no needed to make that right. Pummelling her neck with her fingertips, Anji could feel her body tensing up in preparation for the mountain she was about to climb.

Jeff walked in, all suited and booted with another grim-faced middle-aged man. Everything looked so serious from where she was sitting. Eleanor grabbed Anji's hand in a show of solidarity, and it was as cold as her own. They were both nervous it seemed. Anji glimpsed at her watch. Ten o'clock, read the Rolex that Jeff bought for her some years back. She noticed that it no longer fitted her wrist. It was now way too big. Once this saga was over, she would gift the watch to Omar's wife. She pinched the palm of her hand to make all the pain go in that direction. It was a trick she had learned when going to the dentist, and it helped to transfer the brunt of the pain. But this was so much worse than a visit to the dentist; this was more like open-heart surgery with no anaesthetic.

The judge asked both parties if they were ready to start.

Eleanor stood up and nodded. "Yes your honour," she spoke, while looking at Anji and mouthing 'As ready as we'll ever be'.

Anji had nothing to hide. She had been telling the truth from the very start. Eleanor had told her in the beginning "in order to be credible and believable, we must always remain truthful." She'd also told Anji that the evidence was clear and the truth would shine through. She hadn't said should or could, she'd said would. Anji watched Jeff speaking to his lawyer, a side-mouthed whisper in his ear. She didn't want to look but couldn't help herself. She found herself feeling compassion towards him, and not the hate that she was expecting. He looked half the man he used to be.

Mia was crying outside the room, and the judge looked annoyed. "Why is there a baby here?" he asked Eleanor.

"This is part of the evidence, your honour," she answered, matter of factly.

"Ok," he replied, with both his eyebrows raised. "Let's hurry this up, the baby needs settling."

"The child outside those doors is the love child of Mr Jeff Harris," explained Eleanor. "The child's mother – Mr Harris's former mistress – is outside this court today. A paternity test has been carried out, which proves with 99% accuracy that the child is his. We would of course require a DNA test from Mr Harris to make absolutely sure. The voice recordings and video evidence we present to you today back all of this up."

Jeff's face said it all; he was completely stunned. He hadn't been expecting this.

"What video, what recordings?" Jeff butted in.

"They are all here, the evidence in front of you your honour, including sex tapes, photos, voice recordings of him in the act with the lady who stands outside this door."

Jeff stood up and began shouting: "It's fabricated bullshit, it's all lies, She's the bitch, she's having the affair," he raged, standing up and pointing straight at Anji. "That's not my kid. I only have two!"

"Sit down now!" demanded the judge. "I will have order in this court."

"You're not listening! She's the bitch, she always was. She's been having panic attacks, she is crazy." By this point, Jeff was practically spitting feathers. "You bitch, you fucking bitch. You crazy motherfucking bitch."

"Sit down before you are in contempt of this court," the judge demanded.

Jeff stood up again, burning anger erupting from his insides. He pounded his fists on the desk again and again. His frustration and anger seared across the room like an inferno.

Jeff's lawyers surrounded him, taking hold of his arms, but that did no good; it only managed to enrage him more. Jeff couldn't control himself anymore, and he couldn't cope with having to face up to all of the things he had been running from his mistress, his fear of being left alone, his sadness, the alcohol, and the obvious lack of sleep.

"Control your client please, or we will recess," the judge reiterated.

Jeff looked towards the door where Mia was crying. He pushed himself up on the desk and, forcing the chairs out of the way, he made his way clumsily to the door. Before his lawyers could catch up with him he entered the waiting room to find Sara holding the blonde, blue-eyed baby in her arms.

"She's yours look, she's gorgeous, she looks just like you. Look," said Sara, beckoning him closer but he wasn't interested at looking at the child, he was looking at Sara. His face was a dark red, the vein in the middle of his forehead throbbing painfully,

"You're just another bitch," he said, sneering. "This here today, it's all your fault. You had the audacity to show up here today after stealing two million dollars from me, you whore! You're just a goddamn fucking whore. You were just a number, I lost count what number you were – that's all you were, a fucking number!"

One of the legal team grabbed him, not knowing

what he was going to do next. He managed to drag him away like a stray dog. The rest of his team began helping and it took four men to pull him away while his feet scuffed at the floorboards as he tried his best to wriggle free from their grip.

Anji hadn't uttered a word. She had watched the whole event tumble out of control. It was a shambles, but it was all going her way. His fancy lawyers hadn't done a thing; they had been forced to look on, helpless. Jeff had lied to them about everything and they looked like absolute fools. As they dragged him past the judge, he grabbed all the papers that had taken both sides months to prepare, and started ripping them up and throwing them all over the courtroom. Maybe all the pressure had made his mind snap? Anji held her hand over her mouth, gobsmacked, watching in horror and sadness as everything unfolded.

"Your honour," said Eleanor, swallowing audibly, "my client asks for the money, assets and any other investments to be divided equally. My client asks that the money her husband has paid for his daughter outside the courtroom not to be considered. She feels that the mother of the child will do right by the baby. She would like the current arrangement for their children Max and Georgina Harris to continue, with the children staying with their father every other weekend." Eleanor delivered the message clearly and professionally, cutting through the mayhem that carried on around them. The day's events were nothing to her; she had seen a lot worse. This was just another day at work; only this one was ending in victory.

Jeff's lawyers asked for more time. They were all busy cleaning up the scattered shredded paperwork, which was full of concocted stories that would not stand up in a courtroom; endless hours of rubbish that they would be paid handsomely for, win or lose. It was all so sordid, so embarrassing, so raw and tender. Anji hoped she would never have to cross the paths of these people ever again. She didn't want to be reminded of this day; not in this lifetime.

Anji's eyes followed Jeff as he was escorted from the room. Once the door opened she saw a familiar face. She gathered her senses and blinked her eyes – perhaps she was just seeing things. Doctor Hassan was looking right at her, with an expression that read 'I have no idea what just happened'. There was no way she was going to tell Eleanor that the man outside was someone she'd fucked while she was still married. She had been so honest until that moment, and she wasn't about to mess things up. How had Jeff found out about him? He had obviously been in court to tell everyone about the brief interlude.

As everyone else began to file out of the room, Sara had come in and was acting like a winded footballer. "He didn't even look at his child, not once," she bellowed. "It hurts Anji, it hurts!" she said, rocking Mia in her arms.

"What did you expect Sara?" asked Anji, bluntly.

As Sara got out of the taxi at the hotel, Anji knew it was the last time she was ever going to see her and Mia. She kissed Mia on the forehead; she smelled like sweet milk and baby lotion. Anji prepared herself to say what she'd been planning on the taxi ride back.

"You know, you can keep the two million, but there will be no more payments. That's it. I was prepared to negotiate for more, but you lied about the payoff and I think that amount is more than fair." Sara opened her mouth to protest, then nodded and looked down at her feet.

"Bye Anji."

"Bye Sara."

As Anji arrived back home, Eleanor was calling. She was delighted. "What a result! He acted true to form in court. The judge was totally on our side." Eleanor explained that the judge had ordered a paternity test, and that Jeff's lawyers would have to start dividing everything 50/50. The arrangement with the children would remain exactly the same. "It's certainly not over yet, not by a long shot. But after his behaviour today, it's all looking good. I didn't think for a second it would be that easy," she admitted, the mask of professionalism slipping off for a moment.

"Eleanor, thank you so much, but I'm not feeling so elated," admitted Anji. "It was hard to watch someone I love – someone I used to love, the father of my children – behaving so appallingly. But in the circumstances, I couldn't have hoped for more. For that I'm eternally grateful."

"You're one hell of a strong woman Anji –," Eleanor complemented. "Do you know how many women I've had walk through my door? Victims Anji, victims who will remain victims, then their children become victims. I know it hurts, I'm sure, but you have my admiration. I'm not sure I could've handled it the way you did. I'm saying this as your solicitor and as a friend."

"Thank you Eleanor," said Anji, filling up. "It means a lot coming from you. Thanks for everything. I wouldn't be standing here if it wasn't for you," she confessed.

CHAPTER 60

Anji enjoyed a long, hot bath before heading out to collect the kids. She'd applied natural make-up and dressed in a favourite new outfit – an on-trend leopard print midi dress with a deep V-neck, black biker boots and a leather jacket. It was something she wouldn't have dared to wear in Saudi Arabia but here in London, with the feeling of spring on its way, the new Anji had learned she could pull off any look she wanted. She was starting to learn what suited her new personality. It was perhaps a bit much for the school run, but all the other mums in Kensington managed to appear effortlessly stylish, so why couldn't Anji try the same?

She walked out of the house feeling good, enjoying the fresh air and the gentle warmth of the winter sun on her face after spending so long cooped up in the family court that morning. Anji stood at the school gates filled with gratitude. As she waited for the children, she realised everything could so easily have gone the other way. God knows she'd run the worst-case scenario through her head enough times.

Without warning, she felt a light tap on her shoulder. Instinctively she tensed up, imagining it to be Jeff, ready to rain punches down on her from behind. She expected the worst especially after his performance earlier that day, and wondered how drunk he could've got by now since leaving the court.

"Hello," said a familiar baritone that Anji immediately recognised. His voice sent shock waves down her torso, melting away the frozen nerves that had kept her so tense. "Are you ok?" he asked softly, in his rich, silky tone. She still hadn't turned around, feeling unsure about why he'd been in the courthouse that morning. She was worried that the anger deep in her system might force her to say things she didn't really mean.

"Can you look at me for one moment?" he pleaded. "I want to explain to you – you deserve that much." Anji stood still, looking at her misshapen nails and her worn-out hands. "His lawyers asked me to talk about your incident at the hospital – you know, the anxiety attack. I agreed. That was all." He looked at her back the whole time, searching for an acknowledgement of what he'd just said. But she didn't move, not an inch. "Anji, it was also a chance for me to see you again. I can't get you out of my bloody head," he said, exasperated.

She didn't know if she could trust him she had become so suspicious of everyone and everything. What if he was taping the conversation and it was going to be used in court? She couldn't go through all that again and answered cautiously. "I don't know what you mean, honestly. Do I even know you?" Those words were the hardest words to say, especially as she imagined the hurt in his face and heart, but recent experiences had left her cynical and suspicious. "How did you find me? How do you know where my kids go to school?" she asked, feeling concerned over his motives. "Did Jeff tell you?"

"I followed you here from the court," he revealed. "I didn't want to bother you at your home, so I waited until you left again."

"Please, please," she begged, her back still turned. "Just leave me alone for goodness sake. I've had enough of being bullied." She used her words very precisely and cautiously, knowing if the lawyers were listening, the evidence would be dismissed as harassment. She realised she had become way too good at this.

Max called out "Mum!" from the school steps, and shouted that he needed a few more minutes to get the gym stuff he had left in his locker. Anji acknowledged him with a wave. Then she turned towards the doctor but he was already walking down a side road. She watched his back to see his beige mac blowing in the wind as he turned the corner out of sight, and felt relieved that she wouldn't have to lie to the children about who the tall, dark, handsome man was. Grabbing both of the kids for hugs, they provided instant stress relief. She couldn't get enough of them and snuggled them in tight, as Max wriggled away, embarrassed in case his friends saw the overflow of emotion.

The wind was harsh, and even in her coat Anji still felt frozen. The trees looked forlorn, and the frosted air forced its way into her lungs. She wrapped her scarf around her neck again before they began the march back home. Anji tried to fix Max's scarf, but he wouldn't have it.

"Mum, stop it," he begged. "And you know I can walk home alone from now on," he whispered, shy after his mum's show of affection outside the school gates. Anji laughed and Georgina told her brother not to be so ghastly. Georgie took her mum's hand and squeezed it a little as they walked home.

Anji was able to erase the stresses of the day with the warmth of her children's love. Her head was full of

Doctor Hassan. Why had he turned on her? What had Jeff promised him? Or was he telling the truth? It haunting her a little, she couldn't think about much else. She remembered the small piece of paper he had folded up and placed in her hand, which she had hidden in a very safe place.

CHAPTER 61

In the days that followed, thoughts of baby Mia and her future were painfully chipping away at Anji. She almost wished she'd never seen her; it would have made life easier to write her off. Anji wondered if she had made the right decision by not telling the children they had a half sibling. Maybe when it didn't hurt so much she would let them in on it, but now wasn't the right time.

Internally, Anji was still very much an emotional mess. She worried about Jeff after his ugly meltdown in the courtroom. He had lost every inch of control of the situation and of himself, very unlike him. He also had no job, which must be causing no end of mental anguish to him. Anji really hoped he could keep it together because she didn't want the children to see their father like that. She'd made a positive decision to let go of all the drama and forgive, otherwise all the buried hurt would become toxic to her and end up making her sick.

Anji kept herself busy with the house, since minor tasks still needed to be finished. During the buying process, she had promised Jeff they would install a summerhouse out the back, but she'd now decided against it. Although it would have enhanced the value of the house, she didn't need another reminder of Jeff and the life they could've had in London. She was trying so hard to forget. Anji was also aware that the kids were growing up and busy with school and their new friends.

She would certainly need something to do for herself, but didn't want to go back to recruitment or travel. That period of her life was way behind her. She had re-invented herself and knew she was capable of finding something that would fulfil her while letting her work around the children and their activities.

The landline began to ring, echoing down the spacious halls of the house. Picking up, Anji heard Eleanor's voice. She froze, expecting the worst; maybe Jeff was playing up again, or the Doctor had handed the recording to Jeff's lawyers?

"Hi Eleanor," she answered with a quiver of trepidation.

"Anji, are you sitting down?" she enquired.

Anji's stomach clenched harshly; it didn't help that the knots were still there from the day of the court hearing.

"Anji, you will not believe this but he has agreed to everything. Absolutely everything. The evidence was so substantial literally stacked against him; when his lawyers saw it I'm sure they just wanted to sweep his case right under the carpet. It certainly won't look good for them, but my God it's looking good for you now. Anji, you are brilliant." Anji could practically see her beaming down the phone.

"Say something please!" she continued. "I've never had such an open and shut case. His lawyers were in touch this morning, and I'm happy to let you know that Jeff is being way more generous than expected too. He'll be paying the children's school fees and covering the cost of an annual holiday abroad, plus some smaller details which we can discuss tomorrow if you can pop into the office...?" Her voice trailed off. "I have a proposition for you also, so make sure you come in." Eleanor was buzzing, unable to contain her excitement.

The hate that Anji had been harbouring for Jeff was now thawing out by the minute; a river of difficult emotions flowed out of every vein and orifice. When she had married him, she'd imagined them both soaring across the world together, flying high with their achievements and happiness. But all he'd managed to do was pluck her beautiful feathers and clip her wings. Their relationship had been more akin to that of a master and a slave. The divorce and this settlement would give her the chance to feel free again, no longer bound by her love for him. He was trying to reprieve himself and she was ready to pardon him; there was no benefit to be had by things staying angry and fraught, especially where the children were concerned.

Anji wanted to share the great news with her mum, so she picked up the phone to call Jacky, apologising for not calling sooner. "You must've been worried Mum, but everything is ok," she began. "Jeff has agreed to everything and more. I just got off the phone to Eleanor now and wanted to call you straight away."

Jacky was exasperated, scolding Anji: "Well at least answer your phone! I called twenty times! Your Dad told me to get on a train and come up to you, but I can't leave your Dad right now, you know that."

"Anji, Anji you all right girl?" her father asked through speakerphone.

"Yes Dad, everything is great. He agreed to everything, can you believe it?"

"That's amazing love! Everything will start looking rosier from now on. You're one hell of a girl, I'll give you that!"

"Well, I take after you, right Dad?" she laughed.

As Anji divulged all the details to her parents, everything seemed far simpler and she felt a dark cloud lift from her shoulders. The calm after the storm, her mum reminded her. Anji knew it wasn't over quite yet – Jeff would still be in her life for a very long time – but the settlement had more than satisfied Anji, so that was one argument the ex-couple wouldn't be having any longer.

After she hung up, her next call was to Omar. After five attempts, she finally connected and began telling him her plans before he had the chance to argue back. "I want to offer you, your wife and your family a fully paid trip to the UK," Anji told him. "Whenever you want to come, you'll be welcomed. I will be transferring money to you to say thank you for everything you did for us. I will explain when you come over, but you deserve it, all of it." She'd be sending more money to Omar than he could ever earn in his home country, or in Saudi Arabia. She owed it to him, and it selfishly made her feel better about his deportation and the fact that she couldn't own up to what had really happened when the car had been driven that evening. When Omar heard the amount she was sending, he whimpered down the phone and was rendered speechless for a few moments. She was sure the money would bring him comfort and hope for a better life for his children. It was a promise that something better was now around the corner.

CHAPTER 62

Anji ascended the stairs to Eleanor's office, reminiscing about her first visit there. How things had changed. She smiled as she thought back to the woman she was then –so fragile, broken and afraid, trapped in a mentally abusive marriage. Now she had a new life to build, with lots to look forward to.

Eleanor greeted Anji with a hug. She was ecstatic that the hearing had gone so well. Jeff's lawyers were meant to be the best in London, but Eleanor had been able to wipe the floor with them, thanks to the behaviour of their client and her excellent evidence preparation. Eleanor had already asked her receptionist to update the testimonial section on the firm's website.

"Do you really think we won?" asked Anji honestly. "Is it really a success if my children are living between two homes?"

"What era are you living in?" asked Eleanor, rolling her eyes and laughing jovially. "People get divorced every single day. Children survive separations, and in the majority of cases they come out stronger. You and the kids are more than capable of managing and adapting. Or would you rather be living in an emotionally abusive, coercive relationship?" Anji cast her eyes downwards, shaking her head in response. "I can tell you now, the answer is no. So go and live your life how you want to live it! Your kids will learn from you, how to be warriors, don't worry about them. Kids don't care what happened yesterday; they just need to know they're loved and knowing you like I do now I know you can give them plenty of that."

Anji felt a little more reassured, and knew her solicitor's words were the truth. A few months ago she wouldn't have had the self-confidence to believe her or anyone, but now Anji knew she could make things work and manage alone.

"So, what is this thing you wanted to talk to me about…a proposition?" Anji asked. It had been niggling at her ever since Eleanor brought it up. Eleanor beamed, looking excited.

"I want to offer you a role here in the office Anji, supporting women like you," Eleanor explained once Anji had taken a seat in her office. Anji had been sipping on a bottle of water and spilled a mouthful down her front in surprise.

"Women like me what do you mean?"

"A winner, a survivor. People need to be reminded that they are stronger than they think. Come on Anji, please, you know what I mean," Eleanor continued. "I can get people to support this idea professionals in the field."

"I…thank you but, I don't know," said Anji. She really hadn't thought about her next steps in the UK; she'd just wanted to get the divorce out of the way before she considered a new job or career.

"Just think. Before, you were considered just another statistic of divorce, but you can show others how it's done. You have certainly shown me with your independence and confidence. More than 45% of marriages end in divorce and that percentage is on the rise. The number of people that manage to stay together is becoming now the smaller statistic. You have the power to use your experience to help other women in your situation." Eleanor argued, convincingly. "It's a Foundation we are setting up, well, I'm setting up. A Foundation to help emotionally and physically abused women and men," she said, offering more detail. "I have people who want to join, either to sponsor the program financially or to help in your team. They are literally queuing up," she said, hoping to sway Anji's decision.

"My team?" Anji was amazed. Eleanor had clearly been planning this, and Anji hadn't even agreed to anything yet.

"We need a leader Anji; a hard-working, dedicated leader to bring it to fruition. I know you are the woman for the job."

"Wow. Erm…Can you give me some time to think about it at least?"

"Ok," Eleanor agreed. "But I'm not patient! I've been thinking about this idea for ever and I have the people who are willing to volunteer for free."

Anji churned the information over all day long. It seemed the universe was offering her a solution to her prayers, something to help her fulfil her life's purpose after the death of her marriage. She really could support women to become future winners. She doubted her strength, wondering if she was capable or even professional enough to deal with affairs of the heart. Anji still felt rather disorientated, but she realised that even by winging it, things were slowly falling into place. Divorce felt like an amputation to her – she constantly felt as though something was missing. She hoped her heart would heal soon, and then reminded herself that it was ok to feel raw, hurt and emotional; it was all part of the process.

That night, as she sat with Max and Georgie, helping them with their homework, she couldn't get rid of a nagging voice in her head. The voice was telling her that she was more than just a mum and a divorcee, and she was capable of greater things. At that moment she made the decision. If Eleanor would allow her to name the foundation, Anji would take on the challenge. If she thought it over any longer, she would think of a million reasons and excuses why not to do it.

With his head in his books, Max said. "Mum, Mum, someone's knocking at the door." Strange, Anji thought. No one knocks at the door she didn't have any friends and she hadn't ordered anything. She had a fleeting moment of déjà vu, like when the phone rang with a life-changing call in Saudi Arabia. Little had she known at the time, but that had been a call that would change her life forever.

"Hello?" she called through the front door suspiciously.

"It's me," shouted Jeff through the letterbox. "Can I come in?"

What was to stop her from letting him in? He was allowed to stop by and see his children, but she was scared, worrying what kind of mood he might be in. She didn't want the children exposed to any more unpleasantness.

"What do you want? You should call before you come round," she reprimanded.

"Look, I know. I come in peace, honestly." Anji unlocked the door, opening it slowly to see Jeff standing there holding a bouquet of white roses.

"See, I told you. Peace," he offered, handing over the flowers.

The kids ran through to the hall and hugged their father. Anji was glad to see their attachment for their dad was still strong and his tenderness towards them; it made her smile. She could see the relationship between them hadn't been severed or affected which pleased her; maybe they missed his constant presence in their lives? She sensed that his anger was easing. Maybe it had dawned on him finally that he had been the one who had been an absolute arsehole.

"I am sorry Anji, sorry for everything." He looked in her eyes with honest sincerity. That was all he uttered, all he said, but it was enough to allow the healing to begin on all the open wounds. He was probably healing as much as she was. She hoped they could one day have a good relationship, if not as friends then as the parents of their children.

Anji sat them all down and they shared dinner together. For once, every sentence was directed towards the children, and they chatted away, relishing the attention. There was no bombardment from Jeff's ego, him starting every sentence with 'I', endlessly talking about himself, his needs. This whole situation must have doused his fire, and maybe from out of the glowing embers an authentic Jeff would emerge.

"Mum, does this mean you'll get back together like you promised at Christmas?" asked Max pleadingly, a glimmer of hope in his eyes.

"No," they answered in unison, looking each other in the eye. Both of them knew there was no going back.

"But we will be friends," smiled Anji, looking at Jeff with a softer face.

At the end of the meal, Jeff knew he was outstaying his welcome. Anji walked him to the door to show him out, and he turned to her and said, "I completely under-estimated you. You completely fucked me over." He was smiling as he said it and she gave him a wry smile and shrugged as if to say, 'well, what can I say!'

Steph was obviously working her magic on him, easing all the pain in Jeff's balls, which had been crushed in the courtroom. Would he ever recover from such a defeat? Anji doubted it, but it was a lesson learned. Anji had been feeling guilty about calling Steph after seeing how unhinged Jeff had become, but now, seeing him like this, she felt relieved. It would be good for both of them; the new girlfriend hopefully being showered with affection and gifts from a rich man and he needed a strong woman who would keep him on his toes. Anji hoped Steph would be a good influence on him; after all he had turned up tonight with his tail be-tween his legs, quite a different man. Time would tell, but she hoped her instincts were right on this one.

Anji laid in bed that night and went over the day's events. She could now begin to rebuild her life. Once the settlement was finalised, she would have enough money in the bank to create a life for her and the chil-dren; the life that she had wished for. Thinking of the future made every cell in her body dance. Instead of curling up in the foetal position, as she had done for months, she rolled over onto her belly and kicked and punched the mattress while screaming at the top of her lungs into the pillow. She felt pure exhilaration for the first time in an absolute age.

CHAPTER 63

"Hello Mrs Armstrong, this is Eleanor Watson from Watson and Partners law firm. First of all, may I send my condolences to you and your family? I can imagine it's a very hard time for you now but I have a proposal for you, which I'm putting forward on behalf of a friend of your daughter's and myself. We are currently in the process of creating a foundation for women and men, a refuge for partners who are being abused emotionally or physically, whether that be a bed for the night, someone to talk to or just needing advice. Your daughter's good friend Anji Harris wishes to name the foundation in Karen's honour." Eleanor paused for a moment, allowing Karen's mother to speak. She was met with silence, so continued: "The Armstrong Foundation, if you agree on the name, will be based in London for now. We chose Armstrong as it was Karen's maiden name, instead of her married one."

"It's so kind of you to call," she croaked. "I'm sure you'll understand that Karen's father and I are still dealing with everything that happened. I would have to talk it over with Richard I hope you understand. If you could kindly pop something in the post so we can talk to Steve and the children about it, I would appreciate it. You can't imagine what it's like to lose a child. Maybe if I had been there in Saudi, I could have been there for her, I could've helped her cope with what he did, and stop her from..." Mrs Armstrong broke off, crying heavily into the receiver.

"Ok, Mrs Armstrong," Eleanor reassured sweetly. "We are so sorry for your loss and we hope to hear from you when you're up to it please take time to think over." She gently placed the handset back where it belonged.

"What did she say?" asked Anji.

"They'll have to consult Steve and their children first, to see what they think. I couldn't ask her any more questions, she was sobbing like a baby. The poor woman." Eleanor felt truly sorry for them.

"Oh my God, they're asking that pig?" Anji was shocked, and couldn't begin to understand the kindness of Karen's mum. Here was a lady who understood the bigger picture, still wanting her grandchildren in her and her husband's lives. But they would have to tread carefully now, given that Steve was fully shacked up with Martha. Maybe that's what age brought – wisdom and knowledge; the ability to see beyond their own pain and consider the needs and wishes of others. Still, the Armstrong family must be suffering unspeakable sorrow.

Anji truly hoped that, whatever its name, the foundation would help others to move on with a glimmer of hope. That relationships – and maybe even lives – could be saved through its work. She hoped that Mr and Mrs Armstrong would agree to let them use Karen's name eventually. All the same, Eleanor was determined to make it work, reminding Anji there was no going back now.

They would need psychiatrists, doctors, volunteers, and a huge support team in order to launch a non-profit foundation. Anji knew it was a much bigger project than Eleanor had originally imagined. It certainly had the potential to become a full-time occupation. The foundation would be Anji's way of trying to eliminate domestic abuse in households, whether psychological, physical or financial. She knew Eleanor would be in charge of all the paperwork, enforcements, grants and fundraising, but she needed to create a network with local authorities, the charity sector, and trained employees. She wondered if she could ask a certain someone to help her find professionals in the right fields – after all, Doctor Hassan had a clinic on Harley Street and had worked in Saudi too, so his connections had to be wide-reaching. Anji had treated him so badly at the school gates, and yet here she was considering calling him to ask a favour and a massive one at that. Before she had time to think too much about it, she took the paper from its hiding place and dialled the number hastily before she had time to change her mind using his office line and not his personal number. She reached his secretary or PA or whatever she was and asked ever so politely,

"Hello good morning I'm a friend of Doctor Hassan, I'm calling regarding a business matter. Is he free to take my call?"

"I will check if you don't mind holding? Can I take a name?"

"Anji Harris"

"Hello Doctor" she paused skipping the niceties. "We are starting a foundation for people who've been emotionally or physically abused in relationships. We need people like you with a wealth of knowledge to support us, mainly psychiatrists and doctors on a voluntary basis. Could you help us?"

"Can I ask who is speaking please?"

"Anji Harris' she repeated as if he didn't know already.

"So, given your proposal, I sense you're coming out of everything stronger, and feeling better than I saw you last?" he said hopeful.

"It's been a real uphill battle," Anji admitted. "I fell apart, but I survived. I have to admit, I certainly hadn't forgotten about you. But I didn't need you as an added complication in an already complex situation. I believe you, you know, what you said at the school that day..." She stumbled over her words in embarrassment. "...That you didn't tell anyone about our... Well, you know."

"No need to justify yourself." Anji could almost hear him smiling down the phone. "I'm just happy to hear from you, and even happier to hear that you believed me. I'm always honest, and I mean what I say – even if it scares me sometimes. You'll see that if you get to know me better. I really thought I'd messed up everything, when really my intention was to help you. If supporting you with this venture is the only way of getting to know you better, even as a friend, then maybe we can have dinner to discuss it further?"

"Yes," said Anji, trying to sound cool, when in reality there were butterflies swirling in her tummy. "I don't see any reason why not. We can do it next weekend when Jeff has the children, but only if you promise to help with this little massive project. A promise is a promise," she hinted with a giggle. They both laughed nervously, knowing something could possibly be on the cards, but neither knowing exactly what.

CHAPTER 64

Doctor Hassan held the door open for her, graciously. Anji swept through the restaurant's entrance, the string of pearls around her neck swinging as she turned back to give him a shy smile. Dressed casually in skinny blue jeans and a simple white shirt, she was so out of practice she as giddy as an excited teenager on her first date even though he had been her knickers once. As the maître d' showed the couple to their table, the doctor took Anji's jacket and pulled her chair out. Ever the gentleman, that move was one positive tick already off the list. It was weird. They'd slept together, they'd been intimate once and it her mind maybe a thousand times more. But at the same time, they were strangers who barely knew one another.

Clearing their throats, they each ordered a drink – him Cabernet , she a Sauvignon Blanc – and gazed at each other from under their eyelashes. "Well," he said. "I'll start then." Anji laughed, a tentative giggle, and he smiled back warmly.

"Gosh, this is odd," admitted Anji. "But of course we're here to talk business – about the foundation."

"Absolutely," he replied. "Strictly business." He didn't wink, but he might as well have. They each knew that, in their future together, there'd be both business and pleasure fizzing and mingling like bubbles in a champagne flute. There was too much chemistry between them to just let it go. And besides, if they were going to be working together and seeing more of one another due the foundation, then they wouldn't be able to contain the spark that had ignited between them all those months ago.

"So tell me about yourself, Doctor," Anji invited. She wanted to get to know him, to get more of a feel for what he was all about. And, truth be told, she still felt bad about the way she'd treated him at the school gates, so wanted to put the spotlight on him for a while. Give him something to feel good about.

"Please," he asked. "Just call me Hassan. What do you want to know?" he raised his eyebrow at her invitingly behaving funny and flirtatious. "I'm well-travelled, passionate about my work..." he trailed off, lost for words. "And not a fan of talking about myself, to be honest."

"What about family?" Anji enquired.

"Well, both my parents are still alive, thankfully. They're in Iran, keeping themselves busy in retirement with their clubs and activities. I also have two children."

"You're a dark horse!" Anji interrupted, surprised.

Hassan's face lit up. "I wasn't keeping it from you; it's just we've never had a chance to chat like this," he revealed. "Maziar is seventeen and Elaheh is fifteen. I was married before, but it wasn't a love match."

Anji had spent long enough in Middle Eastern countries to know about arranged marriages, and how they so often don't work out if they're not based on a loving partnership. She felt sad for Hassan that he'd gone through that, clearly at a young age too.

"The children live here in the UK now, with their mother. They were part of the reason for me moving back, so I could spend a little time with them before they both spread their wings and move off to uni. So I see them at weekends, or whenever I can fit around their hectic social lives!" he joked, clearly not fazed by the whole situation. "It works better now. When they were younger and in Iran while I worked all over the world, there was a lot of juggling of time zones so I could call them, and dealing with jet lag when I visited.

They're great kids."

Anji smiled at him. She loved the fact he so clearly loved his children. It filled her with hope over the relationship he may enjoy with her own kids, who could be introduced when the time was right. If, of course, Anji and Hassan's own relationship even got off the ground. She shook her head, annoyed that she was getting ahead of herself.

He shifted in his seat and leaned towards her, asking, "What's up?" There was a real caring tone in his voice.

"Oh nothing, nothing," Anji replied. She felt like he could read her mind and was sure he knew what she was thinking.

"It's a wonderful thing you're doing by the way," he said, changing the subject to put Anji at ease. "Naming the foundation after your friend Karen, I mean."

"Oh, you know about that?"

"Yes yesterday I bit the bullet I called Mrs. Watson to ask her what exactly she required to make the Foundation work so I could be ahead of the game tonight, maybe impress you" they smiled at each other wide eyed "She wanted to tell you herself but I kind of begged her to let me pass on the news – Karen's parents are happy for you to use her name."

"Really, really?!" Anji was buzzing. It meant so much to her and was so symbolic, being able to pay tribute to her friend in this way.

"I can tell you're pleased," Hassan smiled. "So tell me more about Karen," he asked.

"Where do I start? Well, obviously you only met her in sad circumstances," began Anji. "But Karen was a wonderful woman. Glamorous, kind, generous to a fault... She's a great friend." Anji realized what she'd just said. Heat rushed to her cheeks while tears pricked her eyes. "Was – she was a great friend." She sighed, unsure of what to say. Hassan leaned forward, taking Anji's hands in his across the table.

"It's ok, you know? You're allowed to be upset," he reassured her. "Losing someone we love, especially in circumstances like those in which you lost Karen, is something we never get used to. The weeks and years that pass make the pain a little easier to bear but, when someone's been taken too soon, the pain runs deep." Anji looked up at him, blinking her eyes hard to stem the flow of tears, and realizing she didn't need to hold back with Hassan. The tears started to fall easily. "Don't be scared to cry in front of me," he said. "I see it everyday, and I've seen it with you before, after your anxiety attack. It's such early days since Karen's accident. You need to give yourself a little grace. Look what you're doing in her memory." His words were like a balm that soothed Anji's soul. At that moment, she realized that Hassan would be part of her future; more than just a colleague at the foundation, but part of her life. He was so caring and thoughtful, and there was no way she would let that slip from her grasp.

She smiled at him, knowing she didn't need to say anything more. With a sniff, Anji told the good doctor about her plans. "I want to be able to support people like Karen, make them see that their lives aren't over because their partner cheated. I want to provide a safe haven for people like me, people like I was. People who think they're in a loving relationship, when the reality is that they're being smothered by their partner's controlling ways." Anji went on to explain that, although she hadn't proposed her idea to Eleanor, she really wanted the foundation to reach out to expats who were in need of support. "Despite the life we'd built out there, when the chips were down I felt so alone," she explained. "You can have all the friends in the world but, once the gossip starts, people you've been close to for years start snubbing you. I was totally on my own in trying to manage everything, and being in a strict Muslim country and dealing with issues like adultery and domestic violence..." She glanced up to catch his eye.

"Well, it's not easy."

Hassan nodded slowly, paying attention to her every word. "It's wonderful," he began, before trailing off.

"What's wonderful?" Anji asked.

"You're creating something amazing out of something awful. And look how far you've come yourself. I've seen that ex-husband of yours in action; I could hear everything through that courtroom door."

"So stupid," Anji retorted. "I still can't believe I let him treat me that way for so long. I thought it was just the way he showed his love; I felt protected…" Now it was her turn to leave her sentence unfinished.

"It's alright," said Hassan, reassuring her. "It's over now. He can't hurt you anymore. And look how much you've already achieved."

He was right of course, she realized that. From having the balls to get evidence of him in the act, to keeping her shit together in court and setting up a new life for herself and the kids in London, Anji was taking great strides. She'd even partly forgiven Jeff for the way he treated her, knowing that holding on to hatred for him would only hurt her and the children in the long run. And now she could use her experience, along with the help of people like Doctor Hassan, to help others who were in the situation she'd been in only months before. If someone like Karen had been able to phone a helpline for advice, speak to a person who'd been through it and who understood what it was like when your husband ran off with the family maid; what it felt like to want to drown your shame and heartache in copious amounts of gin and vino… Well, perhaps things would've turned out better for Karen. But there was nothing Anji could do to save her friend now, so she must do the best job possible with the opportunity that had been presented to her. And Hassan and all the other professionals involved would be able to help with medical exams, giving evidence in court, carrying out surveillance, providing psychological support and offering legal advice – Eleanor had assembled quite the team of experts. With their input, the Armstrong Foundation would be a shining beacon for men and women enduring the dark times of separation.

The pair continued to chat over dinner, with the conversation flowing as easily as the drinks. Anji felt relaxed and at ease with Hassan, who was proving to be a real gent. He was interested in her as a person, and she felt listened to and valued, which was something she hadn't experienced in a long time.

"I've got to ask something," Doctor Hassan said. "That lady in the courtroom, Sara, is her husband called Fadi?"

"Yes, Fadi. Why?" she asked.

"Well, I know I'm breaking patient confidentiality here, but he and I used to work together. When I moved hospitals about three years ago, he contacted me about doing a routine vasectomy for him. I asked him why he hadn't had it done at his own hospital because he'd get a discount, and he told me it was because he didn't want his wife to know. I'd met her, of course, at social events – when I saw her at court, I recognised her face straight away. It all came flooding back to me, that she'd been clucking around him, asking for a kid, but he said he couldn't afford another one."

Anji held her hand over her mouth to stifle a gasp. She went through every scenario in her head, wondering why Fadi hadn't spoken up. He obviously knew he couldn't possibly be the father, yet there he was acting like the dutiful husband, putting on an amazing show. So he'd had the surgery without her knowing and now had to pay the price by raising someone else's child, right under his nose, in his own house.

Would Fadi love Mia or hate her, knowing what he knew? Can you really love a child that isn't yours? The gorgeous little angelic Mia. Anji hoped she'd have a chance to be innocent and free. She hoped Sara would protect Mia at all costs, make her life colourful, and fill it with love and adventures. She certainly had the money now to make that happen.

They were still talking and laughing when the maître d' came over to suggest they might like to settle up – Anji and Hassan looked round and noticed for the first time that they were the last customers in the restaurant.

After the doctor paid the bill, it was time to head out into the mild spring evening. "Let's flag a cab for you," he said, motioning his arm as he saw an amber light in the distance.

"Well, it's been a wonderful night, it's been great to get to know you better," Anji said, placing her hand on his forearm. At the touch of his skin, both felt the current; the charge was off the charts. All the same, she knew they ought to go home separately.

"And you," he responded, grinning sweetly. He was like a kid in a sweet shop; almost overwhelmed with excitement about what was to come. "But for now I'll say goodnight. As much as I'd like to jump in that cab with you, I think we need to take things slowly."

Anji felt the same. The kids were the most important people in her life right now and for that reason alone, she needed to take things slowly, day by day. Of course Jeff was still happily shacked up with Steph, and Anji was glad for them both. But she'd been hurt enough in her relationship with Jeff, and didn't need to rush headlong into a new one with Hassan. Baby steps, she thought.

As the cab pulled over, they smiled at each other, not saying a word. "Come on," called the cabbie in a Cockney accent, "I haven't got all day, 'arry up you love birds." Even the taxi driver could sense it. Hassan leaned closer towards Anji and gently laid his hand on her cheek. It was a stark contrast to the last time a man had touched her face; when Jeff had held her against the wall in the hotel room on Christmas Day. She shuddered at the thought, with the shudder turning into a shiver of delight as she looked into Hassan's eyes. She was the first to lean in, touching her lips to his to enjoy the sweetest, softest kiss.

As they each pulled away, sharing a smile, Hassan reached for the taxi door and raised an eyebrow. The evening – and the shared kiss – Anji certainly liked everything on the menu so far. Of course, she'd already sampled the main event, and would happily go back for seconds in due course, when the time was right.

CHAPTER 65

The following morning, Anji sat in a plush velvet arm-chair, gazing out of the large window in her lounge. This was the home she'd always dreamt about; in the style she loved, created in her vision and in an area where she'd always wanted to live. Jeff had paid for all the renovations, with no expense spared, because he believed he'd reside there with his family one day. She knew now that she would be much happier without him, and could picture her future taking shape before her – full independence, her own home, and a job and project to focus on. Her children were attending a beautiful private school and they were happy, enjoying their lives back on home turf. Anji's father had been responding well to treatment, and she would soon be paying for him to receive a second opinion privately; the best that money could buy for her dear old dad. The children were rebuilding their relationship with their own father and, although Jeff still hadn't found a job, Max and Georgie gave him more purpose and focus than he'd ever had while working in the hotel trade. He was a different man.

Every time the kids walked through the door, Anji felt happiness. Their chatter about their day's ups and downs, Anji's thoughts about her future plans for the foundation, knowing her parents were only a train ride away, listening to the birds singing in the local streets or heading to the lush, green parks to throw a Frisbee around with the children – these were the things Anji was truly embracing in her new life. She was content, and so happy enjoying the simple things in life. The gossip and shallow glamour of her old life in Saudi seemed a million miles away now.

And things were changing dramatically back in the Kingdom now too. Anji made sure she followed the news reports and kept up to date, and as soon as she had left Saudi Arabia, the country began to transform. Women were now allowed to work. They could drive cars and travel without a man's consent – being able to do those things would've made such a difference to Anji's time there. And the ugly Abaya was becoming a thing of the past too. All the rules that Anji had broken – which could have been punishable with jail time – were being unwritten as society began to open up to see women as equal partners. There was still a long way to go, of course, but it was an era of rapid change. Anji thought about her friends in Saudi often and, as she gazed out of the window in her comfortable London home, she reflected on the fact that her friends' lives were changing in line with hers. They were now allowed to express their individuality, gaining in confidence and beginning to take care of their own affairs, just like she was.

Life was truly a journey, Anji thought. Even though some of the roads on that journey were bumpy and rough, and damn right gruesome at times, the route was capable of change. Instead of fear, she felt excitement about the new path she was taking. Anji was discovering who she genuinely was, and for the first time she was getting to like even love that person. She didn't have to be the person others expected her to be. She'd spent so much of her time wanting to be someone or somewhere else but now, for the first time, she knew she was exactly who and where she was supposed to be. Now she was embarking on this journey of self-discovery – being true, living by her own standards and rules. Emotional scars are raw, as any real burn is, yet they fade like any scar. Learning to love ourselves to look to ourselves for confirmation of real self worth, that's what sets us free.

One book was closing and a new one was opening. She was ready to start over with the next chapters brimming with adventures and colours to enlighten her soul. Whatever life threw at her next, she was ready keeping her eyes on the horizon.

UNTITLED

ABOUT THE AUTHOR

Mary Brown

I have lived a huge part of my life as an Expat wife and travelling extensively. Although I have throroughly enjoyed the journey there are times when the lonliness creeps up in you and you are forced out of your comfort zone which makes you grow in ways you never knew possible. I felt impelled to write about what I knew best. People think you become a lady of 'leisure' but they don't know that you often give up your own career to follow your spouse which can sometimes leave you a black hole of emp- tiness as you somehow lose your identity.

Having said that, I raised three resilient children who never complained about the upheaval and they make me prouder and prouder each and every day. They are capable of making friends on the streets and at the start of each new school they never cried or looked back.

I hope you enjoy the book as much as I enjoyed writing it. All the characters are fictional as are the events.

Printed in Great Britain
by Amazon

67753148R00218